Mentor Coaching
and Leadership

in Early Care and Education

Join us on the web at

EarlyChildEd.delmar.com

Mentor Coaching and Leadership

in Early Care and Education

MARY E. NOLAN

THOMSON

DELMAR LEARNING

Australia Canada Mexico Singapore Spain United Kingdom United States

THOMSON

DELMAR LEARNING

Mentor Coaching and Leadership in Early Care and Education
Mary E. Nolan

Vice President, Career Education SBU:
Dawn Gerrain

Director of Learning Solutions:
Sherry Dickinson

Managing Editor:
Robert L. Serenka, Jr.

Senior Acquisitions Editor:
Erin O'Connor

Acquisitions Editor:
Chris Shortt

Editorial Assistant:
Stephanie Kelly

Director of Production:
Wendy A. Troeger

Production Manager:
J.P. Henkel

Content Project Manager:
Ken Karges

Production Assistant:
Angela Iula

Director of Marketing:
Wendy E. Mapstone

Channel Manager:
Kristin McNary

Marketing Coordinator:
Scott A. Chrysler

Cover Design:
Suzanne Nelson

Composition:
International Typesetting
and Composition

Cover Image:
© Shutterstock Images

For permission to use material from this text or product, submit a request online at http://www.thomsonrights.com

Any additional questions about permissions can be submitted by email to thomsonrights@thomson.com

Library of Congress Cataloging-in-Publication Data

Nolan, Mary, 1956—
    Mentor coaching and leadership in early care and education/Mary Nolan.
        p. cm.
    ISBN 1-4180-0584-3
    1. Early childhood teachers—Training of. 2. Early childhood teachers—In-service training. 3. Mentoring in education. I. Title.

LB1775.6.N65 2006
370.71'5—dc22

2006018565

NOTICE TO THE READER

Contents

CHAPTER 2

Mentor Coaching and Planning 21

CHAPTER 3   <u>Mentor Coaching and Leadership</u> **51**

CHAPTER 6   Mentor Coaching and Learning 101

CHAPTER 9

Mentor Coaching and Creativity and Innovation 159

Foreword

Through the years as an early care and education professional, I have written articles and made presentations about adult-to-adult relationships in the field. Although not specifically discussed or documented, it is believed that, when professionals in child care centers have healthy adult communication patterns and respect for one another, the children thrive. The results of longitudinal studies, such as the Perry Preschool Project, the Carolina Abecedarian Project, or the Chicago Parent–Child Centers Study, include explicit discussions about systematic approaches to working with children and the consistent implementation of curricular goals to support their development and learning. The iterative process of developing each of the settings described in the research studies appears to have included opportunities for staff to discuss and reflect on insights gained relative to the classroom experiences. Although there are no extensive descriptions of the type and quality of adult–adult engagement and communication in each of these studies, it is clear that time was devoted to thoughtful reflection in order to improve classroom practices and, ultimately, outcomes for the children.

Traditionally, educators in early care and education have been so focused on observing children, deciding what is developmentally appropriate, and planning classroom activities that adult–adult relationships received little attention. Furthermore, in order to improve professional practices and ensure that they are appropriately meeting the needs of the children, adults working in classrooms and with families should be able to talk with each other in a thoughtful and productive manner about how they are accomplishing their goals. Staff should develop ways of collecting multiple forms of evidence related to children's progress. This requires adults to engage in systematically recording, collecting, and discussing evidence related to what children know and what they are able to do. In order for this to happen, not only is it important to understand principles of how children learn and develop but also to find professional support to help incorporate principles of adult learning so that effective adult–adult interactions can produce the kind of environment that will result in positive outcomes for children.

Mentor coaching, the process whereby a more experienced person works with, nurtures, and supports a less experienced person, has always taken place in the field. However, based on the theory and an understanding of its importance, organizations now can implement their own unique programs with a better understanding of their rationale and a clearer knowledge of available and appropriate approaches, which will promote success in the organizations. This requires leadership and a vision to create a culture of professional development and learning to support adult–adult relationships that, ultimately, will ensure more positive outcomes for the children and families served.

I have always encouraged participants in programs to allow time for the adults to dialogue and problem solve with one another about their observations of the children and samples of children's work, as well as to share anecdotal notes. Adequate time should be available as well to discuss the family and its role in supporting the child. There should be time allotted for reviewing and rearranging the learning environment in order to keep children engaged, as well as time to allocate tasks, plan special projects, care for pets, and so on in order to provide an interesting and supportive early childhood setting. Years ago when I was a young teacher in the Pacific Oaks Children's School in Pasadena, one of my mentors planned and scheduled what she called "quality adult time." She believed that this not only benefited the children and families but that it also contributed to nurturing the quality of relationships between the caregivers and teachers. The overall goal of a good mentor coaching program should be to heighten the participant's level of understanding, encourage the ability to resolve challenges, and contribute to an attitude of lifelong learning.

As we move forward, these quality relationships and the acknowledgment of the importance of building positive adult–adult relationships will become clearer. This book provides knowledge, understanding, and strategies to help the reader consider ways in which mentor coach programs, if thoughtfully instituted, can foster quality early care and education programs for children and their families. With the challenges in the field, the lack of qualified staff, and a need for leadership, the issues in this book offer valuable contributions to the field.

Ed Greene, Ph.D., early childhood consultant and trainer, former NAEYC board member, community college professor and writer, Princeton, New Jersey

Preface

The purpose of this book is to share with professionals in the field of early care and education the power of mentor coaching, which could ignite its leadership. As a profession, early care and education has been the stepchild in the field of education. Professionals in the field have sought a leadership model; however, as yet leadership has not been clearly defined, and it has not been determined definitively how one becomes a leader or what is expected of a leader. This text is intended to contribute to the knowledge base in the field and present information from a variety of disciplines, including psychology, organizational behavior, business management, and leadership studies, in order to examine and define leadership in the field of early care and education. It is hoped that practitioners in the field of early care and education will move the dialogue forward to think more clearly about their profession and what it takes to be a leader.

In the research and literature reviews, several authors discussed the process of mentor coaching as a journey: a journey that may involve fears but that provides new meanings and, ultimately, a return to where the journey was begun; however, as a result of the journey, people, events, and things are perceived with new eyes and a new heart. Journeys often seem to involve bridges, places where one crosses deep valleys, rivers, and difficult terrain, and that lead to safety on the other side. The notion of a bridge became the metaphor for thinking and writing about the process of mentor coaching.

Cunningham (2005) explains that a stone-arched bridge is an engineering feat from ancient Rome more than 1,000 years ago. The span and the strength of the bridge depend on a center keystone that balances the remaining stones using the theory of weight transferal. Building this type of bridge takes time and requires the skills of a stonemason who is both artisan and artist. It appears to require someone who has the ability to "listen" to stone, someone who sees a haphazard array of stones and knows which one is right for a particular space. There is also the balancing of one stone over two rule, which involves placing the stones in positions such that they work together, and the trimming and chipping and shaping of them to fit.

This description of the art and science of bridge building provides a physical representation and a metaphor for a successful mentor–coach/protégé relationship. The patience, the listening, the connecting of elements, the artistry involved in creating a beautiful structure appears to wonderfully describe the beauty of a successful mentor coach/protégé relationship.

HOW THIS TEXT WAS DEVELOPED

The process of mentor coaching is as old as history and is frequently told and retold in myths and legends. The hero or heroine begins a journey through unknown territory. During the experience, the person inevitably meets a guide or encounters some kind of enlightenment that helps him or her complete the challenging journey. Sometimes those journeying find themselves back at the places from which they began; however, they are not the same; they have new perspectives as a result of their adventures. History has provided many examples, in both fact and fiction, of mentor coaching. People have come to describe a mentor coach as one who guides, facilitates, nurtures, and supports. The mentor coach/protégé process affects many people's lives, sometimes for brief moments and sometimes enduring into long-term relationships.

Sources from the field of business, organizational behavior, leadership, and education provide insights into effective mentor coaching processes. David Stoddard's (2004) *The Heart of Mentoring* introduced me to the concept of mentor partner. The terms *protégé*, *mentee*, and *coachee* have been used interchangeably, and there has seemingly been no single preferred use. However, I was persuaded that *protégé* is the term people currently identify with mentor coaching, so it is the term I use throughout the book. The confusion, I believe, has been that many of these terms connote some sense of inequality; these traditional names for a "protégé" perpetuate the stereotype of the older, wiser person putting his or her arms around a younger, less experienced person and showing him or her the ropes. The English have an apt name for this traditional mentoring experience called "sitting next to Nelly" at whose side was taught the ropes of the position.

The term *mentor partner* perhaps is more reflective of the kind of mentor coaching currently in practice, and I believe it will become the standard term in the future. Mentor coaching originally was more product oriented and was the practice of transferring knowledge. In today's world, mentor coaching has become much more of a process-oriented experience with a facilitator guiding, recommending, and reflecting with a protégé.

This work examines the mentor coaching/protégé relationship as beneficial to both partners. In the field of early care and education, the relationship often becomes a peer relationship.

ORGANIZATION OF THE TEXT

Following is a brief description of the chapter topics. The chapters build on each other; however, according to course needs, they can be studied independently of each other.

Chapter One, "Mentor Coaching: An Overview," and Chapter Two, "Mentor Coaching and Planning," are foundational chapters that should be read consecutively to establish a baseline. Topics for Chapters 3 through 10 can be read in a flexible manner depending on the nature and emphasis of the course as well as student needs and interests.

Chapter One: "Mentor Coaching: An Overview"

Chapter One provides an historical overview of mentor coaching. The general parameters of the mentor coaching process are considered. The discussion includes the importance of mentor coaching in the field of early care and education. Three models of mentor coaching are described. Some of the techniques of reflective practice, the benefits for the mentor coach and mentor protégé, and an overview of the phases of the mentor coach process are discussed.

Chapter Two: "Mentor Coaching and Planning"

Chapter Two focuses on planning for the mentor coaching process. The discussion includes consideration of the stakeholders involved, for example, human resources and fiscal people. There is also a model for the orientation of a new program and a discussion of how, when, and why evaluation should be a part of any program.

Chapter Three: "Mentor Coaching and Leadership"

Chapter Three presents the context for leadership in the field of early care and education, a field that, to date, has not articulated a leadership model and is in search of the parameters of developmental activities, education, and experience that would guarantee a good leader. The difference between leading and managing is discussed. The notions of "leadership without authority" and steward leadership are examined and aligned with the leadership experiences and needs of the early care and education field.

Chapter Four: "Mentor Coaching and Change"

Chapter Four considers how change is an intrinsic part of the mentor coaching process for both the mentor coach and the protégé. Understanding and planning for change, and identifying one's position in the life journey contribute to the process of self-renewal in order to create and sustain an effective mentor coaching process.

Chapter Five: "Mentor Coaching and Communication"

In any kind of educational or personal development process, good communication skills are necessary. Understanding one's own style of communication as well as that of others improves the power and richness of dialogue. Facilitation techniques, including the use of open-ended questions, are discussed.

Chapter Six: "Mentor Coaching and Learning"

Mentor coaching occurs in the context of learning. Chapter Six includes a discussion of what learning is and how to understand one's own and other's learning styles. It explains how the transfer of learning happens. There are also discussions about the important concepts of situated learning and transformational learning.

Chapter Seven: "Mentor Coaching and Values"

Understanding one's own value system and one's motivators may help improve the mentor coaching process. Setting goals and objectives that are not aligned with an individual's personal values or those of the organization may result in failure.

Chapter Eight: "Mentor Coaching and Cultural Competence"

New teachers are often situated in unfamiliar communities and settings. With the support of a mentor coach, a person's feelings of inadequacy and discomfort when working with families who are English language learners may develop more confidence. Children and their families deserve respect for their first language and appreciation for the struggle that acquiring a second language entails. A proven strategy to achieve a comfort level working with others involves first understanding one's own culture, then discovering how family systems work, and finally using that understanding to bridge the gaps.

Chapter Nine: "Mentor Coaching and Creativity and Innovation"

As part of the transformational experience in mentor coaching, there are opportunities to think unconventionally. The mentor coach can provide the tools and environment in which one can take risks and find support for providing services in new ways.

Chapter Ten: "Mentor Coaching and Emotional Intelligence"

Emotional intelligence is an emerging topic in which people consider why some rise to leadership levels and others do not. What combination of traits supports the success of some? The traits discussed include resilience, the ability to make decisions, and the ability to provide emotional support for those being led, as well as setting a vision.

In summary, the one important attribute of the mentor coach/protégé relationship is that the transactions come from the heart. Mentor coaching is about caring. If the mentor coach does not truly care, the process becomes simply a matter of passing on content, and it eludes the power and beauty a true mentor coaching relationship can have.

FEATURES

Mentor Coaching and Leadership includes a number of special features:

- inspirational quotes
- chapter objectives
- case studies with critical thinking questions
- chapter summaries
- key terms
- chapter discussion questions
- mentor coach/protégé interaction exercises

- reflective practice questions and applications
- learning journals
- references
- further readings

ANCILLARY MATERIAL

Online Companion™

The Online Companion™ that accompanies this text contains additional material that will help the reader focus in on understanding mentor coaching and leadership in early care and education. Special features of the Online Companion™ include Web resources, additional case studies with critical thinking questions, and multiple choice quizzes for each chapter. The answers to each quiz, along with the rationale for the correct answers, can also be found on-line.

The Online Companion™ icon appears at the end of each chapter to prompt you to go on-line and take advantage of the many features provided. You can find the Online Companion™ at www.earlychilded.delmar.com.

ABOUT THE AUTHOR

Dr. Mary E. Nolan is an educator and leader in the field of early care and education and has taught for more than 25 years at the university and community college levels. Her course work has been in traditional classrooms as well as on-line and she is a big proponent of distance education.

She has worked in several child care settings, including designing, getting funding, and implementing one of the first adolescent parent/infant–toddler programs in California. The model was used to pass legislation that provides state funding for programs. Dr. Nolan has worked extensively in Head Start programs and is presently the program director for Kauai Head Start. Presently residing in the northwest, she can be reached by e-mail: mentorcoach1@aol.com.

She has seven grown children and six grandchildren. She has presented at many conferences and her previous work includes research and the development of the Learning Success System© software system, which includes a survey that identifies one's learning style.

ACKNOWLEDGMENTS

Many books have lengthy acknowledgments. After you write a book, it is a good idea to remember all the support and love you have received that made it possible. Acknowledgments barely seem enough. For my children and grandchildren, you are all my inspiration, especially my daughter Tricia, who read every word and is a superb editor, catching the misspellings as well as the nuances. Sharon McAfee made sense of the sentences on the pages; her professionalism, diligence, and patience are much appreciated. And for my life partner, Gerry, who always supported my writing and did the cooking and shopping as well, I thank you.

The author and Thomson Delmar Learning would like to thank the following reviewers, whose comments and thoughtful feedback helped to shape the final text:

JoAnn Brager, M.Ed.
West River Head Start
Bismarck, ND

Patricia Capistron
Rocking Unicorn Preschool
West Chatham, MA

Vicki Folds, Ed.D.
Children of America, Inc.
Parkland, FL

Karen Libeler
Adventures in Learning
Tampa, FL

Mary Ann Marchel, Ph.D.
University of Minnesota, Duluth
Duluth, MN

Debra Murphy, MS
Cape Cod Community College
West Barnstable, MA

Marilyn Rice, M.Ed.
Tuckaway Child Development
Richmond, VA

Patricia Weaver, M.Ed.
Fayetteville Technical Community College

Mentor Coaching: An Overview

INTRODUCTION

The process of mentor coaching has the power to ignite leadership in the field of early care and education. When an effective mentor coaching relationship develops, both people in the relationship clearly benefit. Working in the field of early care and education has some rigorous educational requirements; however, there are times when a person must see and experience life events that cannot be learned simply by reading a book or sitting in a classroom.

Ultimately, and as part of its essence, mentor coaching is about caring. It is a matter of the heart. Not only is caring about the other person in the relationship important but also caring about the children and families of the person being mentored in the relationship is important. If there is no heart, a relationship may develop, but the rich and deep relationship possible may be missed.

Mentor coaching involves an experience and a relationship between two people. No two people will have the same experience or outcomes, so there is no formula for being part of a mentor coaching experience. Mentor coaches simply need the willingness to commit time and effort to listen to and learn from another person in order to become better providers for children and their families.

"Whatever you can do, or dream you can, begin in boldness. Boldness has genius, power and magic in it."

GOETHE

Leaders in the field of early care and education increasingly have implemented more rigorous standards for educational requirements in order for a person to be employed in this field. These educational standards are also receiving attention from the No Child Left Behind educational accountability legislation initiated in the Bush era. Fueling these requirements is the realization that children are not being appropriately or sufficiently prepared to enter school. The sooner a child with challenges or developmental delays is identified, the better the opportunity will be to assist the child and help them reach their potential.

■ CHAPTER OBJECTIVES

After reading this chapter, you should be able to:

- Provide the definitions for and describe the fundamental aspects of a mentor coach/protégé program.
- Describe characteristics of a good mentor coach.
- Discuss how and at what stage of a protégé's life and career the protégé is most likely to benefit by participating in a mentor coach program.

THE ANCIENT WORLD OF MENTOR

The figure and myth of Mentor is based in tales of Homer's *Odyssey*. Before Odysseus left for the Trojan War, he consulted Athena about appearing as a tutor and counselor for his son Telemachus. It is thought that the male/female wisdom, as well as the spiritual/practical training for Telemachus, was the strength in his upbringing that assisted Odysseus's wife, Penelope, in warding off the suitors who aspired to Odysseus's kingdom. After many years of wandering and adventure, Odysseus returned home and found Telemachus grown into a young man who was prepared to lead and to assume the responsibilities of his father's kingdom. The meaning of the word *mentor* has traditionally signified a special person in one's life, who, through deeds and words, helps the one being mentored (or the protégé) reach his or her potential.

Mentor, or Athena disguised, provides an instructive view of the subtleties of mentorship. In working with and guiding Telemachus, Mentor acted as a friend, as someone who created a safe **context** for growth. Mentor was sensitive and wise, knowing that his pupil may not be always ready to hear of hard-won wisdom; he understood the resistance the protégé might present.

In his relationship with Telemachus, Mentor exhibited a model that continues to be valid today. A mentor loves learning more than teaching, sharing rather than showing off, and giving rather than boasting. Mentors enthusiastically encourage their protégés. However, the real gift of the mentor involves believing in the dreams and aspirations of the protégé. More importantly,

■ **CONTEXT**
The whole situation, background, or environment relevant to a particular event, personality, or creation

the mentor guides the protégé to help fulfill their dream.

In the 1700s, Fenelon popularized the image of Mentor as the trusted friend, adviser, and counselor to Telemachus. The word *mentor* first appeared as a noun in the *Oxford English Dictionary* as early as 1750. The current *Webster's New World College Dictionary*, 4th ed. (1999) defines a mentor as a wise, loyal, and trusted adviser.

This dictionary definition does not do justice to the magic and intensity of the quality experience two people can enjoy that enables the protégé to grow personally and professionally. Without the mentor coach to prod, challenge, and support risk-taking behaviors and activities, the protégé might remain bound by self-limiting beliefs, remain unchallenged, and, perhaps, even leave the field of early care and education. Mentor coaching is an art and a science. Although it is often believed that mentor coach/protégé relationships should simply occur, the mentor coach relationship actually involves intuition and hunches of the mentor to determine experiences that might provide the protégé with insight and wisdom such that the protégé will develop into a successful professional. There is a mental stereotype of a mentor coach/protégé relationship that involves senior

people putting their arms around younger people, showing them "the ropes" of the organization. In truth, there are specific mentor coach skills that can be learned and that support a quality relationship with a protégé. Also, mentor coach/protégé relationships can occur in many different settings and among a variety of partners, for example, peers or young people working with an older person as the protégé. There are numerous possible gender and diversity combinations. Each mentor coach/protégé relationship is unique and has its own dynamics. There is no formula for this relationship.

WHAT IS MENTOR COACHING?

Mentor coaching, for the purposes of this book, is the facilitated, structured process whereby an experienced person introduces, assists, and supports a less experienced person (the protégé) in a personal and professional growth process. This process, in order to be effective, must occur over time: Sufficient time must elapse for the mentor and protégé to develop action plans, dialogue about issues, and practice and reflect. This guidebook is based on an 18-week course; however, the materials easily could be expanded to cover a program year of staff development.

Mentor coaching is an individualized learning and change process that affects both the mentor coach and the protégé. Both benefit and learn from the process. They learn from the successes as well as the challenges, and both are always part of a **symbiotic** process.

■ **SYMBIOTIC**
An association with mutual advantage among all parties

A mentor coach may take on a variety of roles, and these will vary from program to program. There is no one right model. The mentor coaching program should be tailored to meet the needs of the organization and the protégé. Each mentor coach/protégé relationship will enjoy unique dynamics as a result of the individuals involved.

When identifying and selecting mentor coaches, remember that the roles they fill could be as advisers. Mentor coaches serve in this role as they assist and support the protégé in developing new skills and, perhaps, taking risks. Obviously, the mentor coach will become a confidante. Because of this role, a supervisor should not be a subordinate's mentor coach. The person who evaluates staff has a different perspective, and a protégé may not feel comfortable sharing a dream or vision that does not include staying in a current position. The confidante role demands confidentiality for both the mentor coach and the protégé. Until trust and the realization of the protégé that what is discussed between them is privileged information occurs, the richness of dialogue will not happen.

Another role the mentor coach may take is that of facilitator where the mentor coach assists the protégé in working through challenges. The mentor coach can ask "what if . . ." questions, pointing out alternatives, providing explanations from experience, or directing the protégé to resources. Using the techniques of brainstorming, asking open-ended questions, journal writing, and reflective practice help to support the protégé.

Mentor coaches serve very important roles as connectors and networkers—opening doors for protégés or introducing them to appropriate people, whether inside or outside the organization. These often are critical factors in the successes of protégés, especially in helping them understand whether they want to work in early care and education or in helping them determine future roles in which they may perceive themselves. However, being exposed to successful role models can be the clarifying moment that helps protégés determine that they really want to be somewhere else in their life/career path.

In order to be a successful mentor coach, one must understand that he or she is a change agent, not only for the protégé but also for the organization. This presents situations where challenges can occur that actually disrupt the mentor coach/protégé process. When initiating the program in the planning phase, administration must facilitate it, providing time, resources, and recognition of the process; otherwise, it is being set up for failure. The immediate supervisor of the protégé may believe the mentor coach is a threat or may feel like his or her position is being usurped and that the time involved in the mentor coach process could be better spent by the protégé. As a change agent, the mentor coach must take the time to explain the process to all involved and to get their initial acceptance of the program. Also, the mentor coach and protégé should revisit their organization's goals and objectives. Do

the activities and experiences planned align with the organization's mission? If not, this could present challenges later.

The mentor coach as well as the protégé must be willing to learn. They must be willing to learn from each other in a shared-learning community sense. Part of this requires that the mentor coach not think (or insist) that the protégé do things the way the mentor coach did them. Rather the mentor should encourage the protégé to find his or her own way and unique voice, which may result in the mentor coach rethinking how he or she handled things in the past.

QUALIFICATIONS AND CHARACTERISTICS OF A MENTOR COACH

The qualifications of a mentor coach will vary from agency to agency, but, generally, a mentor coach should have a good educational background, including at least an associate's degree or, preferably, a bachelor's degree. However, there are excellent mentor coaches who do not possess a lot of education who have the heart and the passion to work with children and families and consistently share their experiences with others.

Good mentor coaches have good interpersonal skills; they are amiable, patient, compassionate, and empathetic. It is helpful if they are honest about themselves and their relationships with others. The successful mentor coach tends to be self-confident and to enjoy time spent with others. Being a good listener and being willing to learn are the defining characteristics of a mentor coach. The mentor coach should also be sensitive to the protégé's preferred learning style and flexible in providing content.

The mentor coach must be able to set clear boundaries. Mentor coaching is not therapy, and the mentor coach must indicate immediately when personal matters are not appropriate topics of their sessions together. In addition, they are good listeners and can determine what is not being said as well as what is being said. They are active listeners who frequently ask clarifying and open-ended questions. They understand the techniques of dialogue and share them with the protégé in order to achieve deep and meaningful discussions, regardless of topics, while suspending judgment. Other characteristics of a successful mentor coach include sharing personal expertise as it becomes appropriate as well as a willingness to stay current and update one's self in a broad field of content areas.

When working with the mentor coach/protégé process, it helps to remember that growth means broadening one's knowledge base and learning. Effective mentoring involves clearing an emotional path to make the learning journey as free of boundaries as possible. Change is a door opened from the inside, and the mentor coach provides the key to that door.

The real aim of mentoring is not mastery but "mastering." Mastery implies closure, an ending, or the arrival at a destination. In today's ever-changing world, the goal is "mastering," which is a never-ending, ever-expansive journey of personal growth. It suggests the relationship is more important than the goal, the process more valued than the outcome.

Bell (2002) provides a model of mentoring that has proven useful and easy to remember using the **mnemonic** SAGE, which stands for

- Surrendering
- Accepting
- Gifting
- Extending

■ **MNEMONIC**

A formula or means of improving one's memory

These competencies make up the mentor coach/protégé process. To a mentor coach, the idea of surrendering may sound like a weakness because most mentor coaches are used to leading the learning. However, this kind of surrender really indicates the willingness of the mentor coach to let go of the process and allow the interactions between the mentor coach and the protégé to become a yielding to the process that is greater between them, rather than in either one of them individually. Surrender is the process of leveling the playing field.

Usually, the mentor coach has a higher level of responsibility, and the protégé is in an unequal, lower power position. The risk is that power creates anxiety, and anxiety reduces risk taking. Surrendering encompasses all the action the mentor coach takes to reduce the power and authority in the mentoring relationship so the protégé's anxiety is lowered and his or her courage is heightened.

Accepting involves the act of inclusion. True acceptance is defined as unconditional positive regard. Accepting involves the ability to create a safe haven for learning. As the mentor coach begins to listen to the protégé, demonstrating interest and curiosity about the protégé's ideas and thoughts, the ability to act on their ideas becomes possible without fear of ridicule and failure.

Gifting is another competency that both the mentor coach and the protégé must develop and understand. Gifting is the main event of mentoring. The mentor coach gives unconditionally without expecting anything in return. Mentors give advice, feedback, focus, and direction. They also provide the balance between **intervening** and allowing the protégé to move forward to take a risk. As part of this gifting, it may be natural for the protégé to feel some resistance or to think, "I already know that; why is he repeating himself?" The protégé will benefit by standing back, reflecting, and appreciating the fact that she or he may not think the advice is needed advice now, but the mentor coach is aware of something that may have a positive result or benefit for the protégé later.

Extending is the process of pushing one's self beyond what is perceived as the limit. It is important for the mentor coach to appreciate the fact that the protégé is going to learn from many different sources and to encourage the protégé to be a self-directed learner.

■ **INTERVENING**
To come, be, or lie between

THE EXPERIENCE OF BEING A PROTÉGÉ

Webster's New World College Dictionary, 4th ed. (1999) defines a protégé as the person who is guided and helped by an influential person. This is a limited statement regarding the experience of mentor coaching. Successful, quality relationships have influenced and changed the world, and success is influenced by attitude.

Protégés first need to examine themselves, honestly assessing their abilities to be accepting of learning and their willingness to accept advice from another person. This factor alone, willingness to learn, determines the quality and outcomes of the relationship.

STAGES OF TEACHER DEVELOPMENT

Using the model Lillian Katz (1995) provides in Table 1–1 helps delineate the fact that staff will have different mentor coaching needs, depending on the stages of their personal and professional growth.

Different types of mentoring occur, depending on the individual's as well as the organization's needs. If new teachers are more likely to need support in their first years and **retention** and building capacity are organizational goals, then focusing on new teachers may be the goal of the mentor coaching program.

■ **RETENTION**
Power or capacity to
retain; ability to remember

Stage 1

Stage 1—Mentor coaches may be identified as those who are knowledgeable in the content areas of child development, observation curriculum, and handling challenging behaviors. The focus would be on skill development for mentor coaching, and protégé activities may focus on lesson planning, room arrangement, and working with parents.

Stage 2

Stage 2—The consolidation stage may be characterized by staff members asking to be mentored. Staff members may realize that there are content areas in which they need more experience and knowledge and that their own

---

TABLE 1–1   STAGES OF TEACHER DEVELOPMENT

Stage 1: Survival	**Stage 2:** Consolidation
Year 1—New teacher	Years 2 to 3—Teacher with some experience
Usually feels inadequate, unprepared, and out of control	Begins to feel some level of mastery
Stage 3: Renewal	**Stage 4:** Maturity
Years 4 to 6	Years 7 and on*
Begins to feel stale, repetitive; needs innovation	Has come to terms with self and understands the bigger picture

*The years may vary depending on the individual's experiences.

Source: Katz, L. (1995). Developmental stages of preschool teachers (pp. 1–8). Urbana-Champaign: University of Illinois, Clearing House on Early Education and Parenting (CEEP). Used with permission of Early Childhood and Parenting Technology Group, University of Illinois at Urbana-Champaign.

skill sets are limited in certain areas. Again, this will most likely involve an area of skill development, perhaps a little more complex, for example, when looking at an area such as computer skills, math and science, or how to incorporate and expand the curriculum. The mentor coach and protégé would work on action plans that may be project- or theme-based and developed and added to over time. Outside resource people or workshops and seminars may be suggested.

Stage 3

Stage 3—The renewal stage appears to be a critical time, and it is one ripe for intervention from a mentor coach. At this point, staff are performing routines; nothing is new or sparking their interests. They have grown stale, and they are not seeking help. This could be a challenging situation for the mentor coach; however, if it is approached correctly, the mentor coaching process may be very successful in helping a person through the renewal process.

Stage 4

Stage 4—The maturity stage provides a rich source for mentor coaches. The teachers are still motivated, they are knowledgeable, and they understand why it is important to build quality and capacity for staff.

PHASES IN AN EARLY CARE AND EDUCATION STAFF PERSON'S EXPERIENCE

Whether one is employed in the field of education or in general businesses, human resource professionals recognize the phases that an employee experiences and recognize that different kinds of support are needed at different phases (see Table 1–2). The challenge of phase 1 involves getting the newly employed hired, trained, working, and productive as quickly as possible. In phase 1, a mentor coach could introduce the new employee to procedures and protocols, showing them the ropes and helping them to understand the structure of the organization and move within the culture of the organization.

Phase 2 is the ideal phase where everyone wants the employee to be. Usually, and predictably for most employees, there comes a phase 3 about three to five years after beginning employment. In phase 3, employees know how to do the job, but whether as a result of personal problems or simply because of boredom, they become unproductive and sometimes become problematic for their co-workers. Supervisors need to be alert for this phase and identify what the challenges seem to be. One strategy to improve these

TABLE 1–2	PHASES OF MOTIVATION AND EFFECTIVENESS IN A STAFF PERSON'S CAREER	
Phase 1		**Phase 2**
• New		• Seasoned
• Motivated		• Motivated
• Inexperienced		• Experienced
Phase 3		**Phase 4**
• Seasoned		• Seasoned
• Unmotivated		• Unmotivated
• Experienced		• No longer effective

employees' performances may involve adding new assignments to the employees' responsibilities. This could be a stage for encouraging the employee to become a mentor coach, but, if this is the case, the suggestion to mentor coach must be made before the employee has slipped into phase 4, in which termination of the employee may need to occur.

BEHAVIORAL COACHING

Skiffington and Zeus (2003) describe behavioral coaching as a way of building sustainable personal and organizational strength. Behavioral coaching involves a structured process-driven relationship between a trained professional coach and an individual or a team. It includes assessment, examination of values and motivation, the setting of measurable goals, defining focused action plans, and using validated tools and techniques to help coaches develop competencies and remove blocks in order to achieve valuable and sustainable changes in the personal and professional lives of an individual or team.

In Table 1–3, Skiffington and Zeus (2003) outline the stages of change, five forms of coaching, and how mentor coaching changes through seven steps in the coaching process.

TABLE I–3   SEVEN STEPS IN A CHANGE PROCESS

Stages of Change	Five Forms of Coaching	Seven-Step Coaching Process
Reflective	Coaching education	Education
Preparation		Data collection
		Planning (setting goals, action plans)
	Skills coaching	Behavioral change
	Rehearsal coaching	
Action	Performance coaching	Measurement
		Evaluation
Maintenance	Self-coaching	Maintenance

Source: Skiffington, S., & Zeus, P. (2003). *Behavioral coaching: How to build a sustainable personal and organizational strength* (p. 129). Sydney, Australia: McGraw-Hill. Used with permission.

Behavioral coaching differs from traditional, deficit-based coaching and uses validated behavioral change techniques that enhance learning, performance, and development. Traditionally, coaching examined **extrinsic** motivators, such as the demands of the workplace and performance rewards. Behavioral coaching explores the individual's values and works on the premise that real motivation and change are **intrinsic.**

■ **EXTRINSIC**
Coming from outside

■ **INTRINSIC**
Coming from within

CASE STUDY: INNER-CITY HEAD START TEACHER

Trudy was a teacher in a large, inner-city Head Start program and, after her fifth year, began to feel that she was very isolated. She was so busy each day that she had little time to talk with the other staff members. Her friends from when she started teaching had all left, transferring to other centers or actually leaving the field. Most of the teachers in the program now were very young and new to the field. She was unhappy with the new classroom aide she was assigned, feeling she had to teach her everything. She also felt like she was losing patience with the children more frequently than she used to.

Fortunately, Trudy had a good relationship with her supervisor and had an open and frank discussion with him, telling him how she felt. Her supervisor suggested she register as a protégé in the organization's mentor coach/protégé program and arranged for her to be matched to a mentor coach. Trudy credits her supervisor and her mentor coach for helping her get through this challenging time. As she looks back, she realizes she was very

(Continued)

(Continued)

close to leaving the field and finding another career. Instead, she is reenergized, particularly in the area of literacy, where much of the organization's mentor coach program focused. Now she states she looks forward to each day to see what she can add to the learning centers for the children. She also is much more involved with parents. She invites them into the classroom to volunteer and she sends home book bags to help parents understand the value of reading to their children. Trudy claims the mentor coach/protégé program saved her as a teacher.

Critical Thinking Questions

1. What are some factors that lead to teacher burnout?
2. Why did the mentor coaching program make a difference in Trudy's life?
3. What tends to happen when a teacher gets parents involved?

WHY MENTOR COACHING?

The concept of mentor coaching is not new and has roots in the master/apprentice system of the Middle Ages. As we move into the twenty-first century, this same process of a more experienced person assisting a less experienced person takes on new meanings and new shapes but, ultimately, it is this same process and has similar results.

An organization may consider having a formal, structured mentor coaching process for many reasons, for example, to provide orientation and support for new staff. Additionally, an organization may consider a mentor coaching process as a way to increase productivity and build capacity. Mentor coaching can serve to help staff become more comfortable with one another, especially if they are from diverse backgrounds, or to develop skills and talents that are underdeveloped or that have not been previously recognized. Retention is another significant factor that benefits from the mentor coaching process. As one is recognized and comes to feel valued in an organization, one develops loyalty and identification with the goals and purposes of the organization. Perhaps the most important feature of the mentor coaching process is the fact that a person's self-esteem and personal and professional growth develop, regardless of whether one is the mentor coach or the protégé.

Interestingly, a "tipping point" in mentor coaching was reached in the 1997–98 era as the number of organizations reporting the implementation of formal mentor coaching programs doubled in one year. A tipping point, according to Gladwell (2005), is a number of small, incremental incidences that lead to a change in culture, for example, the sudden popularity of Hush Puppy shoes, which was evidently brought about by a few high-profile people seen wearing them. Suddenly, it seems as if all sorts of organizations simultaneously realized how valuable a formal mentor coaching program could be for them.

Mentor coaching is an honor. It is a rare privilege to help another learn, to have one's relevant wisdom be useful to another, and to partner with someone who can benefit from that wisdom. A marvelous gift in life is to give another the gift of growth.

SOME COMMON TYPES OF MENTOR COACHING PROGRAMS

Just as there are many unique relationships between the mentor coach and the protégé, there are also a wide variety of programs available. Following are three models for implementing a mentor coach/protégé program.

Unstructured Mentor Coach/Protégé Program

As a beginning step to a formal and structured mentor coach/protégé program, agencies have reassigned some staff who have certain levels of experience as mentor coaches. A list of available mentor coaches is published and protégés self-select with whom they want to work. In this model, it is recommended that the mentor coach not be assigned more than three protégés. The mentor coach goes to the protégé's site, observes, and provides feedback. Then an action plan is developed that usually has a duration of three to six months. This level of programming is useful for skill building.

Structured Mentor Coach/Protégé Program

In the structured mentor program, staff are assigned full time as mentor coaches and are matched to between 10 and 12 protégés. This model works well when the agency is working toward implementing a literacy program with an emphasis on outcomes, has hired a lot of new staff, or is building capacity among existing staff. This model has been used when collaborating with an educational program using vocational education or service learning credits as incentives to the participants.

Formal Leadership Mentor Coach/Protégé Program

Formal leadership programs have been implemented successfully in organizations that are considering transitioning existing staff into more responsible and, eventually, leadership positions. This model is based on the traditional, individualized relationship and involves a more intense relationship. The balance of this text is devoted to the kind of in-depth organizational leadership topics that help develop leadership skills for these individuals. Formal leadership programs involve intense growth, and individuals in these programs should be provided a minimum of a year for the experience. The opportunity for a fellowship, sabbatical, or some type of leave greatly enhances the process, especially if there is the opportunity to shadow the mentor coach. As part of a higher education program, it could become the capstone event in which a project or program is designed and implemented with the assistance of a mentor coach.

From these brief descriptions, many variations can be drawn, and they always should be determined by the needs of the protégé, the agency, and the commitment of time and resources available.

A MENTOR COACHING MODEL FOR AN ORGANIZATION

Crane (2001) developed an effective mentor coaching model. Although most of Crane's work has involved the corporate world, the model lends itself to any organization with little, if any, modification. Early care and education programs must be capable of change and adaptation in order to respond to a variety of environmental, political, and consumer demands. This requires leaders who are adaptable, passionate, and committed to winning the hearts and the minds of the community, parents, and staff; have high energy; and provide an encouraging environment. Table 1–4 lists characteristics of mentor coaches.

TABLE 1–4   MENTOR COACH CHARACTERISTICS

A mentor coach is a person who

- Gets to know another person easily.
- Sets clear expectations about purpose, direction, and needed results.
- Understands human behavior and temperament theory.
- Understands the roles and responsibilities of his or her own position as well as those of the protégé.
- Provides consistent and specific feedback.
- Supports concrete commitments to change.
- Empowers people to contribute at an increasingly higher level of performance.

TRANSFORMATIVE COACHING MODEL

In the transformative coaching model, there are three phases. These are described in Table 1–5.

Without continued mentor coaching and support, new information may not be internalized and the protégé may stumble at the first setback or the information may not be acted on until there is commitment. Crane (2001) comments that the higher-level transformative learning only takes place over a period of time. As one comes to understand the purpose of mentor coaching, it becomes clear that no two mentoring experiences are alike. Mentor coaching must include an individualized approach, which means that each organization, as well as each pair, in the mentor coaching relationship will have its own dynamics and evolutionary path to follow.

TABLE 1–5   TRANSFORMATIVE COACHING MODEL

Phase I: Foundational

The relationship is established in phase I. It is important for the coach and the protégé to meet often enough to establish rapport and appropriate ways of communicating. It is important in this phase to establish the expectations for both parties. What are the goals? What does the protégé expect as a result of the experience? Is the mentor coach prepared? Does he or she have the time to support and nurture the protégé to achieve the expected goal? As with many things, it is important to begin with small, specific, and achievable goals. Build in early successes. If goals are too lofty, the experience may be more likely to fail.

It is always advisable during this phase to actually observe the protégé in the workplace; at meetings; and dealing with children, families, and co-workers. In this phase, it is also important to begin drafting an action plan with timelines that can be modified but that also set the parameters of the experience.

Phase II: Transformative Learning

In phase II, the real "heart" of transformative learning occurs. While the protégé has been listening, observing, reading, and accepting of learning and when the content and process become internalized, the protégé has reached a higher level of performance and understanding.

Phase III: Reflective Dialogue

In phase III, reflective dialogue takes place and the commitment to integrate and act on the new learning becomes apparent.

Source: Adapted from Crane, T. (2001). *The heart of coaching: Using transformational coaching to create a high performance culture.* San Diego: FTA Press. Used with permission.

CASE STUDY: MONTEREY COUNTY MENTOR COACH PROGRAM

"Staff Learning–Children Achieving" is the motto of the Monterey County Office of Education Head Start Mentor Coach Program. Sylvia Campos is one of 11 assigned mentor coaches for an 1,100-children program of whom 80 percent are English language learners. These mentors spend a great deal of time planning. Their basic approach includes the following:

- All new staff and site supervisors have a mentor coach.
- Protégé's choose their mentor coaches.
- Each mentor coach has no more than five protégés.
- Site supervisors meet with mentor coaches at sites different from the one they supervise.
- Mentor coaches and protégés develop appropriate schedules for themselves.

Campos added that observation and reflective practice are the basic tools of the program.

Critical Thinking Questions

1. How would a mentor coach help a new staff member?
2. Why is the ratio of 1:5, mentor coaches to protégés, suggested?
3. Why do site supervisors work with mentor coaches at sites other than the ones they supervise?

SUMMARY

This chapter covered the basics of formal mentor coaching programs. The SAGE model by Bell for mentor coaching was presented. The role of the protégé was discussed. In the present work environment, mentor coaches must keep current in the field. It has been proven that the mentor coach/protégé relationship can be one of the most effective and satisfying means of building capacity in an organization.

Chapter 1 discussed mentor coaching. Chapter 2 provides some suggestions for planning and implementing a mentor coach/protégé program in an early care and education program. Chapters 3 through 10 address topics, such as communication, learning, values, cultural competence, creativity, and emotional intelligence, that might initiate discussions and lead to learning activities.

Someone once described entering the twenty-first century as similar to living in permanent white water. Early care and education staff know the feeling well and, depending on their dispositions, put their energies into damming the waters, ferociously paddling to keep up, or actively scanning for the optimal balance between challenge and safety. Helping staff cultivate dispositions in anticipation of continuous change and challenge enhances their responsiveness to classroom dynamics and sustains their abilities to endure the continual demands and frustrations of their work.

The basic premise of this book is to encourage educators to know themselves, feel valued, and understand the joys of working with young children and their families.

KEY TERMS

Context

Extrinsic

Intervening

Intrinsic

Mnemonic

Retention

Symbiotic

CHAPTER DISCUSSION QUESTIONS

1. What are some of the benefits of participating in a mentor coach relationship?
2. Describe the stages, as presented in the Katz model, that teachers typically experience.
3. Give three reasons for developing a mentor coach/protégé program.
4. Describe three possible challenges of a mentor coach/protégé program.
5. Explain the SAGE model of mentor coaching.
6. Why is it important to set goals and timelines in a mentor coach relationship?

MENTOR COACH/PROTÉGÉ INTERACTION

The beginning of the special relationship between a mentor coach and a protégé should involve the simple opportunity for them to get to know each other. Initial discussions may include both personal and professional information, such as family, educational, and career information. The next step is to explore appropriate goals and activities for the protégé. This also is the time to set up the mechanics of the process: when and where the mentor coach and protégé will meet and how much time can be devoted to the process.

REFLECTIVE PRACTICE

Review Katz's (1995) developmental stages of preschool teachers and determine in what stage the protégé is. What are the demands and expectations of this stage? Then determine what stage the mentor coach is in and discuss this person's demands and expectations of this stage.

■ LEARNING JOURNAL

Write a couple paragraphs about what you have learned as the result of reading this chapter. Can you apply any learning, personally or professionally? Describe any insights or "ah-has" that you have experienced as the result of reading and doing the activities suggested in this chapter.

_____

_____

_____

_____

_____

_____

_____

■ REFERENCES

Bell, C. (2002). *Managers as mentors: Building partnerships for learning.* Mumbai, India: Magna Publishing.

Crane, T. (2001). *The heart of coaching: Using transformational coaching to create a high performance culture.* San Diego: FTA Press.

Fenelon, F. (1994). Riley, P., *Telemachus* (Cambridge texts in the history of political thought). Cambridge University Press.

Gladwell, M. (2005). *Blink: The power of thinking without thinking.* New York: Little, Brown & Company.

Katz, L. (1995). Developmental stages of preschool teachers (pp. 1–8). Urbana-Champaign: University of Illinois, Clearing House on Early Education and Parenting (CEEP).

Skiffington, S., & Zeus, P. (2003). *Behavioral coaching: How to build a sustainable personal and organizational strength.* Sydney, Australia: McGraw-Hill.

Webster. (1999). *New world™ college dictionary* (4th ed.). New York: Macmillan.

■ FURTHER READINGS

A training guide for mentors. (2003). Clemson, SC: National Dropout Prevention Center.

Bellm, D., Whitebrook, M., & Hnatiuk, P. (1997). *The early childhood mentoring curriculum: A handbook for mentors.* Washington, DC: Center for Child Care Workforce.

Carter, M., & Curtis, D. (1994). *The visionary director: A handbook for dreaming, organizing and improvising in your center.* St. Paul, MN: Redleaf Press Resources for Child Caring.

Cohen, N. (2000). *A step-by-step guide to starting effective mentoring program.* Amherst, MA: HRD Press.

Daloz, L. (1986). *Effective teaching and mentoring: Realizing the transformational power of adult learning experiences.* San Francisco: Jossey-Bass.

Gilligan, C. (1982). *In a different voice.* Cambridge, MA: Harvard University Press.

Hart, K., & Schumacher, R. (2005, July). Making the case: Improving Head Start teacher qualifications requires increased investment (Paper 1). Washington, DC: CLASP (Center for Law and Social Policy).

Hayden, J. (1996). *Management of early childhood services: An Australian perspective.* Wentworth Falls, NSW: Social Science Press.

Johnson, W., & Ridley, C. (2004). *The elements of mentoring.* New York: Palgrave Macmillan.

Jorde-Bloom, P. (1997). *Leadership in early care and education.* Washington DC: NAEYC.

MENTOR/National Mentoring Partnership. (2005). *Elements of effective practice: A tool kit* Alexandria, VA: National Mentoring Institute.

Murray, M. (2001). *Beyond the myths and magic of mentoring: How to facilitate an effective mentoring process.* San Francisco: Jossey-Bass.

Nolan, M. (1982). *The effect of mentoring on the life/career paths of California community college administrators.* University of LaVerne, CA: Unpublished manuscript.

Putting the pro in protégé: A guide to mentoring in Head Start and Early Head Start. (2001). American Institute of Research Contract #105-94-2020. Washington, DC: U.S. Department of Health and Human Services Administration on Children, Youth and Families Head Start Publications.

Schein, E. (1972). *Career dynamics: Matching individual and organizational needs.* Essex, England: Pearson Ed EMA Harlow.

STEP-Notes: An instructional design for early literacy mentor-coaches in Head Start and Early Head Start. (2004). Washington, DC: U.S. Department of Health and Human Services Head Start Bureau.

Stoddard, D. (2005). *The heart of mentoring.* Colorado Springs: NavPress.

Zachary, L. (2000). *The mentor's guide: Facilitating effective learning relationships.* San Francisco: Jossey-Bass.

For additional information on research-based practice, visit our Web site at http://www.earlychilded.delmar.com

Additional resources for this chapter can be found on the Online Companion™ at http://www.earlychilded.delmar.com. Special features of this supplement include Web resources, additional case studies with critical thinking questions, and multiple choice quizzes for each chapter. The answers to each quiz, along with the rationale for the correct answers, can also be found on-line.

CHAPTER

2

Mentor Coaching
and Planning

INTRODUCTION

This chapter offers some suggestions for planning a mentor coach/protégé program for an organization. Planning is a necessary part of the process to ensure a successful program because it gives structure and support to the participants and exposes any challenges or unforeseen obstacles. Including top administrators, human resources personnel, and fiscal people as resources in the planning process is important, and staff job descriptions may need to be modified. Obviously, this planning effort should be completed before staff is assigned or hired. Working with an advisory board can significantly contribute to ensuring an effective and successful program by providing resources and helping with training and technical assistance as well as being part of the evaluation process.

■ CHAPTER OBJECTIVES _____

After reading this chapter, you should be able to:

• Identify the key elements in planning for a mentor coach and protégé program.

> "It is good to have an end to journey towards, but it is the journey that matters in the end."
>
> **URSULA K. LEGUIN**

21

- Describe the importance of defining the roles and responsibilities of the mentor coach and protégé.
- Understand the importance of involving and getting the acceptance and approval of the individual's supervisor and the organization's administrators.

THE IMPORTANCE OF PLANNING IN THE MENTOR COACHING PROCESS

■ LITERATURE
A body of written works, selected readings

In an ideal situation, a minimum of three months, and preferably at least six months, should be devoted to the planning phase. There are three distinct phases before implementing a mentor coach/protégé process. In the first phase, participants should allow enough time to research the **literature,** visit existing programs, talk with participants of mentor coaching situations, examine best practices, and decide on a model that works in a particular situation. Every mentor coach/protégé relationship is unique.

■ STAKEHOLDER
A person with an interest in an activity or process

In phase 2 the model is set up. Ideally, there will already have been some dialogue about the process among all the **stakeholders.** Although the core issue of mentor coaching is the relationship, there are always a variety of other considerations. Time and availability for the mentor coach process planning is always an issue. Time and availability then translate into personnel costs and often release time for the protégé, which may mean finding a substitute to cover a classroom. These issues involve budgeting and personnel **allocation.** (See Appendix A for a Sample Budget.) In phase 3, the plan is implemented, which includes developing orientation activities, developing action plans, setting goals and objectives, and determining ways to self-assess, as well as preparing a formal organization evaluation plan before the process begins.

■ ALLOCATION
A portion of resources that are identified and reserved for a purpose

QUESTIONS TO ASK BEFORE STARTING A PROGRAM

When deciding to implement a mentor coach/protégé program, a good place may be to start with the Head Start training manual *Putting the Pro in Protégé: A Guide to Mentoring in Head Start and Early Head Start* (2001). It includes a wealth of resource materials, such as descriptions of several successful programs that are operating nationally, planning strategies, and sample curriculums.

The Head Start Act, as amended October 27, 1998, includes a section (Sec. 648A [b]) describing mentor teachers.

(1) The definition of a Mentor Teacher is an individual responsible for observing and assessing the classroom activities of a Head Start program and providing on-the-job guidance and training to

the Head Start program staff and volunteers in order to improve the qualifications and training of the classroom staff, to maintain high-quality education services, and to promote career development in Head Start programs.

(2) Requirement—In order to assist Head Start agencies in establishing positions for mentor teachers, the Secretary shall:

    (A) Provide technical assistance and training to enable Head Start agencies to establish such a position.

    (B) Give priority consideration in providing assistance pursuant to Subparagraph (A) to Head Start programs that have substantial numbers of new staff, that are experiencing difficulty in meeting applicable education standards, or that lack staff of a similar cultural background to that of the participating children and their families.

    (C) Encourage Head Start programs to give priority considerations for such positions to Head Start teachers at the appropriate level of career advancement in such programs.

    (D) Promote the development of model curricula, designed to ensure the attainment of appropriate competencies of mentor teachers in Head Start programs.

MENTOR COACHING AND THE LOGIC MODEL

A useful planning tool used by universities, nonprofit organizations, and businesses involves a process called the *logic model*. This entails a systems approach of identifying who will be involved, who the recipients of services will be, who will provide services, what will happen and when, and what the outcomes and benefits will be. The University of Wisconsin-Extension, Cooperative Extension, Program Development and Evaluation Department uses the model extensively for program planning and evaluation. The model is illustrated in Table 2–1.

THE MENTOR COACHING LOGIC MODEL

Using this model for a mentor coaching program in a simpler format might look like Figure 2–1.

STRATEGIC PLANNING FOR A MENTOR COACHING PROGRAM

When deciding to implement a mentor coach/protégé program, the key to success is **strategic planning**: Allow a sufficient amount of time for planning before beginning the program. If possible, allow approximately six months to

■ **STRATEGIC PLANNING**
Planning for the future using key elements and timelines

TABLE 2–1   PROGRAM ACTION: THE LOGIC MODEL

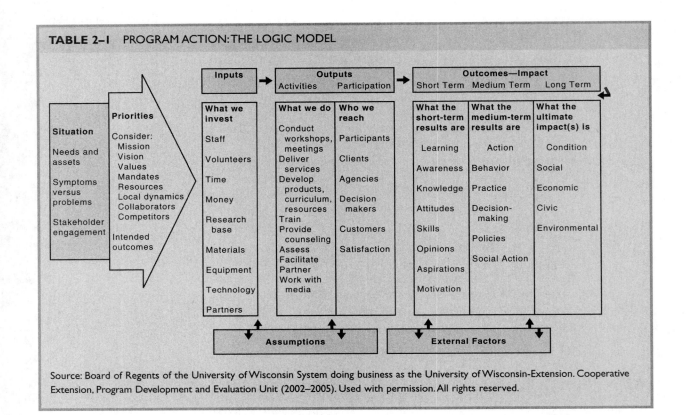

Inputs	Outputs		Outcomes—Impact		
	Activities	Participation	Short Term	Medium Term	Long Term
What we invest	**What we do**	**Who we reach**	**What the short-term results are**	**What the medium-term results are**	**What the ultimate impact(s) is**
Staff	Conduct workshops, meetings	Participants	Learning	Action	Condition
Volunteers	Deliver services	Clients	Awareness	Behavior	Social
Time	Develop products, curriculum, resources	Agencies	Knowledge	Practice	Economic
Money	Train	Decision makers	Attitudes	Decision-making	Civic
Research base	Provide counseling	Customers	Skills	Policies	Environmental
Materials	Assess	Satisfaction	Opinions	Social Action	
Equipment	Facilitate		Aspirations		
Technology	Partner		Motivation		
Partners	Work with media				

Situation

Needs and assets

Symptoms versus problems

Stakeholder engagement

Priorities

Consider:
  Mission
  Vision
  Values
  Mandates
  Resources
  Local dynamics
  Collaborators
  Competitors

Intended outcomes

Assumptions   **External Factors**

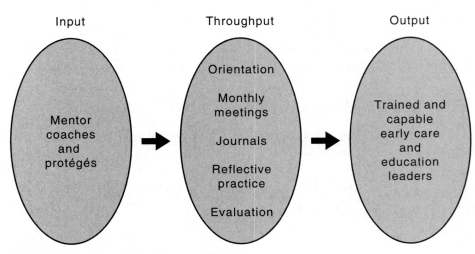

Input   Throughput   Output

Mentor coaches and protégés

Orientation

Monthly meetings

Journals

Reflective practice

Evaluation

Trained and capable early care and education leaders

FIGURE 2–1   Mentor Coaching Logic Model

design the program, implement it, inform stakeholders of the plan, and develop an advisory committee. Three months prior to implementing a program should be allocated to identify the mentor coaches and then match them to the protégés. Allow for some **orientation** and training before the process actually begins.

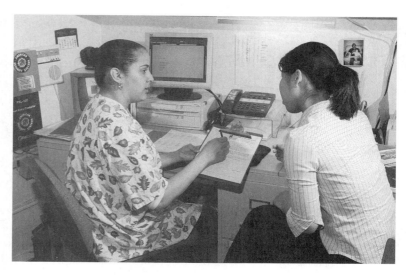

QUESTIONS AND CONSIDERATIONS IN PLANNING FOR A MENTOR COACHING PROGRAM

■ **ORIENTATION**
An overview and introduction

Putting the Pro in Protégé: A Guide to Mentoring in Head Start and Early Head Start (2001) provides a strategic planning tool called "Take Stock!" in which questions and considerations are considered in the following categories:

CASE STUDY: THE TEACHER NEXT DOOR

I have heard the expression: "Good teachers are not born; they are created by the teacher next door." I was really floundering, the children were out of control, and I went home crying just about every day. Gently, Sally, the teacher next door, began to give me quiet little suggestions on how to redirect the children and how to spot a "meltdown" ready to happen. Generously, she met with me once a week over a cup of coffee to listen to my latest woes. Sally always complimented me on something I did well and then offered some constructive feedback on how to do something even better the next time.

Now, 15 years later, I look back and realize if it hadn't been for Sally, my informal mentor, I would probably have left the field and missed 15 wonderful years of working with children and families.

Critical Thinking Questions

1. What seemed to be the most important part of this mentoring relationship?
2. What does the strategy of providing a compliment before providing constructive feedback do for the protégé?
3. What was Sally learning about the mentor coach and protégé process?

■ **EVALUATION**
Criteria for judging
program activities

- planning, coordination, and **evaluation** of mentoring
- identification, selection, and matching of mentors and protégés
- the mentor coach/protégé relationship
- professional development and support for mentors
- identification of individual protégé needs
- organization's commitment and support

Planning, Coordination, and Evaluation of a Mentoring/Coaching Program

Taking the time to plan adequately is essential for a successful mentor coaching program. Six months should be long enough to establish a quality mentor coaching program. If less time is taken, the research, buy-in from stakeholders, and proper orientation will be rushed. Planning is an important first step in establishing a vision and the mission statement for the project.

Identifying and orienting key personnel, as well as setting up a coordination and communication process, is important. It is also valuable in the planning phase to establish an evaluation process that is simple to maintain and yet substantial enough to provide meaningful data. (See Table 2–2.)

When members of an agency take the time to work together, include stakeholders, and diligently answer each of these questions, the project has a better chance of being effective. Using chart paper and having a "recorded memory" of items discussed will assist as time goes on and challenges occur. This recorded memory can assist in determining where the project may have deviated from the original plan.

Identification, Selection, and Matching of Mentor Coaches and Protégés

Along with establishing the vision and mission statement, a system of matching mentor coaches and protégés should be determined. Consider such factors as level of responsibilities, work and learning styles, and time and geographic constraints. (See Table 2–3.)

The matching of the mentor coach and protégé may become more a matter of logistics, time, and geography than really having the ideal partnerships. It is recommended that some type of Learning Styles Survey© or behavioral assessment, such as the DiSC instrument, be used.

It is hoped that some training has been provided for both the mentor coach and the protégé. As part of this training, the importance of relationship building should be stressed with some role modeling, and tips on how to build respect, trust, and good communication should be provided.

TABLE 2–2 PLANNING, COORDINATING, AND EVALUATING
A MENTOR COACHING PROGRAM

Questions	Considerations
How can a mentor coach/protégé project enhance the quality of the program?	Consider ways in which the agency can use a mentor coach/protégé program. Consider how teachers, systems within the agency, and children and families can benefit.
Where can the agency get information to help identify goals for mentoring? How can these resources help?	Consider sources such as performance standards, monitoring reviews, Head Start initiatives, accreditation requirements, and staff and community recommendations.
Based on the assessment, what was learned about the agency's goals for mentoring? How can these sources help?	Consider several goals: retaining qualified teachers, building career ladders, helping teachers develop new skills, and gaining National Association for the Education of Young Children (NAEYC) accreditation.
If a mentor coach/protégé advisory committee is formed, who can serve on it to help the agency develop or strengthen the mentor coach/protégé program? What contributions would they bring?	Consider individuals, such as agency staff or supervisors, community partners, families, parents, and outside consultants.
How can the agency evaluate the mentor coach/protégé process? Who should be involved?	Consider the following: • What kind of information can be collected from mentor coaches, protégés, supervisors, mentor coordinators, families, and outside consultants? • Who can evaluate it? • How can the information be used to improve the program?
How can the agency determine whether goals have been met for the mentor coach/protégé program?	Consider the following: • What kind of information needs to be collected and from where can this information be gathered, for example, performance evaluations, community needs assessments, self-assessments, client satisfaction surveys, and other documents? • Who can conduct the evaluation? • How can the information be used to enhance outcomes?

■ COMPETENCIES
Set of skills that defines
capabilities in a staff
person

TABLE 2–3	IDENTIFYING, SELECTING, AND MATCHING MENTOR COACHES AND PROTÉGÉS
Questions	**Considerations**
What **competencies** and backgrounds will mentor coaches in the agency have?	Consider the following areas: educational background, experience, content knowledge, and mentor coaching skills.
What are some of the issues the agency may face in selecting mentor coaches?	Consider the following: insufficient number of staff to serve as mentors with the agency and having mentors that are classroom teachers or full-time staff, such as supervisors.
How will the agency identify and select mentor coaches?	Consider informal and formal selection procedures.
How will the agency identify and select protégés?	Consider informal and formal selection procedures. Who could benefit the most?

Mentor Coach/Protégé Relationships

Not only is training important in the beginning but it is also important along the way. (See Table 2–4.) Both content and process training should be made available so that all parties can grow in the relationship. Determining the

TABLE 2–4	MENTOR COACH/PROTÉGÉ RELATIONSHIPS
Questions	**Considerations**
What mentor coach/protégé ratios will the organization use?	Consider factors that determine different ratios, such as size of the program, available staff, geographic locations, and use of technology.
How will the organization match mentor coaches and protégés?	Consider criteria and procedures that the agency can use in making matches.
What will be the duration and frequency of the mentor coach/protégé relationship?	Consider factors such as the needs of the protégé, availability of staff, and geographical location.
How can the organization support communication between mentor coaches and protégés?	Consider factors such as time, distance, meeting place, and financial resources.

ratio of mentor coach to protégé is significant. If a mentor coach is over-loaded in the initial stages, the program may be a target for failure. A mentor coach should work with one protégé until he or she feels comfortable. At that time, the mentor coach may wish to add additional protégés; however, a maximum of three protégés to one mentor coach is the recommended ratio.

Professional Development and Support for Mentors

It is important to plan for ongoing professional development and support for both the mentor coach and the protégé. (See Table 2–5.) Mentor coaches have commented that their work can be a lonely business. Identifying resources and building in and compensating for time is key to a successful program. The quality of the program will be commensurate to the level of professional development and support provided.

The planners for each program will design and deliver a mentor coach program in their own unique ways. There is no right or wrong way to run a program. When an organization is beginning a mentor coach program, it may consider using an outside consultant to initiate and provide a "train the trainer" session for an internal staff member and provide materials and technical assistance to help get the program up and running. If an agency uses internal staff to design and implement a program, the planning process may prove to be time consuming and costly.

TABLE 2–5   PROFESSIONAL DEVELOPMENT AND SUPPORT FOR MENTORS

Questions	Considerations
What are the different ways in which the organization can provide mentor training?	Consider the advantages and disadvantages associated with different ways of providing training, such as in-house, by an outside consultant, or by a technical or community college, as well as whether training should be provided to mentor coaches only or to both mentor coaches and protégé.
On what topics should the training focus?	Consider the needs of the protégés and the program and the skills the mentor coaches need.
What kind of ongoing support can the organization provide the mentor coaches?	Consider how to address mentor coach needs, such as resources, time for networking, and further professional development.

Identification of Individual Protégé Needs

Protégés have different needs, depending on the teaching stage of their lives. Is this person only beginning a teaching career? Is he or she a mid-career teacher or preparing to assume a leadership role in the agency? The individual needs of the protégé should begin with the protégé's own assessment of what is needed, and then those needs should be validated and added to by the mentor coach. (See Table 2–6.) If the protégé does not believe that the mentor coaching process is important at this point in her or his career, the process will fail. It is important for the protégé to embrace the program and not simply to accept participation in a program.

As indicated, it is important that the protégé define and state his or her needs. Validating these needs and developing an action plan with support from the mentor coach are necessary to achieve the desired results. If the mentor coach is a senior staff member, the protégé may experience feelings of intimidation and inadequacy that should be addressed early in the process.

The Organization's Commitment and Support

One of the biggest downfalls of programs occurs when well-intentioned staff begin a mentor coaching program without full organizational commitment. Without organizational commitment, the program will falter. All members of the organization must be thoroughly committed to the program. Not only is it important to get approval but it is also critical to keep all staff informed and to provide consistent, timely information on the program's progress.

■ **REFLECTIVE PRACTICE**
Activity in which a mentor coach, supervisor, or peer takes time to listen to another's observations, interactions, or experiences and processes them for appropriateness or makes suggestions on how things might have been handled better

TABLE 2–6   IDENTIFICATION OF INDIVIDUAL PROTÉGÉ NEEDS

Questions	Considerations
What strategies can the organization use to identify mentor content?	Consider how to use the various types of assessments (observations, supervisor recommendations, performance evaluations, and self-assessments) and the value that each brings to the process.
What mentoring strategies will work for this organization? What can the organization do to support these mentoring strategies?	Consider a variety of strategies that would support **reflective practice,** such as using a journal, discussing case studies, and problem solving, and the resources needed to implement them.

TABLE 2–7 ORGANIZATION'S COMMITMENT AND SUPPORT

Questions	Considerations
How can the organization integrate mentor coaching into its overall operations? What financial resources are available to build and strengthen the mentor coach program?	Consider how other organizations can collaborate to support this effort.
What are the potential monetary resources?	Develop a budget in order to allocate any available funds.
Who can be responsible for coordinating the mentor coach program for the organization?	Consider creating a full-time mentor coach **coordinator** position—or at least a part of a position. Consider what qualifications and responsibilities would be involved.

■ **COORDINATOR**
Designated person responsible for a program's activities

Mentor coaching should not be considered an "add-on." Rather, it should be integrated into the program and management design and be reflected as part of the agency's self-assessment and community needs assessment. What identified needs will be filled by having a mentor coaching program? (See Table 2–7.)

SUMMARY OF A PLANNING PROCESS

Each organization will have other considerations in addition to those provided in the preceding tables. It is important to involve a human resources staff person in the planning of a mentor coaching program because these activities affect job responsibilities and may suggest the need to alter job descriptions. There are also important considerations involved if there is labor union representation. It is important to consider a budget. Has money been allocated for the program? Often, it will be necessary to approach outside funding resources. There are real costs involved and ignoring them could set the stage for failure of the program.

STEPS IN A QUALITY MENTOR COACHING PROCESS

During the planning phase, it is important to decide on a model or process that works for each unique mentor coach/protégé relationship. There is no one right way, and several different approaches could be combined to accommodate the goals and objectives desired. Following is a five-step process that covers everything from starting the process to completion.

Five-Step Mentor Coaching Process*

■ INITIATION

Beginning of an activity without instructions or direction

1. The **initiation** process considers the following:
   - Why are we doing this?
   - What are the goals and objectives?
   - What are the constraints and barriers to this effort?
   - What are the roles and responsibilities of both parties?
   - What learning and skill development will take place?
   - How will change affect the mentor coach and the protégé?
   - How will change affect the early care and education classroom?
   - How will change affect the organization?
   - What kind of feedback and evaluation are needed for whom and when?
   - How should differences be resolved and the process terminated?

   Some of these questions probably will not be answerable until after the process begins; however, they should be referred to and answers developed.

2. Observation strategies should include having a dialogue about the following:
   - The mentor coach observes the protégé in some type of action or practice.
   - The protégé observes the mentor coach in some type of action or practice.
   - The protégé involves self in some type of self-assessment.
   - The mentor coach and protégé observe aspects of the system and environment.

   Another source of dialogue can be developed by participating in some kind of action. This could include the following suggested strategies; however, many others could be developed that provide a rich dialogue between the mentor coach and protégé.

3. Some actions that could take place include the following:
   - The mentor coach could model a skill for the protégé.

*Adapted from Hanft, B., Rush, D., & Shelden, M. (2004). *Coaching families and colleagues in early childhood* (p. 60). Baltimore, MD: Paul H. Brookes Publishing Co.

- The protégé could practice using an existing or new skill after discussing it with the mentor coach.
- The protégé could experience a behavior, issue, or situation that results in a dialogue with the mentor coach.
- The mentor coach could anticipate a behavior, issue, or experience to discuss with the protégé prior to the event.

4. Reflective practice as a learned skill can be one of the richest areas of learning and capacity–building. Using this strategy, the mentor coach assists the protégé in determining what he or she already knows or what can be discovered by the mentor coach asking the right questions. These open-ended questions can be as simple as the following:

- What do you want to accomplish?
- How did you decide where to focus?
- What have you tried? What did you do?
- How could you do it differently?
- How will you know when you are successful?

The mentor coach can open the dialogue with the protégé using some of these questions as well as other open-ended questions in order to stimulate the protégé's thought processes and add a dimension that allows for new learning.

5. Be sure to include evaluation. Following are some additional suggestions for the mentor coach/protégé interaction. The value of this process is to "stretch" both the mentor coach and the protégé to try new ways of doing things, not to repeat things previously used. In the spirit of continuous improvement, constantly ask what could be done differently, what could be added, or what could be removed to make the children's and the teacher's experiences better.

- Provide feedback on observation and/or action.
- Share information, resources, and supports (as necessary).
- Confirm the understanding of the protégé.
- Review what has been accomplished.
- Plan new observations or actions and strategies to implement between mentor coaching sessions.

Journal writing as a tool for self-reflection has proven to be very effective for several reasons. It is one of the ways that the protégé can bring dreams into reality. There are different formats for journal writing. At the end of each chapter, there are brief directions for a "Learning Journal," a very simple running log capturing what has been learned both from readings and meeting

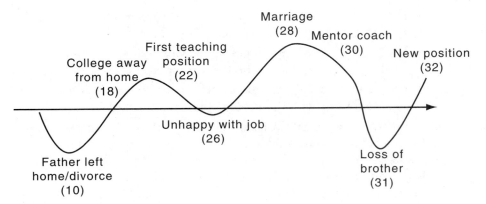

FIGURE 2–2 Journaling with a Lifeline

with the mentor coach. This will serve as a way to record the discussions and ideas that are covered during the mentor coaching session.

A decision up front needs to be made about whether this journal will remain a private matter for the protégé only or whether it will be something shared with the mentor coach. This is a decision that the protégé should make.

There are additional types of journaling that can enrich the protégé's experience. One type of journaling involves an autobiographical look at identifying moments, such as educational experiences, marriage, and child raising (see Figure 2–2).

This type of journaling requires reflecting on events, writing about how one coped with various situations, for example, what did not work in a first teaching position, what was involved in the positive times, and what was learned during the mentor coaching process that will assist in being successful in the new position?

Other exercises with journaling can encourage a person to transcend self-limiting beliefs and emotions. This kind of journaling is best when shared with the mentor coach to help evaluate actions that are merely reactions to life or those that involve proactive learning.

Evaluation includes the following:

Review—Decide what the goals and objectives of the program are and decide on a timeline for completion of them as well as when reviews will occur. Decide who needs what kind of information and when.

Self-assessment—Take a "slice in time" periodically just to update and see if the process is moving in a forward direction.

Periodic informal and formal feedback—Let the supervisors and administrators share in the informal and formal feedback sessions or provide them with written summaries. Keeping them informed will ensure the availability of resources needed to continue the project.

Final report—The final report should be personal and directed to administration, including human resources and fiscal. Being able to present a return on investment (ROI) is helpful in supporting the continuation of the program. It is important to decide before beginning a mentor coach/protégé program, perhaps with the assistance of an advisory group, when and what items and data will be needed for normative reports along the way and a summative report at the end.

EVALUATION TOOLS

Mentor coaching as a process is difficult to define because it cannot be quantified. As previously indicated, each mentor coach/protégé relationship is unique and the participants will experience the process in unique ways. One standard way of evaluating process outcomes involves interviews. The mentor coach can conduct interviews at the beginning of the process, during the process, and then six months after closure. The variables need to be decided on, as well as the method of recording them.

Self-reports—Self-reports can be included as part of the learning journal, adding specific topics asking the protégé to identify personal views that have shifted or new ways of responding to daily issues.

Rating by others—The use of learning instruments and 360-degree feedback could be useful for providing constructive feedback for the protégé and an objective way for the mentor coach to redirect activities.

Direct observation—In direct observation, the protégé is actually shadowed, or observed while engaged in performing specific tasks. The mentor coach then provides critiques and feedback on these activities.

FREQUENTLY USED TRAINING TOPICS AND ACTIVITIES

During the planning phase, it is advisable to set some goals and objectives for the overall program. Goals and objectives are part of the mentor coach/protégé action plan. Identifying resources for providing training and technical assistance can help the developing relationship in the program proceed smoothly. Following are some basic considerations that will assist organizations in implementing programs.

Introduction to Mentoring

In the beginning, it is important to discuss with the staff their perceptions of mentoring. Most people have encountered some type of mentoring, and not all of their experiences will have been positive; these views should be expressed and discussed. Other items to define and discuss include the following:

- goals and purposes of the mentoring program
- definition of mentoring
- roles and responsibilities of mentor coaches and protégés
- balancing mentor coach responsibilities with other responsibilities
- assessing mentor coaching behaviors

Adult Learning Theory

An awareness of adult learning theory will differentiate the mentor coaching relationship from a training or staff development exercise. Adult learning theory ensures that multiple learning approaches are used, thereby limiting the amount of lecture and maximizing experiential activities. Examples of topics to be discussed include the following:

- stages and phases in adult development
- teacher development
- characteristics of adult learners
- learning styles

Reflective Practice

Reflective practice is an excellent habit to establish early in the process. It encourages the development of rich dialogue that creates opportunities to explore thoughts and feelings in depth; to look at things differently; to understand and manage challenges; and to discuss what went well, what did not happen that the teacher hoped would happen, and what could be done differently the next time. Following are a few items to consider when introducing reflective practices:

- definition
- journal writing
- reflective dialogue

Diversity

In the close interpersonal relationships that develop in a classroom, the adults need to appreciate each other's backgrounds and customs. Similarities between backgrounds are the best place to start a discussion and come to an understanding and appreciation of each other. Two other items for discussion include the following:

- recognizing the importance of diversity
- understanding differences in order to respect differences

Change Process

It is important to discuss and understand how change will be a part of the mentor coach/protégé process. How and when will change occur? What will it look like? How will you know things have changed? Change is a core topic and happens as the result of an effective mentor coach relationship. Change always infers some kind of loss. Discuss the following topics, emphasizing that change can cause strong feelings, but that, in the end, change helps everyone grow and develop and is a positive part of the process:

- the mentor coach as change agent
- understanding and managing change
- changes in the mentor coach process

PROTÉGÉ SKILLS

Identifying and validating the protégé's skill sets can provide a good starting point for additional work and assist in establishing an action plan. Spending time exploring the protégé's strengths and establishing a baseline to measure growth is important for the protégé's acceptance of the mentoring process. Following are several topics for discussion:

- strategies for understanding self
- determining goals and objectives for self
- examining expected outcomes and results

Mentor Coach Skills

The mentor coach drives the mentoring process. Role modeling effective priority setting, time management, organizational skills and leadership, and expertise are crucial. The mentor coach should not be the protégé's supervisor. The person responsible for evaluating staff is not the same one with whom the protégé will want to share personal weaknesses and fears. If the supervisor is the only one available, then a discussion to set parameters distinguishing the two functions will be needed. Alternating with another supervisor is another strategy that has been used to avoid pairing a mentor coach with someone he or she supervises. A mentor coach needs to bring the following supervisory skills into her or his interactions with the protégé:

- understanding how to set effective long- and short-term goals
- understanding boundaries
- reinforcing mutual respect and trust
- collaborating for conflict resolution
- providing and receiving feedback
- time management and schedules

Communication Skills

Perhaps the single most important skill for the mentor coach and protégé to work together on is establishing clear written and spoken communications. Ultimately, this will determine the success of the relationship and is a key skill for leadership in the field. Communication involves two people; one is the sender and the other is the receiver. Clear messages with clarification questions will promote healthy, in-depth dialogue. Critical points to consider when discussing the importance of communication include the following:

- active listening
- assertiveness
- conflict resolution
- collaborative problem solving
- writing and observation skills
- sharing information verbally and nonverbally

■ MODELING SKILLS
Activities that demonstrate how to correctly perform or teach

Modeling Skills

The most subtle and least understood gift that the mentor coach can pass on to the protégé is that of being a role model. The importance of appearance, how to behave in a one-to-one relationship as well as in group and community settings, is vital. The mentor coach must realize how powerful this modeling can be. Often, it is as powerful as the spoken word, if not more so. Mentor coaches should learn how to

- understand and observe role modeling
- receive effective feedback

Observation and Conferencing Skills

Knowing how to observe and assess children's behaviors is the key to effective classroom management. The mentor coach and protégé should agree on and explore different ways of observation and assessment while working with children. What methods and assessments will be used? Are they targeted to the outcomes and results desired? Discuss the following and establish clear guidelines:

- pre- and postobservation conferences
- data collection and analysis
- observation
- assessment strategies

■ **CONFERENCING SKILLS**
A two-way conversation that allows each person to contribute ideas

Self-Assessment Skills

Self-assessment should continually be a part of the self-reflection process in order to validate and support the mentor coach/protégé process. There are many different methods and instruments that can be used. Following are some self-assessment tools that could be considered:

- strategies for self-assessment: journal writing, portfolios, checklists.
- classroom and environmental ratings, Early Childhood Environmental Rating Scale (ECERS) by Harms, T., Clifford, R., & Cryer, D. (2005), revised ed.
- the Program Administrator's Scale (PAS) by Talan, T., & Jorde-Bloom, P. (2004).
- the Learning Success System© by Nolan, M. (1998) (discussed in further depth in Chapter 6)

■ **SELF-ASSESSMENT SKILLS**
Methods of looking at how one is viewed by others as well as understanding one's own work and behavioral style

Leadership and Advocacy Skills

The path to leadership in early care and education is clearly defined. Mentor coaching is the one strategy and process that can successfully ignite leadership and advocacy in the field. The mentor coach can introduce the protégé to appropriate people, situations, or events; provide networking opportunities; and sponsor the protégé in professional organizations. Following are some of the ways that this can be done:

- advocating in the community
- making board presentations

- using the media, newspaper, radio, and television
- developing *capacity* and quality in the field of early care and education

Curriculum

Once a mentor coaching program has been implemented and is running successfully, other **initiatives** and curriculum can be introduced more easily. A few to consider are as follows:

- literacy
- parent–mentor programs
- fatherhood initiatives

This list of topics is, of course, in no way exhaustive; however, it includes some of the most frequently covered topics in mentor coach/protégé programs.

■ INITIATIVES
Set of authorizations promoted by an organization for programs and activities that support an approach

SOME RECENT MENTOR COACH/PROTÉGÉ INITIATIVES

In April 2002, President George W. Bush launched an early childhood initiative known as Good Start, Grow Smart. The effort addressed three issues: strengthening Head Start; partnering with states to improve early childhood education; and providing information to teachers, caregivers, and parents. Good Start, Grow Smart identifies children's early literacy as the key focus for Head Start program improvement. In response, the Head Start Bureau developed and implemented a comprehensive, multifaceted, and sequential professional development endeavor known as Strategic Teacher Education Program (STEP). Its purpose is to ensure that all teachers engage in research-based strategies to support children's early literacy and social and emotional development, which, in turn, will lead to positive child outcomes and school readiness. STEP was designed to enhance the quality, **intentionality,** and effectiveness of staff interactions with children and families. During the summer of 2002, a major training effort occurred for more than 3,000 Head Start staff and 100 state early childhood administrators nationally. The participants experienced 32 hours of training covering the following topics:

■ INTENTIONALITY
Having a focus or an intention

- phonological awareness
- book knowledge and appreciation
- print awareness and concepts

- listening and understanding
- speaking and communicating
- early writing
- Alphabet knowledge

The participants, known as early literacy mentor coaches, were charged with returning to their programs to provide similar training to their classroom colleagues. In fall 2002, the Head Start Bureau reconvened the participants from the first effort, STEP I. Building on their knowledge and experience, there was a renewed focus on the mentor coach process as well as two additional strands. The first strand was a 32-hour training program, "Developing Children's Social and Emotional Competence," the topic of which was thought to be an essential piece to any early literacy efforts. This program was designed and presented by the Center on the Social and Emotional Foundations for Early Learning at the University of Illinois. The training has four components:

- building positive relationships
- classroom prevention practices
- social and emotional teaching strategies
- individualized intensive interventions

In the second strand, STEP II, training was designed and presented to mentor coach attendees by the National Center for Family Literacy. This program was initiated and described in a Head Start Information Memo (IM) ACYF-IM-HS-00-25. According to the initiative, Head Start agencies were to assess the family literacy activities in which they were presently engaged. Participants were asked to consider four family literacy elements. Does your program provide all four family literacy elements?

1. interactive activities between parent and child
2. training for parents, as the prime educators for their children
3. age-appropriate education for their child
4. literacy training for parents that leads to economic self-sufficiency

Is the program taking advantage of opportunities to connect and integrate these elements:

- Is discussion of family literacy needs, assets, goals, and available resources a regular part of the family partnership agreement process in the program?
- Does the program make active efforts to support children and families so that they participate in family literacy services with sufficient intensity and duration to make sustainable impacts?

- Does the program monitor and assess the progress of families and children in terms of increasing confidence and competencies in family literacy and emergent literacy?
- Are there identifiable gaps in family literacy services, missing connections among components, or a need to improve the quality of services?

As a result of the family literacy initiative and along with the Good Start, Grow Smart efforts, the Head Start Bureau contracted with the National Family Literacy Center to design and deliver a 32-hour family literacy training program. The training focused on supporting parents in their roles as their children's most important teachers. The stated goals for the program were as follows:

- to develop a better understanding of family literacy services
- to become more familiar with and increase utilization of relevant research and strategies in the development of family literacy services
- to support and enhance services to children that promote language and early literacy development
- to support and enhance services to parents that support them in providing meaningful language and literacy experiences for their children
- to support and enhance the capability to better identify quality adult education/English as a second language (ESL) services in local communities
- to support and enhance program capability to develop stronger partnerships with adult education providers to ensure that retention strategies are identified, developed, and implemented and to better integrate adult education with other literacy services
- to support and enhance the capacity of programs to integrate family literacy goals, including adult education, into the ongoing family partnership agreements

There are four components of the training. The first focuses on age-appropriate early literacy practices in the classroom; the last three focus on parents and their roles in developing their children's language and learning.

1. Early literacy practices in the classroom: This section examines the environment, assessing the environment with a literacy checklist, understanding and providing age-appropriate resources, and affirming the good practices that are already in existence.
2. Parents and children learning together: This section emphasizes interactive literacy activities between parent and child, as well as the importance of the parent as the primary teacher in the child's life and as the full partners in the education of the child.

3. Importance of parents' literacy backgrounds: This section addresses the importance of education and parents' literacy training in their economic self-sufficiency. It also addresses connecting and developing partnerships with adult education and community college offerings.

4. A systematic approach: Finally, "putting it all together," or taking the pieces and developing a systematic process for the program to coordinate, plan for, and deliver family literacy services.

In June 2004, in the next phase of the STEP process, the National Center for Family Literacy introduced their Parent–Mentor Program and, since then, has been crisscrossing the country with parent training sessions of 35 to 50 parents at a time. (See Figure 2–3.) This two-and-a-half-day seminar explores with parents and their children, using the acronym and icon of an apple, the following concepts for developing early literacy:

- **a**lphabet knowledge
- **p**honological awareness
- **p**rint awareness and book knowledge
- **l**anguage development
- **e**arly writing

After training, the parent-mentors are expected to return to the Head Start programs and communities and, in small groups or even one-on-one, share the early literacy techniques they have learned.

STEPS TO SUCCESS: 2005/2006 MENTOR COACHING INITIATIVE

In a February 2005 Webcast, E. Dollie Wolverton, Chief of Educational Services, Head Start Bureau, announced a program called Steps to Success that is an extension of the previous STEP efforts. Wolverton provided an instructional framework for early literacy mentor coaches. This Webcast has since been followed up with an IM of October 10, 2005, from the Head Start

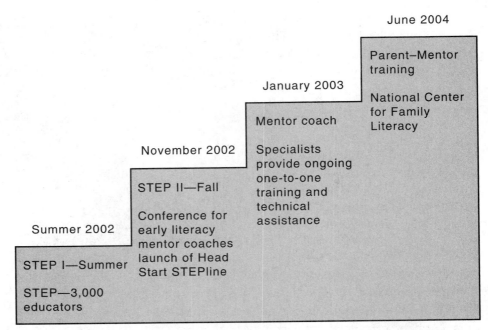

FIGURE 2–3   Steps to Success: Mentor Coaching Initiative for Head Start and Early Head Start

Bureau outlining the purposes and the expectations for the mentor coach program. At this time no additional funds have been appropriated to continue the initiative; however, all Head Start programs are expected to attend training sessions and implement a mentor coach program. The stated vision of the *Steps to Success* program is as follows:

1. to prepare mentor coaches and help them refine their mentor coaching skills and increase their knowledge about effective interactions with protégés and other adults
2. to promote positive early literacy and language development outcomes for children from birth to age five

The *Steps to Success* program includes four units in the instructional design, a tutored video instructional supplement, and a Decision-Maker's Guide. (See Table 2–8.)

STEPS TO SUCCESS DECISION-MAKER'S GUIDE

The Steps to Success Decision-Maker's Guide has been designed to assist those involved in preparing and implementing programs. The guide has five topics as outlined in Table 2–9.

TABLE 2–8   STEPS TO SUCCESS INSTRUCTIONAL DESIGN

Unit 1: Building Relationships to Promote Child Literacy Outcomes

      Module 1: Getting ready for early literacy mentor coaching (ELMC)

      Module 2: Effective ELMC and protégé relationships

      Module 3: Supporting protégés in changing practice

      Module 4: Early literacy mentor coaching and supervision

Literacy Focus: Book knowledge and appreciation

                Print awareness and concepts

Unit 2: Observation and Staff Analysis

      Module 1: Getting ready for observation and analysis

      Module 2: Observation and analysis

      Module 3: Making some observations/data/postobservations

      Module 4: Achieving reliability in observation

Literacy Focus: Early writing and alphabet knowledge

Unit 3: Reflective Practice

      Module 1: Getting ready for reflection

      Module 2: Using reflection

      Module 3: Reflective writing strategies

      Module 4: Building communities of learners

Literacy Focus: Listening and understanding

              Speaking and communicating

Unit 4: Using Child Assessment Information to Guide Instruction

      Module 1: Getting ready for assessment

      Module 2: Helping staff use child and classroom information for planning

      Module 3: Individualizing instruction for children

      Module 4: Adaptations for children

Literacy Focus: Phonological awareness

Each module has a cover page that outlines the context, learning outcomes, and exercises. The modules also contain

- presentations
- videoclips
- group discussions and activities
- on-line discussions
- exercises

TABLE 2–9   STEPS TO SUCCESS DECISION-MAKER'S GUIDE

1. Selecting a model for an early literacy mentor coach program

2. Finding financial resources for an early literacy mentor coach program

3. Selecting and matching mentor coaches and protégés

4. Orientation and training for mentor coaches

5. Linking an early literacy mentor coaching program to an existing program management system

(See Appendix B, Steps to Success Decision-Maker's Checklist.)

MENTOR COACH/PROTÉGÉ ORIENTATION

Participants in mentor coach/protégé programs often consider the amount of planning time, resources, and an orientation session that contribute to a successful program. Orientation can be as brief as a couple of hours or as involved as a three-day comprehensive orientation session. The modules are designed for two-hour segments to allow for flexibility in the presentation. This orientation is also designed to provide a hybrid learning session that includes a combination of on-site and on-line training. Following is a sample module.

Module 1: Introduction to the Mentor Coaching and Protégé Program

Day 1

Introductions and overview of program

Energizer: "Dinner Party" Activity (The facilitator asks the group to work in pairs.)

Directions: Think about a famous person you would like to sit next to at a dinner party. This person can be dead or alive, famous or unknown. What would you talk about and why does this person interest you?

Have participants report back and post answers on a flip chart. Comment on types of questions and trends. Relate these to leadership traits.

The following modules may be scheduled as parts of day 1, at other convenient times, or as on-line work.

Two-hour module

- Definitions of mentoring
- Handout

- List experiences with mentoring. What did it feel like? What results and changes in life or work occurred? In a second column, list experiences that involved mentoring someone else. What did it feel like? What results or changes in the protégé's life occurred?

Two-hour module

- Examine the role of the organization.
- Have an administrator lead a discussion on the vision and mission of the organization.
- Have participants work in small groups and generate three to five strategies for mentor coaching and the reasons they will align with the vision and mission of the organization.

Two-hour module

- Understand yourself and others.
- Use a self-assessment profile, and discuss the mentor coach's and the protégé's personal and work behavioral styles.
- Match the mentor coaches to protégés and allow time to discuss goals and objectives.

Two-hour module

- The mentor coach and protégé meet and work together to develop an action plan and a presentation to administrative staff.

Two-hour module

- Present the action plan to the advisory group and administration.

Two-hour module

- Develop an evaluation process, timeline, and recognition ceremony.

■ **PRO FORMA BUDGET**
A budget that estimates future costs

SUMMARY

This chapter covered several aspects of planning that may be beneficial for a mentor coach/protégé program. The use of an advisory board is recommended. Several items were presented for consideration as well as topics frequently used for orientation and training. Planning for evaluation and using a combination of tools is effective in helping others see the value of a mentor coach program.

■ KEY TERMS

Allocation	Literature
Competencies	Modeling skills
Conferencing skills	Orientation
Coordinator	Pro forma budget
Evaluation	Reflective practice
Initiation	Self-assessment skills
Initiatives	Stakeholder
Intentionality	Strategic planning

■ CHAPTER DISCUSSION QUESTIONS

1. Describe why planning is an important part of a mentor coach program.
2. What line items might be used in a **pro forma budget** for a mentor coach/protégé program?
3. List and briefly describe three training topics that might be used for both the mentor coach and protégé.
4. Why is journaling an important tool in a mentor coach program?
5. Describe three evaluation tools.
6. How could an advisory board assist the mentor coach program?

■ MENTOR COACH/PROTÉGÉ INTERACTION

The mentor coach and protégé can develop an action plan. The action plan should include a minimum of three goals and objectives. In addition, timelines should be included, along with resources that may available and when the two meet again.

■ REFLECTIVE PRACTICE

A mentor coach coordinator is in the middle of giving a presentation to 10 top administrators in an organization. Cell phones begin to ring and the administrators start getting up and leaving the session. What are your recommendations to the coordinator?

■ LEARNING JOURNAL

Write a couple paragraphs about what you have learned as a result of reading this chapter. Can you apply any learning, personally or professionally? Describe any insights or "ah-has" that you have experienced as the result of reading and doing the activities suggested in this chapter.

_____

_____

_____

_____

_____

_____

■ REFERENCES

Hanft, B., Rush, D., & Sheldon, M. (2004). *Coaching families and colleagues in early childhood.* Baltimore, MD: Paul H. Brookes.

Head Start Act. (Amended 1998). Washington, DC: U.S. Department of Health and Human Services, Administration for Children and Families, Head Start Bureau.

Putting the pro in protégé: A guide to mentoring in Head Start and Early Head Start. (2001). Washington, DC: American Institute for Research. Head Start Bureau Publication #105-98-2080.

Steps to success: An instructional design for early literacy mentor-coaches in Head Start and Early Head Start. (2005). Washington, DC: U.S. Department of Health and Human Services, Head Start Bureau Publications.

■ FURTHER READINGS

Bell, C. (2002). *Managers as mentors: Building partnerships for learning.* Mumbai, India: Magna House.

Bellm, D., Whitebrook, M., & Hnatiuk, P. (1997). *The early childhood mentoring curriculum: A handbook for mentors.* Washington, DC: Center for Child Care Workforce.

Carter, M., & Curtis, D. (1994). *Training teachers: A harvest of theory and practice.* St. Paul, MN: Redleaf Press.

Content-Focused Mentoring Program. (2000). [Pamphlet]. Newton, MA: Education Development Center, Inc.

Dodge, D. T., & Colker, L. J. (1988). *The creative curriculum for early childhood teaching strategies.* Washington, DC: Teaching Strategies, Inc.

Wincek, J., & O'Malley, C. (1995). *Taking hold of the future: The abc's of strategic planning.* Washington, DC: National Catholic Educational Association.

For additional information on research-based practice, visit our Web site at http://www.earlychilded.delmar.com

Additional resources for this chapter can be found on the Online Companion™ at http://www.earlychilded.delmar.com. Special features of this supplement include Web resources, additional case studies with critical thinking questions, and multiple choice quizzes for each chapter. The answers to each quiz, along with the rationale for the correct answers, can also be found on-line.

CHAPTER

3

Mentor Coaching and Leadership

INTRODUCTION

Leadership is one of those difficult concepts to capture in a summary sentence. However, everyone has the opportunity to be a leader in the home, workplace, and community. Leadership involves many things in many different settings, as the context and the nature of work differ. Leadership, even in the field of early care and education, can be quite varied. Leadership, simply stated, is the process whereby two people are involved in reaching a goal—one leads, the other follows.

Is leadership an innate quality with which a person is born, as identified in the "great person" theory, or can leadership be developed? This remains a topic for discussion. What is known is that there is no one, clearly defined model of leadership; there is no clear path of how leadership is developed in the field of early care and education. In fact, most leadership seems to emerge accidentally as responsibilities are thrust on a person.

The position of this author is that leadership can and must be developed, even though society tends to support only the status quo: Do not try anything new, it may fail. Yes, new ideas may fail, but new experiences serve to promote growth and innovation.

> "We were born to make manifest the glory of God that is within us, it is not just in some of us; it is in everyone. And as we let our own light shine, we unconsciously give other people permission to do the same. As we are liberated from our own fear, our presence automatically liberates others."
>
> **NELSON MANDELA**

■ LEADERSHIP
A set of skills that allows a person to lead a team of individuals to collectively work toward a goal

Consciously developing and working with a protégé toward successful leadership can be one of the most rewarding opportunities experienced by both the mentor coach and the protégé.

■ CHAPTER OBJECTIVES

After reading this chapter, you should be able to:

- Understand and describe how the mentor coaching/protégé process and leadership are linked.
- Understand and describe the leadership skills needed in order to be a successful leader in the field of early care and education.
- Understand and describe the cycle of leadership development.

HISTORICAL VIEW OF LEADERSHIP

■ ORGANIZATIONAL BEHAVIOR
A unified group of elements creating a systematized whole that describes behaviors in an organization

According to a historical perspective of leadership in early care and education, most of the theory building and understanding of leadership is based on business and **organizational behavior** models. There are some key concepts and models on which early care and education can expand. Borrowing from these fields sheds light on how to effectively develop managers and leaders.

In the 1920s, business management was associated with Frederick Taylor's scientific management, a command-and-control approach that focused on management style, personnel production, and finance. Fayol (1916) built on Taylor's (1919) scientific management theories and contributed the concepts of systemizing work, job roles, and responsibilities with time and motion studies. Organizations today still reflect some of these basic concepts.

World War II ushered in an era of assembly lines, mass production, and women working shoulder-to-shoulder in the workforce. The dynamics of the war demands for airplanes, ships, and equipment fueled the need for child care centers near or at the work sites, for example, at the Kaiser Steel Company.

In the twenty-first century, technological and world changes are creating new types of and concerns about leadership styles. What is leadership? Can leadership be developed? Leadership now is multifaceted and requires many skills. The skills include, but are not limited to, managing people, sales, and marketing, as well as paying particular attention to return on investment (ROI), including increasing profits by adding value, measuring results, and attending to financial issues. These components all contribute to the present-day field of management and leadership.

Organizational behavior was marked initially by management efforts to increase productivity through time and motion studies. Eventually, the research showed that the difference in productivity had less to do with equipment and environmental arrangements than how workers were organized and treated by management. Studies evolved that considered trait styles of managers and leaders. An overarching question revolves around the "great person" leadership theory, which suggests that some people are genetically disposed to being great leaders. Some favor the theory that a crisis or situation creates a leader. The discussion continues on these two ways of thinking about leadership.

According to Sullivan (2003), leadership in its simplest form involves two people, one person leading and the other following. A leader intentionally must want to influence another person in order to have some change take place. Early care and education staff are predominantly women. Women on the whole are not educated or acculturated to consider themselves as leaders, yet the traits needed for leadership are the same that a good teacher uses with her children. This is an argument for leadership development and having a mentor coach program. Another reason for a mentor coach program is the fact that the early care and education field is often undervalued by society. The pay is low and static, there are few entry requirements, and there are even fewer opportunities for professional development and training.

The early care and education community has not developed a clearly articulated view of leadership, and few classroom staff understand that they are already operating with the traits needed for leadership. Teaching staff provide encouraging, empowering, and supportive learning environments so each child in a classroom has the opportunity to learn. In the mentor coaching/protégé process, the veteran teacher guides newcomers along. This leadership model fuels the generational process of giving and improving child care.

Myths abound for leadership in early care and education. For instance, it is a myth that anyone can be a program director, that all you need is some teaching experience in a classroom and to be a nice person. Much more is required of a director, who must fill multiple roles and handle the daily interface with a variety of people. There is also a myth that there is one right way to be a supervisor because the nature of the work is supervising people. The program director has to be flexible: Some teachers want a lot of directions; others prefer to find solutions to their own challenges. The type of setting, the children and families served, the behavioral style of the program director, as well as other variables, all affect how a program operates.

Leaders are described in many ways—from servants to those who forge ahead guiding the way. Leaders can be described as architects, catalysts, advocates, prophets, mediators, and coaches. Leaders may be considered poets, looking at their work settings from a variety of perspectives. Leaders can be designers and stewards building the community. Leaders are learners, performers, power brokers, and role models.

A leadership development process in early care and education can be enhanced greatly by using the mentor coach/protégé process. In trying to delineate the leadership development process and develop successful leaders, many factors must be considered. One of the first issues to understand is the difference between a leader and a manager in an organization. According to Bennis and Goldsmith (1997), a good manager tends to do things right; a leader does the right thing. Successful leaders try to understand and conquer context. Leaders investigate reality and develop plans, goals, and visions; managers accept others' directives and implement them without questioning. Leading is about effectiveness; managing is about efficiency. Leadership is about innovating and initiating; managing is about maintaining the status quo. A leader is her own person; a manager is a "good soldier." A leader has an eye on the horizon; a manager is looking at the bottom line. A leader has the capacity to bring people to a new place through a vision of what can be. This "pull" kind of leadership attracts and energizes people.

Leadership is about the reinvention of self. Each leader is unique, and there is no one direct path to a leadership position. Most leaders have experienced failure at some point as part of the development process. A failure tempers the soul and develops in a person the resilience to access and execute successfully even bigger challenges.

"Leadership is about knowing oneself and being able to re-invent oneself for the tasks on hand. It can be an intense journey softened by a mentor coach who guides and encourages while lighting the path along the way." According to Bennis and Goldsmith (*Learning to Lead: A Workbook on Becoming a Leader,* 1997, p. 22), during the self-reflection process, a person is encouraged to review both successes and failures, resolving to learn from both. Keeping a journal is helpful in the self-reflection process. A journal can be as simple as a running log of thoughts and events; it need not be concerned with format or even grammar. Simply writing down thoughts and ideas is helpful. The first thing in the morning is often a good time to do this. After awhile, as you review your notes, you will see patterns and repeated events emerging that will have meaning for you.

Mentor coaches can be extremely helpful in defining self-limiting beliefs that are restraining. Through this self-reflective process one can become more congruent (whole, if you will) and develop a consistent vision and goal for oneself and the organization's mission. A successful leader creates a vision in which others in the organization can believe. See Table 3–1.

TABLE 3–1   A LEADER SETS THE VISION

The vision

- Engages one's heart and spirit.
- Taps into embedded concerns and needs.
- Asserts what you and your colleagues want to create.
- Is something worth going for.
- Provides meaning to one's work and organization.
- Is a little cloudy and out of focus—otherwise, it wouldn't be a vision.
- Is simple.
- Is a living document that can always be expanded.
- Provides a starting point that gets to more.
- Is based on human needs, quality, and dedication.

Source: From *Learning to Lead* by Warren G. Bennis. Copyright © 1997 by Warren G. Bennis and Joan S. Goldsmith. Reprinted by permission of Basic Books, a member of Perseus Books, L.L.C.

Each vision is unique to the leader. The essential qualities for successful leadership are highlighted in Table 3–2. The challenge is to understand how to embed these essential qualities of leadership into a leadership development process for early care and education.

TABLE 3–2   ESSENTIAL QUALITIES OF A SUCCESSFUL LEADER

- Knowing oneself through reflection and self-observation.
- Understanding one's history and environment.
- Clarifying one's values and goals.
- Knowing and applying your learning style.
- Being willing to be a lifelong learner.
- Taking risks and being open to change.
- Accepting mistakes and failures as necessary to creativity and innovation.
- Creating a vision and seeing oneself as a part of it.
- Maintaining trust, through empathy, constancy, and integrity.
- Translating intention into reality through committed action.

Source: From *Learning to Lead* by Warren G. Bennis. Copyright © 1997 by Warren G. Bennis and Joan S. Goldsmith. Reprinted by permission of Basic Books, a member of Perseus Books, L.L.C.

A HISTORICAL PERSPECTIVE OF EARLY CARE AND EDUCATION

Looking back at the past can help people understand the present and help them project future trends. Gordon and Browne (2004) suggest that, by understanding the origins of the early care and education profession, people come to understand that what they are doing today has roots in the past. Schooling for children began thousands of years ago, and teachers still use the works of Socrates, Plato, and Aristotle as part of the educational philosophical background. Educators in both Rome and Greece taught the sciences, art, and literature. These became the backbone of northern European studies, which in turn heavily influenced educational programming in the United States.

In ancient Greece and Rome, teachers in schools tutored the sons of wealthy families and trained these young men in the arts, finance, and military strategies. Life in the Middle Ages was much about survival, and children were expected to accept adult responsibilities at early ages. Child labor played an important part of the Industrial Revolution of the 1400s and 1500s, and the concept of apprenticeships and training through guilds appeared for the first time.

It was not until the early 1900s that the concept of "nursery schools" and out-of-home care became national practices. These learning centers were concerned with whole-child development and served the children of middle- and upper-income families only. During the 1920s and 1930s, researchers in laboratory schools at universities began to study child development. These schools facilitated the observation of children and provided insights into child development. They also served as training grounds for teachers.

During World War II, the Kaiser Child Care Centers became industry-based facilities and were located at the entrance to plants. They were subsidized by Kaiser and also parent fees. During the late 1960s, as part of the war on poverty of the Kennedy–Johnson years, Head Start was developed. Originally, it was meant to serve as an impetus to help welfare mothers obtain some training and education while caring for small groups of children. The program has steadily grown and has enjoyed several decades of providing educational, social, medical, dental, nutritional, and mental health services.

At the beginning of the twenty-first century, people in the United States seem ambivalent about what the proper care for children should be. Parents are believed to be the most important educators of children; however, because many mothers now work outside the home, the role of child care in family and community life needs to be established. Who should be responsible for paying for child care—parents or taxpayers? How can worthy wages be provided for caregivers?

Research has led to the study and examination of competencies that have application in early care and education. Boyatzis (1982) states that competencies are the underlying characteristics of an individual that are causally related to effective and superior performance. Competencies can include motives, traits, self-concepts, attitudes, values, and content knowledge of skills. In the field of organizational behavior, there has been discussion about "transformational leadership" and "transactional leadership." Transformational leaders are described as visionaries who deal with complexity, ambiguity, and uncertainty. Transformational leaders are persuasive and have the ability to influence and inspire others. According to Bennis and Nanus (1997), transformational leadership is concerned with values rather than facts and is an art rather than a science.

Transactional leaders facilitate the development of a mutually supportive community. They are described as value driven, persuasive, strong, predictable, essential to team building, and skilled in anecdotal communication. Transactional leadership is more a science than an art. Experts agree that outstanding leaders combine both transformational and transactional skills.

It is widely understood now that one style of management/leadership is not appropriate for all. An organization's culture and environment shapes the requirements of the work of the organization. If an organization is highly participatory, change requires different skill sets than if the environment tends more toward individualization. Going forward, workers in this era of knowledge-based organizations as well as new technologies certainly require new skill sets, and it is generally acknowledged that women tend to be better multitaskers as well as more adaptive in their management/leadership styles than men.

In the 1950s, Bertanffy (1968) developed and popularized a general systems theory that changed perceptions of organizations. Rather than viewing organizations as flat and linear, organizations are now perceived as textured, or layered, when viewed from different vantage points. According to the general systems theory, organizations are complex and constantly changing, which, in turn, creates a level of instability. This complexity and continual change requires that the leadership within an organization help staff accept the work environment as part of a naturally evolving system. In fact, Wheatley (1992) suggests that analogies from nature can illustrate for people how to comprehend and deal with change. Change for many is a painful experience and suggests a sense of loss. However, when people move successfully through the stages of change, new ways of existing become possible. After successful change, people frequently become more productive and satisfied with their lives and career situations.

Self-renewing organizations are those organizations that embrace errors, risk taking, innovation, goal setting, and goal revision. Managers in these organizations value creativity and intuition in their decision-making processes. Leaders in these organizations accept paradox and put less emphasis on using pure power and authority.

LEADERSHIP DEVELOPMENT IN EARLY CARE AND EDUCATION

Leading and managing in the field of early care and education is inextricably intertwined. The early care and education manager operates within a context that has as its central mission ensuring the quality of children's (and their families') day-to-day experiences that support their learning, growth, and development. For a manager, this means no two days are alike: Each day, the manager handles specific details of daily practice. However, the leader moves beyond day-to-day operations to understand and embrace the bigger picture and her or his role in moving the early care and education agenda forward (Culkin, 1997).

In a landmark collection of essays, *Leadership in Early Care and Education,* Kagan and Bowman (1997) gathered some of the leading researchers and practitioners in the field of early care and education to present a collection of articles on "The Five Faces of Leadership."

Pedagogical Leadership

According to Katz (1966), a noted University of Illinois educator, there are two main sources of information: data and action research. Data comes from practitioners in the field. Action research comes from the ivy-clad halls of the university researcher. The two visions frequently do not agree. Working with young children, securing reliable data, and analyzing the data do not form a large part of the daily activities of early care and education practitioners. With national attention focused on accountability and standards, there is an increased effort to collect reliable data. The challenges that occur in collecting data involve questions about the validity of some instruments used as well as the fact that the usefulness of the instruments for the classroom teaching staff appears to be limited. Nonetheless, practitioners in the field of early care and education need to set an agenda of topics and issues for research and data collection. It is then important for the information and results of the research to be widely disseminated in order to provide positive implications for the day-to-day services provided to children and their families.

Administrative Leadership

In a field where leadership is barely defined, the lack of **consensus** about the parameters of the role as well as the fact that there is no clearly defined way of assuring qualified leadership presents a vacuum and shotgun approach in how to achieve this important mission. Culkin (1997) suggests that there are three main avenues to building stronger pathways to leadership. Interestingly, they all lend themselves very nicely to a mentor coaching process.

■ CONSENSUS
Agreement among all parties on an issue or activity

The first strategy enlists a **mediated entry** process, where a fledgling administrator works with a mentor/supervisor and gradually assumes new responsibilities. In organizations with tight budgets, this is not always an available option because it requires paying two people for the same position.

■ MEDIATED ENTRY
The medium that initiates and brings about results

The second strategy includes a requirement for a credential or licensing process. This approach at least ensures a level of **competencies** that can be verified. During the process of acquiring a credential or license, a mentor coach obviously can be very helpful.

The third strategy requires improving higher education offerings to ensure that appropriate management and leadership course work is available in all degree programs. Again, it would be advantageous to have a mentor

■ COMPETENCIES
Condition or quality of being competent; ability, fitness, or legal capability; power or justification

coach component as part of field-work or as a capstone assignment. This higher education, community college and university level, could play a significant role in developing quality and capacity in early childhood education.

Culkin (1997) discusses seven competencies first identified by Morgan (1997) for consideration in early care and education leadership development. As competencies are discussed and understood, one can begin to see how complex and demanding an early care and education leader's position is. Table 3–3

TABLE 3–3   EARLY CARE AND EDUCATION PROGRAM DIRECTOR COMPETENCY REQUIREMENTS

Competency 1: The early care and education leader must develop and maintain an effective organization. Organizations are systems of components that include legal and regulatory processes. Leaders in organizations develop mission statements and management strategies based on teamwork, ongoing evaluation, and strategic planning.

Competency 2: The early care and education leader must plan and implement administrative systems that effectively carry out the program's mission, goals, and objectives.

Competency 3: The early care and education leader must effectively administer a program of personnel management and staff development.

Competency 4: The early care and education leader must develop and maintain good community relations and influence the community about child care policy that affects the program.

Competency 5: The early care and education leader must identify, develop, and maintain facilities that are safe and healthy as well as licensable.

Competency 6: The early care and education leader must have the legal knowledge necessary for effective management.

Competency 7: The early care and education leader must have financial management skills necessary to operate.

Competency 8: The early care and education leader must ensure self-development.

Competency 9: The early care and education leader must market the program.

Source: Culkin, M. L. (1997). Administrative leadership. In *Leadership in Early Care and Education*, eds., S. L. Kagan & B. T. Bowman (pp. 23–33). Washington, DC: NAEYC. Adapted, with permission, from the National Association for the Education of Young Children.

■ **EMOTIONAL INTELLIGENCE**
A set of behaviors that enables a person to survive and succeed, even in challenging and negative environments

■ **DESCRIPTOR**
Describes, classifies, or identifies something

provides a list of competencies required for an early care and education program director credential as presented by the National Child Care Association, which is an organization whose members are primarily employed by private providers.

In reviewing these competencies, note that most focus on content knowledge; however, content knowledge alone is not enough. As a leader develops, **emotional intelligence** must develop. Emotional intelligence is a **descriptor** for a set of behaviors that enables a person to survive and succeed, even in challenging and negative environments. Some of the behaviors include empathy, resilience, and the ability to communicate with people of diverse backgrounds and interests. Emotional intelligence develops early in life as the result of a person's interactions with caring, involved adults who model successful behaviors.

Beyond these competencies and the content knowledge required, one must also master the processes. These processes are the ones that are "caught" not "taught"; they create the synergy that results in a successful mentor coach relationship.

A HIERARCHY OF LEADERSHIP AND MANAGEMENT COMPETENCIES

In an in-depth examination of these leadership competencies, Bloom (1997) asserts that a **hierarchy** exists that is important to understand and appreciate. If the building blocks for these competencies are unavailable or nonexistent, the organization will fail. This hierarchical concept of competence-to-excellence is based on the work of Sergiovanni and Hayden (1984), and it has since been reexamined and adapted by Hayden (1996). Take a look at the hierarchy depicted in Figure 3–1.

According to the hierarchy, technical skills are at the base; this is where a leader must start. Technical skills include those necessary tasks for operating

■ **HIERARCHY**
A group of persons or things that are rank ordered from the most to the least important

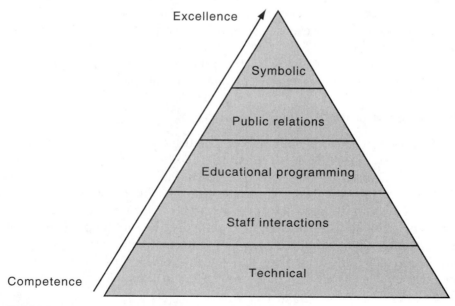

FIGURE 3–1   Hierarchy of Competence to Excellence

Source: Reproduced from P. J. Bloom's Commentary on M. L. Culkin's Administrative leadership in *Leadership in Early Care and Education,* eds. S. L. Kagan & B. T. Bowman (Washington, DC: NAEYC. 1997), 36. Reprinted with permission from the National Association for the Education of Young Children. Adapted from Sergiovanni & Hayden (1984) and Hayden (1996).

a program: budgeting, record keeping, facilities management, scheduling, and developing and implementing policies and procedures to meet state and local regulations. Moving up the hierarchy, staff interactions involve the communication skills and knowledge to cultivate positive interpersonal relations and motivate staff to achieve high levels of performance Specific competencies include supervision, mentor coaching, team building, professional development, and performance appraisal. The next level is educational programming. This is the level at which the new leader excels because she or he was a successful teacher and was then promoted to this management position with little previous training or experience. The skills of educational programming and the client-oriented functions of dealing with children and their families, curriculum planning, staff development, and assessment are usually in the comfort zone for a new director.

Once the mentor coaching opportunity is in place, the technical and staff-relations skills can be acquired on the job. Of course, a leader should try to avoid costly mistakes along the way. Once the technical, staff relations, and educational programming issues have been addressed, the public relations issue needs to be addressed; this issue is critical to quality programming. Efforts in community outreach, advocacy, networking, membership in professional organizations, special events, and fund-raising are all part of the leader's work. Once these four levels of competency have been reached, the stage of being the program's "symbolic" leader evolves. Becoming a symbolic leader requires depth and passion in order to serve as the symbol for the collective identity of the group by articulating a vision, promoting reflection and introspection, and creating a norm of continuous improvement and ethical conduct.

From Competence to Excellence

In reviewing this hierarchy of competence-to-excellence as a leader in early care and education, it is evident that the technical, staff relations, and programming levels need to be in place and running smoothly before beginning the community relations and symbolic leadership aspects.

Directors of exemplary programs are trend watchers; they seek out and evaluate pertinent data that are important to the future of their organizations. According to Bloom (1997), these exemplary directors focus on the present and future simultaneously. They know how to define problems, weigh creative alternatives in solving those problems, and then take appropriate and timely action to implement changes.

Implications for Training and Credentialing

Based on the preceding discussion, it is apparent that a new manager will need to tackle the skills associated with the lower part of the hierarchy initially. The technical, staff relations, and programming skills are more easily acquired and can be addressed in focused training sessions because they are skill based and easy to evaluate. The competencies that will benefit most from mentor coaching are the public relations and symbolic skills. They are more "caught" than "taught" and are less content focused and more process oriented.

Advocacy Leadership

Another aspect of leadership is **advocacy.** Advocacy is the process of educating policymakers as well as the public in the important issues of family and the care of children. Leaders receive little preparation for advocacy and there is limited understanding about how critical the role of advocacy is. Early care and education people must continually keep the message about family needs in the forefront on the local, state, and national level. In order to accomplish the mission of advocacy, early care and education managers and leaders must move beyond day-to-day operations and responsibilities to forward the early care and education agenda.

> ■ **ADVOCACY**
> The act of writing or speaking in favor of something

Strong leadership and advocacy have brought wages in the field of early care and education to their current levels; however, there is more work to be done in the field until workers are compensated appropriately. It has been said about the field that it is the only consumer service where the provider pays part of the burden. In other words, child care is affordable for many families only because the caregivers are paid so little.

Advocacy is needed not only to increase wages for caregivers but also to ensure accountability and quality as standards for staff. In addition, quality environments are needed for children. Most child care facilities are in remodeled church basements, storefronts, commercial buildings, or modular classrooms rather than classrooms designed specifically with young children in mind.

Community Leadership

Directors should present themselves as community leaders, moving out of their offices and into the community. An early care and education leader must be involved in all aspects of community life, not only early care and education. It is important for the leader to have a "story," a vision, to which the minds and hearts of the people can relate. The leader should be able to describe the current situation as well as the potentials that are possible with the vision.

Carter and Curtis (1998) believe a leader should begin by creating the vision and then provide the community with a taste of the possibilities it could provide. Then it is important for people to collaborate in order to share this vision. Reaching out strengthens individual community members as well as the collective group. Initially, it may be impossible to address all the issues presented in the vision, so it is important to focus on a clear set of attainable

goals. In order to succeed, a leader must understand the interconnections between how things work to maintain or change inequalities of power. It is also important to attend to the means of change and the processes used for coming together and accepting challenges related to the goals sought.

A mentor coach could be the catalyst for bringing together like-minded people to address community issues, find ways to change policies, discover new sources of funding, and bring issues to the forefront in communities. The synergy of the mentor coach and protégé can produce amazing results when both are committed and persistent in the mission.

The environments in the centers and programs in the community should be as homelike, inviting, safe, and secure as possible. Children now spend as many hours of their preschool lives in school settings as they spend in the home settings. When entering the center, a parent should feel welcomed and relieved rather than stressed. Personal greetings and a welcoming interest in their lives should create a sense of community for parents and children.

Centers should be perceived as the places where support and resources are available. The teachers (and, if available, the family advocate) should be caring listeners for the challenges and issues that parents wish to discuss.

Conceptual Leadership

Conceptual leadership is also needed in the field to develop new ideas and ways of doing business. According to one dictionary definition, a concept is an "idea or thought, especially a generalized idea or class of ideas" (Webster, 2003). In other words, for the field to advance, practitioners must be willing to do things in new ways, to challenge existing assumptions, and to anticipate situations and issues and think broadly.

These rather abstract ideas may seem to be a luxury for the not-enough-hours-in-the-day managers and leaders. However, it is the leaders who must carry the torch, anticipate the future, and strive for improvements. A mentor coach can significantly influence the conceptual leader in creating a vision that leads to continuous improvement. Leaders should be aware that each day need not follow existing standard routines; rather, the leaders should

CASE STUDY: MALE TEACHER

Rickie, a male teacher with several years of experience, shared with his mentor coach, June, the fact that males always seem to feel out of the loop and not part of the group in early childhood settings, and, although he had gotten used to it, he still was not happy about it. Rickie asked June for some suggestions on how to become more a part of the group.

June had to admit that this was an issue for males throughout the profession. Among her suggestions was one to start a male involvement group with his colleagues' support. He discussed this idea with an administrator and managed to arrange for a minigrant of about $5,000 to support the extra activities. He then set up a committee of intergenerational males that included grandfathers, uncles, biological dads not living with their children, other males involved with children at the center, and dads living with their children. As a result, a series of Saturday events was arranged, including a fishing day, an ice cream social, an athletic field day, a car rally, and a shopping center scavenger hunt topped off with a pizza meal. At each event, a picnic meal was provided, a literacy activity was shared, and books and art supplies were given to each child.

Looking back over the year, Rickie complimented June on providing a great suggestion. He believed that he had benefited almost more than anyone else because he had developed leadership skills, including organizational and time management skills. He had also become known and respected in the community and with his colleagues for what he had accomplished for the children and the men in their lives.

Critical Thinking Questions

1. What are some strategies for getting more men interested in the field of early care and education?
2. Why are men underrepresented in early care and education?
3. Why is it important for children to have males involved in their lives?

question (and ask staff to question) themselves about improving policies, procedures, and the system in general.

THE ROLES OF MENTOR COACHING AND LEADERSHIP

The following discussion leads to the understanding of where early care and education leadership has traditionally been and into what kind of a new "transformative" type of leader a person could grow into with support and validation. Table 3–4 lists the beliefs of "old-style" early care and education leaders and the beliefs of new "transformative leaders."

TABLE 3–4   OLD-STYLE EARLY CARE AND EDUCATION LEADERS VS. NEW STYLE TRANSFORMATIVE LEADERS' BELIEFS

Old-Style Early Care and Education Leaders Believe:	New Style Transformative Leaders Believe:
• Their job is to push people or control them.	• Their purpose is to lift, support, and make the burden lighter every day.
• They should talk at people by telling, directing, and lecturing.	• They should engage in dialogue with people by asking, requesting, and listening.
• In controlling others by the decisions they make.	• In facilitating others to make decisions and empowering them to make their own decisions.
• They know the answers.	• They must seek the answers.
• In triggering insecurity by administering a healthy dose of fear as an effective way to achieve compliance.	• In using purpose to inspire commitment and stimulate creativity.
• That their job is to point out errors.	• That their job is to facilitate others to solve problems and make decisions.
• In delegating responsibility.	• Modeling accountability.
• In creating structure and procedures for people to follow.	• In creating a vision and promoting flexibility through values as guidelines for behavior.
• In doing things right.	• In doing the right thing.
• That their power lies in their knowledge.	• In their vulnerability.
• In focusing on the bottom line.	• In focusing on the process that creates a bottom-line result.

Source: Crane, T. (2001). *The heart of coaching: Using transformational coaching to create a high-performance culture.* San Diego: PTA Press.

THE NEW TRANSFORMATIVE EARLY CARE AND EDUCATION LEADER

The transformative model of leadership requires change and resistance may result. The mentor coach can provide the vision and support to sustain the change process for the protégé. Refer to Table 3–5, which presents the beliefs of transformative early care and education leaders.

TABLE 3–5   TRANSFORMATIVE EARLY CARE AND EDUCATION LEADERS' BELIEFS

Transformative early care and education leaders believe

- Staff is inherently good, and they want the best for children and their families.
- Staff is doing the best they can with what they have been given.
- Staff make mistakes, but they usually do not make them on purpose.
- Staff can learn from mistakes if they are framed positively.
- Staff's own limiting beliefs keep them from doing all they can do.
- Staff working together can create a successful learning environment beyond anything that could be done individually.
- Staff supports changes they create, not those imposed on them.
- Staff usually does want to improve.

An important quality for a mentor coach who is working on developing leadership skills involves the ability to understand and respect others for their uniqueness. Along with this quality, it is critical to support the protégé's values and purposes, even if they do not match the mentor's, and to realize that the mentor coach process takes a serious commitment of time to be effective.

Perhaps one of the more difficult transitions for a person moving into a management position is to understand how the dynamics of relationships change.

Employees want bosses, not coffee-buddies. They do not want the same peer relationship once experienced with a co-worker with the new boss. This can cause misunderstandings. An employee's expectation is for an efficient, consistent, organized supervisor. Equity is extremely important, and a supervisor should be perceived as dealing with all employees equally.

CASE STUDY: THE RELUCTANT PROTÉGÉ

Jeannie and Nancy were a teaching pair for five years. They were good friends and worked well together, providing a wonderful learning environment for their children. They were compatible and enjoyed working together. Because of staffing needs, the agency administrator decided to place Nancy at a new center located further from her home.

When the administrator announced the news about the new assignment to Nancy, she immediately said she would quit before moving. The administrator shared the news about Nancy's resistance with human resources personnel and asked for suggestions on easing the transition. The human resources person recommended using a mentor coaching process.

A seasoned teacher, Wini, was identified as an appropriate mentor coach from another site. Wini had been trained as a mentor coach and had worked with several new teachers as part of their first-year orientations; the process had been very successful and meaningful.

Both Nancy and Wini were provided release time to meet away from their classrooms on a regular basis. Nancy resented being assigned a mentor coach and failed to show up for the first meeting. However, Wini was prepared for this and followed up with a telephone call to Nancy, gently encouraging her at least to meet and then decide if the mentor coaching process would be helpful. Reluctantly, Nancy finally met Wini, and slowly, with attentive listening, Wini encouraged Nancy to direct the conversation. An agreement was prepared between them that indicated they would meet once a week. Wini asked Nancy to identify changes she had made in the past: What had worked for her and what had not worked for her. This helped Nancy identify some coping strategies and understand some feelings of loss, which proved helpful because Nancy felt uncomfortable and unsure in her new surroundings.

As time passed, Nancy began making excuses for not meeting with Wini. At this point, Wini became frustrated and returned to the administrator and the human resources person to ask for advice about what she was doing wrong. After reviewing the process, they realized that although Nancy had been assigned a mentor coach, she had never accepted the process. When she was asked why she did not participate, she indicated that she believed that she was being punished for her attitude and that Wini could not change her assignment, which was all she really wanted.

Critical Thinking Questions

1. What went wrong with this mentor coach/protégé relationship?
2. What strategies could have been used to assist Nancy through this transition in assignments?
3. What could the program director have said and done to ensure a successful mentor coach/protégé relationship?

THE EARLY CARE AND EDUCATION LEADER AND TEAM BUILDING

A critical task, and one that generally results only from experience, involves building a team. This is one of the categories of learning that has to be "caught" rather than "taught." A team with a vision is needed to accomplish the tasks of the organization. It is one thing to have a staff of people ready to work for an organization; it is quite another to have people work with their managers. This level of team development is achieved over time by working with people to earn their trust and communicating with them openly to win their respect. According to Scholtes, Joiner, and Streibel (2003), there are 10 ingredients for a successful team. See Table 3–6.

TABLE 3–6   CRITERIA FOR TEAM BUILDING

- Clarity in team goals: A team works best when everyone understands its purpose and goals. If there is confusion or disagreement about the purpose and goals and how to reach them, these issues must be cleared up.
- A plan for improvement: This always implies change and what goes with change.
- Clearly defined roles: Create an efficient system where everyone's talents are tapped into and all members understand their duties and know who is responsible for engaging in issues and tasks.
- Clear communication: This ensures that information is disseminated across the board.
- Beneficial team behaviors: This includes having meeting agendas, keeping notes, and maintaining a schedule of upcoming meetings.
- Well-defined decision procedures: This includes knowing who will make which decisions and when, as well as pushing that decision-making down whenever possible.

(Continued)

> **TABLE 3–6** (*Continued*)
>
> - Balanced participation: Everybody is given an opportunity for input and feels included in the decision making.
> - Established ground rules: It is important to set up ground rules early in the process.
> - Awareness of the group process: Be able to see, hear, and feel the group dynamics, staying focused and in the moment.
> - Work with scientific processes: Use data and ask to see back-up reports. Work to avoid short-term fixes instead of long-term solutions.
>
> Source: Scholtes, P., Joiner, B., & Streibel, B. (2003). *The team handbook* (3rd ed.). Madison, WI: Oriel, Inc. Reprinted with permission.

Beyond organizing and implementing these criteria to develop a successful team, there are predictable stages that the team will experience, which should be carefully facilitated. If possible, secure the support and services of outside technical help. Otherwise, the leader needs to be aware of, and sensitive to, moving the team successfully through the stages.

The first stage is known as forming. During this stage, the team members ask themselves, "How did I get included? What is going to be expected of me? and Who will give me direction?" They may also be wondering, "What is in it for me?"

The second stage is about storming. As the group members begin working together, their different expectations become apparent and they are unclear about their roles and responsibilities.

The third stage focuses on norming, which is the turning point in the success of the team. All talents and expertise should be identified, and a sense of cohesiveness and respect for each other should have developed as well as a sense of forward movement in the process.

The fourth stage produces performing. The team members are working together cohesively, have looked at the data, have developed an action plan, and are moving forward; results can be seen.

In a service profession such as that of early care and education, clients are simply offered the employees' services. Therefore, it is important to hire, train, and retain good employees. Turnover produces stress on everyone in the organization. Hiring and training new people strains all parts of the system, including the children and their families.

The industry, as Caruso and Fawcett (1999) explain, is about caring. The word *care* is embedded throughout the titles of employees, such as *care* givers and child *care* providers. Services are provided at child *care* centers.

Noddings (1992) has proposed that education be organized around centers of care. Thinking about early childhood programs as centers of care would help broaden conceptions of caring. Centers of caring would place emphasis not only on caring for children but also caring for the adults who care for children as well as their families.

Leadership and supervision should involve caring. Mayerhoff (1971) defines caring for another person as helping the other to grow and actualize the self. According to Mayerhoff (1971), there are eight major ingredients in sincerely caring for another person. The first is knowing. Knowing involves first of all knowing oneself and then knowing about the employees, children, and families for whom one cares. Early care providers also must have "know-how," which requires knowing how to care for employees, children, and families.

The second ingredient calls for alternating rhythms. The leader or supervisor must know when to step back, reflect, and learn as well as when to direct, take action, and insist on certain behaviors.

Patience is the ingredient of caring that requires taking time to achieve the changes desired. This might include letting caregivers forgive themselves. Honesty and trust are the next ingredients. Honesty involves confronting the truth as well as developing trusting relationships. Humility happens when one learns about care from those for whom one cares. Care produces hope for those who begin to perceive possibilities. Caring involves courage; neither the caregiver nor the cared for are quite sure where their journey will take them. So, if there is only one thing to learn in a mentor coach/protégé relationship, it is about caring and bringing one's heart and spirit into the work.

SUMMARY

This chapter examined the background and settings of both early care and education and the field of leadership, and how the process of mentor coaching enters into them. The definitions of mentoring and coaching were given, as well as a description of the types of mentors. Also, there was a discussion about the old type of early care and education and the new transformative leader and how their views affect the staff they supervise. In addition, the five faces of early care and education and leadership were reviewed: pedagogical, administrative, advocacy, community, and conceptual. The chapter concluded with a list of benefits and challenges for both the mentor and the protégé.

■ KEY TERMS

Advocacy

Competencies

Consensus

Descriptor

Emotional intelligence

Hierarchy

Leadership

Mediated entry

Organizational behavior

■ CHAPTER DISCUSSION QUESTIONS

1. Name three competencies expected of an early care and education program director.
2. What kind of leadership is needed now in the field of early care and education?
3. Describe how mentor coaching can support the development of leadership.
4. List three criteria of team building.
5. Describe three types of mentors.
6. List three beliefs of a transformative early care and education leader.

■ MENTOR COACH/PROTÉGÉ INTERACTION

During the beginning phase of the mentor coach/protégé relationship, it is important to take time for the people involved to discuss their hopes and expectations. This is also the time to set up the mechanics of the process: where and when to meet, how much time will be available to meet, whether the meetings will be face to face or by telephone, e-mail, and so forth. Finally, summarize the preliminary meeting with the beginning of an action plan that will be finalized at the next meeting.

■ REFLECTIVE PRACTICE

The personnel interview committee has come back with two recommendations for your final decision for a supervisor's vacancy. One is a good friend who has several years of experience, is not great at the job, and has not continued with her education. The second candidate has some experience and has completed her educational requirements. As a mentor coach for this protégé, prepare a summary of your suggestions about which candidate to choose and why.

■ LEARNING JOURNAL

Write a couple paragraphs about what you have learned as a result of reading this chapter. Can you apply any learning, personally or professionally? Describe any insights or "ah-has" that you have experienced as the result of reading and doing the activities suggested in this chapter.

_____

_____

_____

_____

_____

_____

_____

■ REFERENCES

Bennis, W., & Goldsmith, J. (1997). *Learning to lead: A workbook on becoming a leader.* Cambridge, MA: Basic Books.

Bennis, W., & Nanus, B. (1997). *Leaders: The strategies for taking charge* (2nd ed.). New York: Harper.

Bertanffy, L. V. (1968). *General systems theory.* New York: George Braziller.

Bloom, P. (1997). Commentary. In S. Kagan & B. Bowman (Eds.), *Leadership in early care and education* (pp. 34–37). Washington, DC: NAEYC.

Boyatzis, R. E. (1982). *The competent manager: A model for effective performance.* New York: Wiley InterScience.

Caruso, J., & Fawcett, M. (1999). *Supervision in early childhood education: A developmental perspective* (2nd ed.). New York: Teacher's College Press, Columbia University.

Carter, M., & Curtis, D. (1998). *Visionary director: A handbook for dreaming, organizing and improvising in your center.* St. Paul, MN: Redleaf Press.

Crane, T. (2001). *The heart of coaching: Using transformational coaching to create a high-performance culture.* San Diego: PTA Press.

Culkin, M. (1997). Administrative leadership. In S. Kagan & B. Bowman (Eds.), *Leadership in early care and education* (pp. 23–37). Washington, DC: NAEYC.

Fayol, H. (1916). Administration industrielle et generale. (1930) ed., English. London, UK: Pitman & Sons.

Gordon, A., & Browne, K. (2004). Timeline for early care and education: Good beginnings. *Beginnings and beyond: Foundations in early childhood* (pp. 645–648, Appendix A). Clifton Park, NY: Thomson Delmar Learning.

Mandela, N. (1994). *Long walk to freedom*. Boston: Little, Brown & Company.

Mayerhoff, M. (1971). *On caring*. New York: Harper & Row.

Merriam-Webster's Collegiate Dictionary. (2003). 11th ed. New York Merriam-Webster Publishing.

Morgan, G. (1997). In S. Kagan & B. Bowman (Eds.), *Leadership in early care and education.* Washington, DC: NAEYC.

Noddings, N. (1992). *The challenge to care in schools: An alternative approach to education.* Berkeley: University of California Press.

Scholtes, P., Joiner, B., & Streibel, B. (2003). *The team handbook* (3rd ed.). Madison, WI: Oriel, Inc.

Sergiovanni, T., & Hayden, J. (1984, February). Leadership and excellence in schooling. *Educational Leadership*, 5–13.

Sullivan, D. (2003). *Learning to lead: Effective leadership skills for teachers of young children*. St. Paul, MN: Redleaf Press.

Taylor, F. (1919). The principles of scientific management. New York: Harper & Brothers Publishers.

Wheatley, M. (1992). Leadership and the new science: Learning about organizations from an orderly universe. San Francisco: Berrett-Koehler.

■ FURTHER READINGS

Daloz, L. (1986). *Effective teaching and mentoring*. San Francisco: Jossey-Bass.

Hennig, M., & Jardin, A. (1997). *The managerial women*. New York: Pocket Books.

Levinson, D. J., et al. (1978). *The seasons of a man's life*. New York: Knopf.

Mintzberg, H. (1973). *The nature of managerial work*. New York: Harper & Row.

Murray, M. (2001). *Myths and magic of mentoring*. San Francisco: Jossey-Bass.

Senge, P. (1990). *The fifth discipline: The art and practice of the learning organization*. New York: Doubleday.

Zachary, L. (2000). *The mentor's guide: Facilitating effective learning relationships*. New York: John Wiley.

Zigarmi, D., Blanchard, K., O'Connor, M. K., & Edeburn, C. *The leader within: Learning enough about yourself to lead others*. New York: Prentice-Hall.

For additional information on research-based practice, visit our Web site at http://www.earlychilded.delmar.com

Additional resources for this chapter can be found on the Online Companion™ at http://www.earlychilded.delmar.com. Special features of this supplement include Web resources, additional case studies with critical thinking questions, and multiple choice quizzes for each chapter. The answers to each quiz, along with the rationale for the correct answers, can also be found on-line.

4

Mentor Coaching and Change

INTRODUCTION

Understanding and working with the process of change can greatly improve the quality and success of a mentor coach/protégé relationship. An understanding of how change occurs, whether it is an informal mentor coach/protégé one-to-one relationship or a mentor coach program formally implemented in an organization, are extremely important to the success of the relationship.

■ CHAPTER OBJECTIVES

After reading this chapter, you should be able to:

- Understand and describe the developmental stages in one's life.
- Identify stages in a teacher's life.
- Describe phases in a protégé's life/career path that a mentor coach may be effective in facilitating.

> "For everything there is a season, and a time to every purpose under the heaven, a time to be born and a time to die, a time to plant and a time to pluck up that which is planted."
>
> **PSALMS, OLD TESTAMENT**

MENTOR COACHING AND CHANGE

Change is a universal thread of life. Change can happen unexpectedly or it can be predictable, as, for example, graduating from college, getting married, or having a baby. Although one can prepare for predictable change, this type of change does not always involve an easier transition than that for unexpected change. However, generally speaking, the better prepared for change one is, the more likely it is that the change will be smoother and that it will stabilize quickly. Working with change, identifying the stages of change, and understanding the feelings and emotions that accompany each stage are important for the mentor coach/protégé relationship.

CHANGE AND LIFE TRANSITIONS

William Bridges (1980), in his work *Transitions,* identified and described how individuals experiencing life cycle stages can benefit from the assistance of a counselor or a mentor coach. One of the first things to understand is that change is an inevitable part of life, and it is not a vertical human experience. In the process of life cycles, an individual first begins at an "ending." This ending, according to Bridges (1980), actually serves as notice for the real "beginning." Once the ending has been identified and internalized, a person enters a kind of neutral zone. After experiencing this stage, the individual may feel a sense of loss and uncertainty about the future. These feelings have been compared to those of a person walking on a tightrope without a safety net or as a person who is out of balance; how one falls will have a significant impact on one's life.

Eventually, but not in any predictable way (for example, following the acceptance of a new position, a relocation, or at the beginning of a new relationship), the actual beginning takes place, and obstacles that once seemed insurmountable are transcended. This new beginning often results in a better situation or more satisfying experience. One of Bridges' (1980) strategies for working with change involves asking the individual how he or she handled change in the past. What were the person's reactions to loss? How did this individual embrace or avoid change?

Could the person identify those action steps that helped him or her understand and accept transitions? When one reflects on change, patterns and reactions become apparent, and one can predict likely reactions to future change. A skillful mentor coach can identify for the protégé some of the limiting self-beliefs that may have prevented successful transitions in the past and assist the protégé through a passage of renewal and effective change management.

THE COMPLEXITY AND PACE OF CHANGE

Organizations now are faced with unprecedented complexity and an increasingly fast pace of change. For individuals to succeed in an organization, a guide or mentor coach may be useful. When many changes are occurring and decisions are being made almost simultaneously, an individual may feel overwhelmed or immobilized simply by the intensity of the issues and the situation. A mentor coach can suggest shortcuts for the protégé and assist in helping the protégé focus his or her energies and efforts.

In the 1980s and 1990s, managers in business began using a process called **reengineering** in order to meet the demands of competition and deal with the effects of technological advances. The major reengineering theorists, Hammer and Champy (1990), acknowledged in the *Wall Street Journal* that, with all of their reengineering designs, they really had forgotten about the people, and the people are what make an organization work. With the increasing availability of technology, the amount of information available to the average person is doubling every five years. No one has all the answers. This complexity and potential opportunity is causing leaders in organizations to consider dismantling traditional organizational structures and policies in favor of a broader sharing of information and increasingly more people involved in decision making. This provides challenges as well as opportunities. There is currently a flattening of organizations, and, as a result, the traditional hierarchical form of management is disappearing in favor of more shared decision making and teamwork in accomplishing the goals and activities of the organization.

■ **REENGINEERING**
Retooling and refining all systems; eliminating redundant reporting and work

THE ART OF SELF-RENEWAL

In *The Adult Years: Mastering the Art of Self-Renewal,* Hudson (1999) presents an in-depth change model for individuals that prescribes using a mentor coach to facilitate movement through **discernible** life cycles. Everyone experiences developmental life cycle stages as they age, and ups and downs of the change cycle inevitably occur in everyone's life. Mentor coaching can be extremely effective in facilitating and helping one negotiate through these changes and in identifying the life cycles.

■ **DISCERNIBLE**
Able to see and examine separately

Hudson (1999) identified 10 life skills that represent the most important challenges a person must master in order to reach the dreams for which a person strives (see Table 4–1). Adults experience the cycle of change as a renewal cycle. As one proceeds through the cycle, one experiences growth and development,

TABLE 4–1   FRAMEWORK OF LIFE SKILLS

Phase 1: Go for It. The Heroic Self—Outer Work

- A dream or vision provides conviction, inspiration, and energy for constructing a life chapter.
- Launching requires personal commitment, perseverance, and adaptations—social and economic alignments.
- Plateauing sustains and deepens a successful, functional life chapter.

Phase 2: The Doldrums. The Disenchanted Self—Out of Synch

- Managing the doldrums comes to terms with decline, negative emotions, and feeling trapped in an increasingly dysfunctional life chapter.
- Sorting things out results in a personal plan for what to keep, what to eliminate or change, what to add, and how to move into a revitalized life chapter.
- Ending a life chapter with dignity and care requires an adult to say farewell with gratitude and clarity, leaving you free to consider your next options.

    There are two possibilities at this point: restructuring or making a life transition. Restructuring conducts a mini-transition back into a refurbished life chapter. Restructuring is like minor surgery, with a strategic plan to make the life chapter work better—a new location, a new partner, a new job, or a new home. The same basic goals and values prevail, but the action steps setting players in the drama are altered.

Phase 3: Cocooning. The Inner Self—Transformation from the Inside Out

Cocooning is the first activity of a life transition—turning inward to take stock, to find one's own basic values, and to disengage mentally and emotionally from the life's chapter that one finds himself or herself in. A life transition is like major surgery, usually resulting in personal development, new life options, and transformations.

Phase 4: Self-Renewal—Follows from Successful Cocooning

It is the ability to be self-sustaining—producing confidence, energy, purpose, and hope. Self-renewal also involves a reevaluation of core issues and beliefs. Experimenting, the final and tenth skill of the cycle, engages one in being creative, learning, exploring, risk taking, and networking. When the self is ready to venture back into a life chapter, it takes on this skill.

Source: Bridges, W. (1980). *Transitions*. Cambridge, MA: Da Capo Press, Perseus Books, L.L.C. Copyright © 1980 by William Bridges and Associates, Inc. Reprinted by permission of Da Capo Press, a member of Perseus Books, L.L.C.

■ **COCOONING**

Withdrawing; enclosing protectively

renewal, and evolution. The very movement through the cycle keeps a person on the learning edge. No one place on the cycle is better or worse than another. Each has its time, place, and lesson to be experienced. Each place challenges the individual to extend himself or herself toward completion.

Although each person is challenged with a life skill at a particular time in the cycle, it is important for a person to master all 10 abilities. In experiencing minitransitions involving the life skills, the individual, to some degree, is simultaneously experiencing all the parts of the cycle. Each life skill leverages one through a particular portion of the cycle of change and prepares the individual for the next part of the journey. Knowing which competencies to favor at various points of one's personal cycle reveals the wisdom of adult life.

TYPES OF MENTOR COACHING USED IN CHANGE MANAGEMENT

There is no one model or right way to be a mentor coach or a protégé. What each person brings to the relationship makes it unique. Another aspect of the mentor coach/protégé process involves realizing that some of these relationships may last only for an hour or a relatively short period of time yet constitute a profound life-changing event. Other relationships may last a

CASE STUDY: AN INFANT AND TODDLER TEACHER

Karen, a fifth-year teacher of infants and toddlers, had been working with a mentor coach, Wilma, for about three months. During this time, no real progress had been made; each of their biweekly sessions ended with Karen crying and indicating that she was at the end of her rope with her co-teacher Kate. This was the first year they had worked together, and they had very different working styles. Karen was organized, neat, and rather quiet in her communication style. Kate was flamboyant, dressed outlandishly, and talked loudly and incessantly. Kate also did not clean up after herself and was messy. She made the children nervous, they cried all day, and she had no idea how to soothe them.

Critical Thinking Questions

1. What are your recommendations to Wilma, the mentor coach, in assisting Karen in getting through this phase?
2. What is Wilma's role as a mentor coach?
3. What appropriate topics and activities are part of the mentor coach/protégé process?
4. What are Karen's options?

longer period of time and provide some skill building or other results but are not as meaningful.

A one-to-one informal mentor coaching relationship frequently occurs as a result of a personal and professional goal development—a life/career-pathing process. The mentor and protégé will benefit from discussing the stages of the life cycle and how it affects a particular period in one's life. If the protégé is in his or her twenties and just starting a career, the skills and decisions to be made are much different from those for the protégé who is in his or her thirties and experiencing a successful life/career path rather than a dead-end job or a debilitating relationship. In their forties people should find themselves at some level of career mastery and family balance. This seems to be a period when individuals begin to search for a mentor coach because they have reached a plateau, have a feeling of emptiness, and are sensing restlessness in both their careers and relationships. Obviously, this becomes a critical period for clarifying one's values and vision for the future. By their fifties, people usually have experienced some accomplishments and they begin searching for quality of life rather than striving for the next raise or promotion. Increased life span and good health for many during their sixties provides a sense that there is additional time and financial resources for people to choose active retirements and become flexible with their time and commitments. At this time they may find rewarding ways to contribute in their fields and communities. People in their sixties also find time to follow passions, to develop avocations for which there was no time during a busy career. The seventies through the nineties can be a rich time for mentoring, writing memoirs, and savoring family and friends. Unfortunately, it becomes a time of bitterness and sadness for some. Throughout all the stages of life, there are critical choices and passages that can be greatly enhanced with the guidance of a wise mentor. During these life cycles, different kinds of mentor coach/protégé relationships may be beneficial, but choosing a mentor coach who has recently successfully negotiated the stage preceding the anticipated life cycle seems to work well.

Once they understand the developmental life/stage in which the protégé and the mentor coach find themselves, they should begin to examine the inner workings of the protégé's day-to-day life and reflect carefully on what is happening. Is this a period of energy, of excitement, for example, perhaps the protégé has recently received a promotion or accepted a new position. Events such as these can provide the mentor coach and protégé with the opportunities to consider what kinds of planning and actions helped the protégé reach the situation. They can think about how energy is being used to accomplish the tasks of this phase of the life cycle.

A mentor coach at this phase may assist the protégé by using any of the activities presented in Table 4–2.

The protégé may be experiencing a sense of boredom. This usually occurs three to five years into a teaching assignment A level of sameness becomes apparent. There seems to be no new path for working toward or achieving the next stage, relationships seem unfulfilling, and life feels out of control. A mentor coach, in this phase, may assist the protégé by recommending that the protégé try the activities in Table 4–3.

This leads into another cycle of development and time for renewal. A mentor coach can facilitate how this phase in the protégé's life can help prepare for the next phase.

In the next phase of development, the mentor coach might recommend that the protégé do one or more of the activities listed in Table 4–5.

The mentor coach can play a significant role in working with the protégé during this phase. The protégé should reflect on and reexamine his or her life purpose and value system. The mentor coach may help the protégé during this assessment to determine what is really important. Some activities suggested may include writing an autobiography, journal writing, identifying patterns of choices, and examining relationships. As difficult as this may seem, sometimes it is necessary to transcend relationships that have been outgrown. People's lives change; they change directions. It is important to develop new relationships; widen circles of friendships; do unconventional

TABLE 4–2   LIFE/CAREER PATH PHASE I ACTIVITIES

- Developing a set of personal and professional goals
- Understanding and enjoying the success one has reached
- Stabilizing one's finances and planning for the future
- Identifying and being able to use creativity to advantage
- Solidifying relationships and networking
- Accepting leadership positions in professional/community organizations

Source: Hudson, F. (1999). *The adult years: Mastering the art of self-renewal.* Hoboken, NJ: John Wiley. Copyright © 1999 by John Wiley & Sons, Inc. Reprinted with permission of John Wiley & Sons, Inc.

TABLE 4–3   LIFE/CAREER PATH PHASE 2 ACTIVITIES

- Accept that all life/career paths do not follow a straight line
- Assess what the strengths of the position are and the challenges
- Assess if it is time to move on
- Decide what strategies can help one move through this phase

Source: Hudson, F. (1999). *The adult years: Mastering the art of self-renewal.* Hoboken, NJ: John Wiley. Copyright © 1999 by John Wiley & Sons, Inc. Reprinted with permission of John Wiley & Sons, Inc.

TABLE 4–4   LIFE/CAREER PATH PHASE 3 ACTIVITIES

- Stand back and assess the situation
- Plan some travel, preferably alone
- Begin developing an exit plan
- Quietly begin assessing other opportunities
- Take a **sabbatical,** if feasible

Source: Hudson, F. (1999). *The adult years: Mastering the art of self-renewal.* Hoboken, NJ: John Wiley. Copyright © 1999 by John Wiley & Sons, Inc. Reprinted with permission of John Wiley & Sons, Inc.

TABLE 4–5   LIFE/CAREER PATH PHASE 4 ACTIVITIES

- Redefine one's life/career purpose
- Go back to school
- Prepare for a specialization
- Reach out for support from others

Source: Hudson, F. (1999). *The adult years: Mastering the art of self-renewal.* Hoboken, NJ: John Wiley. Copyright © 1999 by John Wiley & Sons, Inc. Reprinted with permission of John Wiley & Sons, Inc.

■ **SABBATICAL**
A period of rest that occurs in cycles

things; and contribute to the community by volunteering at a homeless shelter, working with the Sierra Club, or donating time and skills to the Habitat for Humanity.

Other recommendations for this phase might include reducing activities or participation levels, limiting day-to-day responsibilities and activities, and trying to gain some insight into the next phase. This is a great time for a sabbatical or a leave of absence, if possible, because, as the saying goes, "doing what you are doing is going to get you what you got." However, be careful: Making rash decisions may not solve the problem. As the individual reflects, asking personal, probing questions and redefining life's purpose, it may be time to recreate a current job or search for a new one. Looking for a new position may require some training or relocation. Allow time to prepare for the next big step. This cycle can take three to five years to accomplish, or there can be minitransitions along the way.

Once ideas begin forming, an individual's mood will change, energy will start returning, and a clear path will become evident. As the individual finds he or she has more time for personal and professional activities, he or she will find classes that are available that could lead to higher degrees or some recreational classes, such as those in art or music, may be attractive. There is less a sense of urgency in this phase than in others, and the individual's confidence will begin returning—as long as the individual has a goal in mind.

With each phase, there are significant questions for the mentor coach to pose and for the protégé to consider and respond to. Level of activity during the phases of change include

Phase 1—High-energy phase

Phase 2—Spinning phase

Phase 3—Reflective, quiet-time phase

Phase 4—Renewal, redefining purpose phase

Some of the benefits of a formal mentor coach/protégé program, when properly implemented and change is consciously managed, are that they result in significantly higher productivity, better morale, and a reduction in lost staff time and resources. Often change is perceived negatively. However, change actually can be very positive. It is the basis for growth. Some basic understanding of the change process should be explored in one of the early sessions between the mentor coach and protégé.

APPRECIATIVE INQUIRY

A recent approach to change management called **appreciative inquiry,** or AI, takes a different approach. Forgoing the negative and focusing as much as possible on the positive, this approach has been used for individual as well as large-scale organizational change. Appreciative inquiry can be described in different ways, but, in essence, it is a radically affirmative approach to change that completely disregards problem-based management. Summing up

■ **APPRECIATIVE INQUIRY**

The cooperative search for what is best in people

appreciative inquiry is difficult. Some consider it a philosophy of knowing; others, a methodology for managing change; still others might describe the process as an approach to leadership and human development. Cooperider and Whitney, as presented in Holman and Devane (1999), define appreciative inquiry as the cooperative search for the best in people, their organizations, and the world around them. AI involves the systematic discovery of what gives a system "life" when it is most effective in economic, ecological, and human terms. Appreciative inquiry involves the art and practice of asking questions in order to strengthen a system's capacity to improve positive potential. It mobilizes inquiry through crafting an "unconditional positive question," often involving hundreds or sometimes thousands of people. In appreciative inquiry, **intervention** gives way to imagination and innovation instead of negativism, criticism, and circular thinking. Those who agree with the philosophy of the appreciative inquiry approach assume that every living system has untapped, rich, and inspiring accounts of the positive. Link this "positive change core" directly to any change agenda, and changes never thought possible are suddenly and democratically mobilized.

■ INTERVENTION
To provide an activity, idea, or strategy that affects an outcome for someone

An important insight from the appreciative inquiry process is that human systems grow toward that which they persistently question. The single most important action a group can take to liberate the human spirit and consciously construct a better future is to make positive change commonly and explicitly available to all.

SUMMARY

Change is a process, not a single event, and it takes time. It takes time to plan for change, and even after the course is set, the change will not occur overnight. People involved in the change process experience different levels of activity. Change can be exciting, difficult, unpleasant, or all of these at once. People involved in the change process can be exhilarated, relieved, or hopeful. Not everyone welcomes change; resistance often occurs. Being prepared and understanding how to resolve resistance is an important skill.

Change begins with the individual. When a course is set for changing in an organization, one individual at a time accepts the change until a groundswell or critical mass occurs, which will move change forward. Often sharing and dialoguing are necessary before staff will accept change. Change is a highly personal experience. People react differently to change; each situation will involve particular motivators and perspectives, which the mentor coach and protégé should attempt to identify and classify. There is no single right way to manage change—no road map for success. But there are some guidelines for assessing needs, setting parameters, and keeping communication open. Change is best understood and accepted when it is clearly defined. Individuals need to know what will be different as the result of change.

The more definitive the discussion about what changes the protégé would like to attempt and clarify, the more beneficial the assistance of the mentor coach can be. Writing out the proposed changes, engaging the stakeholders in discussions, and preparing an action plan with timelines will greatly enhance the process and chances of success.

KEY TERMS

Appreciative inquiry

Cocooning

Discernible

Intervention

Reengineering

Sabbatical

CHAPTER DISCUSSION QUESTIONS

1. Does change occur in predictable ways?
2. Can one be prepared for change? Explain.
3. What role can the mentor coach provide for a protégé in a change event?
4. What is appreciative inquiry?
5. How could appreciative inquiry be used in the mentor coach/protégé process?

MENTOR COACH/PROTÉGÉ INTERACTION

Arrange a session with the protégé to examine Hudson's (1999) model of life transitions. Identify where both the protégé and mentor coach are at this particular time. Discuss transition times and how they were handled in the past. Develop an action plan and timelines for working through the current life transitions.

REFLECTIVE PRACTICE

Share both the positive and negative experiences of how an individual handled life's transitions in the past. Then identify how previous strategies and coping skills can successfully assist managing and experiencing current life transitions.

■ LEARNING JOURNAL

Write a couple paragraphs about what you have learned as a result of reading this chapter. Can you apply any learning, personally or professionally? Describe any insights or "ah-has" that you have experienced as the result of reading and doing the activities suggested in this chapter.

■ REFERENCES

Bridges, W. (1980). *Transitions.* Cambridge, MA: Da Capo Press, Perseus Books, L.L.C.

Hammer, M., & Champy, J. (1990). Reengineering the corporation. New York: HarperCollins.

Holman, P., & Devane, T. (Eds.). (1999). *The change handbook: Group methods for shaping the future.* San Francisco: Berrett-Koehler.

Hudson, F. (1999). *The adult years: Mastering the art of self-renewal.* Hoboken, NJ: John Wiley.

■ FURTHER READINGS

Bellm, D., Whitebrook, M., & Hnatiuk, P. (1997). *The early childhood mentoring curriculum: A handbook for mentors.* Washington, DC: Center for Child Care.

Conger, J., Spreitzer, G., & Lawler, E. (Eds.). (1999). *The leader's change handbook: An essential guide to setting direction and taking action.* San Francisco: Jossey-Bass.

Miller, C., Aguilar, C., Maslowski, L., McDaniel, D., & Mantel, M. (2004). *The non-profit's guide to the power of appreciative inquiry.* Denver: Community Development Institute.

Newton, A., et al. (1994). *Mentoring: A resource and training guide for educators.* Andover, MA: The Regional Laboratory for Educational Improvement for the Northeast and Islands.

For additional information on research-based practice, visit our Web site at http://www.earlychilded.delmar.com

Additional resources for this chapter can be found on the Online Companion™ at http://www.earlychilded.delmar.com. Special features of this supplement include Web resources, additional case studies with critical thinking questions, and multiple choice quizzes for each chapter. The answers to each quiz, along with the rationale for the correct answers, can also be found on-line.

CHAPTER 5

Communication

INTRODUCTION

This chapter provides a discussion of the importance of communication in a mentor coach/protégé program. Communication is an essential ingredient in a successful mentor coach/protégé program. Developing good communication skills should be one of the first tasks mentor coaches and their protégés undertake. Protégés should examine and understand themselves and others. During the orientation and the assigning of protégés to mentors, activities may include training sessions designed to facilitate particular communication styles.

■ CHAPTER OBJECTIVES

After reading this chapter, you should be able to:

- Understand and define communication and describe its importance in the mentor coaching/protégé relationship.
- Understand and describe the difference between dialogue and discussion.
- Understand and describe an outline of work/behavioral styles based on Carl Jung's four-quadrant model.

> "Seek first to understand . . . and then to be understood."
>
> **STEPHEN COVEY**

A DEFINITION OF COMMUNICATION

■ **COMMUNICATION**
Two-way process that
requires one person to
provide a message or a
stimulus and another
person to receive the
message and respond

Communication is a two-way process that requires one person to provide a message or stimulus and a second person to receive the message and respond. Developing good communication skills should be one of the primary efforts addressed in the mentor coach/protégé relationship. The mentor coach should consider the setting that will facilitate the best opportunities for good communication. If the mentor coach/protégé meetings occur in the classroom setting, the protégé will tend to be distracted by activities in the background. However, if one of the tasks of the project is to have the mentor coach observe the protégé in the classroom or have the mentor coach role model an activity, a classroom environment would enhance the activity. However, if the mentor coach and the protégé meet in the mentor coach's office, the effect of who is in charge and has more authority might influence the interchange. Choosing a neutral location to meet and using technology to communicate can help to eliminate the geographic and location problems.

In his classic book *The Seven Habits of Highly Effective People,* Stephen Covey (2004) describes communication as a competency of a successful person. People spend much time, especially in organizational settings, communicating with one another. The key to good communication is listening. The interesting thing about listening is that people do not spend educational time learning about it.

Understanding active listening and reflective listening may help a person become an effective listener; however, when one is actively listening, it may seem as if the person is mimicking, which may inhibit any possible probing for deeper meaning. Covey (2004) suggests that the successful person learn to become an empathetic listener, a person who can suspend judgment in order to understand what another person is really trying to communicate. How does this person feel? Why does this person hold these beliefs? What can be learned from this person? Empathetic listening involves the intent to understand another person's frame of reference.

The lowest level of communication, which results from low-trust situations, is characterized by defensiveness, protectiveness, and, often, legalistic language. This kind of communication creates win/lose or lose/lose situations. However, as indicated in Figure 5–1, there is a middle ground of respectful communication. Respectful communications work in independent and interdependent situations where compromise and collaboration are possible. Ideally, real creativity and **synergy,** the synergy that occurs in high-trust communications, is the level for which the mentor coach and the protégé will want to strive.

■ **SYNERGY**
Interaction to accomplish
tasks

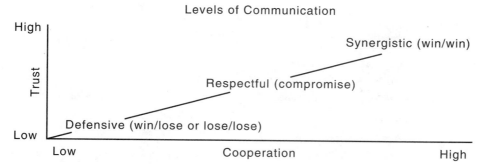

FIGURE 5–1 Levels of Communication

Source: Reprinted with permission of the publisher. From *The change handbook: Group methods for shaping the future,* copyright © (1999) by P. Holman & T. Devane (eds.). Berrett-Koehler Publishers, Inc., San Francisco, CA. All rights reserved. www.bkconnection.com

DIALOGUE

An important communication skill to understand and appreciate the value of in the mentor coach/protégé relationship is the art and science of dialogue. **Dialogue** is a form of communication that is used to gather information, learn from it, and discover new ideas without seeking to convince or persuade another person (Gonzalez-Mena, 2001). According to Gerard and Ellinor (1999), dialogue has a variety of meanings, but it is primarily characterized by honor, respect, and trust. The experience of dialogue should involve careful listening even if the listeners do not agree with the speaker. Instead of arguing, listeners try to ascertain the position of the speaker and why he or she holds a particular view. The word *dialogue* stems from the Greek: *dia* meaning "through" and *logos* for "meaning." The essence of dialogue involves the search for shared meanings so that people will be able to appreciate and understand the foundations, values, and reasons for these beliefs. This means that dialogue goes beyond mere words and discussion to reveal nonverbal communication with deep meanings, feelings, and values. Listeners suspend judgment on what is being said and try to imagine themselves in the other's position (see Table 5–1).

Although people experience dialogue and discussion daily, the conscious decision to use dialogue can greatly enhance the mentor coach/protégé relationship. Much of the work of mentor coaches and protégés should involve helping protégés find their "voices," their personal styles of leadership and of teaching. A protégé may enter the relationship expecting to mimic the mentor coach. This expectation should facilitate an important dialogue about focusing on the protégé's needs and expectations.

■ **DIALOGUE**

A form of communication used to gather information and learn from it

TABLE 5–1   THE CONVERSATION CONTINUUM

Dialogue	Discussion/Debate
• Seeing the whole that encompasses the parts	• Separating issues/problems into parts
• Seeing connections and relationships	• Seeing distinctions and differences
• Inquiring into assumptions	• Justifying/defending assumptions
• Learning through inquiry and disclosure	• Persuading, selling, and telling
• Creating shared meaning among many	• Choosing one meaning among many

Source: Reprinted with permission of the publisher. From *The change handbook: Group methods for shaping the future,* copyright © (1999) by P. Holman & T. Devane (eds.). Berrett-Koehler Publishers, Inc., San Francisco, CA. All rights reserved. www.bkconnection.com

Dialogue is useful for focusing on learning and developing a systems view of an organization. Dialogue can help members of an organization or other group move beyond polarization to discover alternatives that build shared meaning and aligned action. Dialogue can facilitate the development of communication skills that foster an environment of cooperation and shared leadership founded on trust and respect. Finally, dialogue can help generate some unconventional thinking.

Using dialogue makes conversations more intimate and encourages both the mentor coach and the protégé to practice communication skills that will

lead to long-term culture change. In addition, dialogue helps groups move toward shared leadership. Dialogue is unique in its application of a higher level of awareness, which helps leaders in organizations choose optimal, long-term, and systemic actions. Managers can examine underlying assumptions behind group decisions and perhaps substitute or alter those decisions for better, more effective ones.

MENTOR COACHING AND COMMUNICATION

In addition to the suggestion that the protégé need not mimic the mentor coach are the ideas of identifying the protégé's personal work and behavioral styles in order to improve the quality of the dialogue and communication between the mentor coach and the protégé and build trust and respect. Several learning instruments are available that can be self-administered to help identify personal and **behavioral** work styles.

Following is a brief discussion of DiSC Classic Instrument (1986), a self-assessment tool based on Carl Jung's (1964) **four-quadrant behavioral model,** which is also the basis for the Myers–Briggs and other instruments for behavioral assessments. Jung **hypothesized** that there are deep-rooted psychological types, or patterns, in the human **psyche** that are consistently revealed over time. These patterns may even be passed on **genetically** and exist in the **collective unconscious** of each individual. Variations of Jung's (1964) theories have been incorporated into user-friendly self-report instruments that are available electronically. The letters of the acronym, DiSC, refer to the four dominant **dispositions** of the model: dominant, influencing, steady, and conscientious.

OVERVIEW AND DESCRIPTORS OF FOUR BASIC BEHAVIORAL STYLES

In successfully working closely with someone, taking the time to self-assess and share with each other personal work and behavioral styles will help prevent misunderstandings in the future. It is important to remember that the protégé is in the process of discovering his or her personal voice. The protégé is discovering new ways of doing things, and they may be quite different from those of the mentor coach. Table 5–2 through Table 5–5 presents a widely distributed four-quadrant behavioral model based on Carl Jung's (1964) theory of dispositions.

Directive-dominant ("D") individuals are dynamic, forceful, and results oriented. They enjoy challenges, want to be creative, and show strong wills to achieve their goals. They tend to strive for concrete results, contribute long hours to achieve those results, and at times, pay a high price for success in

---

■ **BEHAVIORAL**
Describing the way a person acts

■ **FOUR-QUADRANT BEHAVIORAL MODEL**
A theory that has four major premises of observable behavior

■ **HYPOTHESIZE**
To form groundwork, a foundation, a supposition

■ **PSYCHE**
The mind considered as a subjectively perceived, functional entity, based ultimately on physical processes but with complex processes of its own

■ **GENETICALLY**
Having to do with genetic (biological) inheritance

■ **COLLECTIVE UNCONSCIOUS**
Carl Jung's theory involving the part of the unconscious mind that each human being inherits along with all other human beings; it contains certain patterns or archetypes

■ **DISPOSITIONS**
An individual's customary frame of reference

■ **CHARACTERISTICS**
Distinguishing traits,
features, or qualities

■ **PESSIMISTIC**
Expecting the worst

■ **EXTROVERTED**
Outgoing personality

TABLE 5–2   DOMINANT COMMUNICATION STYLE
The "D" behavioral disposition tends to be directive and dominant.

"D" **characteristics**

• Direct	• **Extroverted**
• Controlling	• Change oriented
• Risk taking	• Fight oriented
• **Pessimistic**	
• Judging	

their personal and social lives because they choose getting results over developing relationships. "Ds" tend to take control of tasks and outcomes. They seek bottom-line results. They like to win and may challenge current expectations or rules to achieve desired results. They can display impatience, **aggressiveness**, anger, and **combativeness** when stressed or thwarted.

"D's" preferences often result in their being powerfully direct forces in organizational settings. They may not always be right, but they will be out in front leading. Their extroverted, direct need for control can have either a positive or negative influence, depending on the situation and other variables. "Ds" can be tremendous assets to organizations because of their desires to take risks and look for creative solutions to new challenges. "D's" communication style tends to be fast paced, looking for results, and not particularly good at listening.

"I" character types prefer to be liked by people; relationships are more important than tasks. They display optimistic outlooks on life and people. They find being with others energizing, almost regardless of the context. They seek frequent approvals and affirmations from others and easily give it. Much of their psychic energies are used in understanding the emotional reactions of individuals

■ **AGGRESSIVENESS**
Initiation of action

■ **COMBATIVENESS**
Ready to fight

TABLE 5–3   INFLUENCING COMMUNICATION STYLE
The "I" behavioral disposition tends to be direct and accepting.

"I" **characteristics**

• Direct	• Perceiving
• Accepting	• Extroverted
• Risk taking	• Change-oriented
• Optimistic	• Flight-oriented

and groups. The "I's" are concerned with giving and receiving interpersonal acceptance. A person with this dispositional type enjoys talking more than listening but will observe the social norms enough to listen when necessary. They will strike up a conversation with almost anyone and often show a keen sense of humor. They influence others with optimistic, friendly conversations in social and work environments. They establish wide networks of friends and build alliances in order to be included and accepted. An individual with an "I" disposition shows an expression of interpersonal warmth and down-to-earth congeniality.

"I" character type preferences may cause them to become the interpersonal glue of an organization. They are sensitive to the emotional lives of those around them and act as lightning rods for the general feelings generated by organizational life events. Their extroverted, direct need for relationships can be either a positive or negative force, depending on the situation. They demonstrate tremendous value to the organization because of their optimism; enthusiasm; sense of humor; and ability to promote ideas, strategies, and products.

The "I" communication style is fast paced. "I's" seek relationships and are not good listeners until maturity or training helps them understand the importance of listening, which can help them be very effective in reflective and empathetic listening.

"S's" dispositional type is typified by the behaviors of accommodation and steady-paced follow through. They tend to care about people. They also tend to focus on building trust, with the goal of establishing long-term personal relationships. They prefer stable, constant environments that are familiar and in which they can work at a relatively relaxed pace, earning the confidence and sincere personal attention of their co-workers. They have patience, staying power, and stick-to-itiveness. They are indirect accepters who commit themselves to and work hard at making relationships work.

"S's" prefer low-key, relaxed, steady-paced actions that result in consistent predictable follow through on work tasks. Their value to the organization

---

TABLE 5–4   STEADY COMMUNICATION STYLE

The "S" behavioral disposition tends to be steady and stable. Their behavioral preferences are as indirect accepters.

"S" characteristics

• Indirect	• Perceiving
• Accepting	• Introverted
• Risk assessing	• Continuity oriented
• Optimistic	• Flight oriented

■ **INTROVERTED**

Passive, inwardly focused
personality

derives from producing consistent, predictable results over time. They may not be innovative, but they can incrementally improve what already exists. Their **introverted,** indirect need for relationships can be either a positive or a negative force, depending on the situation. They can provide tremendous value to the organization because of their accommodating service and team orientation.

The "S's" communication is the best of all the behavioral types when it comes to listening. They are natural, reflective, and empathetic listeners, as well as natural helpers, dedicated to assisting others while sacrificing their own needs.

"C" dispositional types are recognized by their introverted and controlling tendencies. They tend to look at the whole picture or system, while honing in on the main critical factors or issues that increase the efficiency or quality of the output. They like to solve problems in a deductive, precise, and logical manner. They want products and services to be produced under specific, controlled conditions. They act as if subjectivity and emotions distort reality. They believe that there is a proper procedure for doing things. The way to improve outcomes is through logical, tested policies, procedures, and practices, which eliminate risk and allow for further testing and improvement. They use rationality and analysis in a nondemonstrative fashion to focus on tasks at hand.

"C's" preferences may lead them to become the most technically proficient people in their chosen fields of interest because they perceive that power comes from the acquisition of systematically proven knowledge. With this knowledge, organizational work can be logically ordered and structured for maximum efficiency and output. "C's" believe that if the job is done by the book, but the desired results are not forthcoming, then appropriate databased modifications need to be made after logically examining where the breakdowns occurred. Their introverted, controlling preferences can have positive or negative influences in the organization, depending on the situation. "C's" offer tremendous worth to the organization because of their logical, databased, systematic approach to the operation of organizational work.

TABLE 5–5   CONSCIENTIOUS COMMUNICATION STYLE

"C's" cautious and conscientious behavioral preferences are as indirect controllers.

"C" characteristics

• Indirect	• Judging
• Controlling	• Introverted
• Risk assessing	• Continuity oriented
• Pessimistic	• Fight oriented

"C's" communication styles can be inflexible, responding only to a systems or data approach to work. Appealing to their desires for quality control keeps them involved. They are often loners, resisting teamwork. They will be the most resistant to the mentor coaching process from both aspects: This behavioral type is not interested in being a mentor coach or a protégé. But if the mentor coach is an expert in a field of interest for the protégé, the process can work.

CRUCIAL CONVERSATIONS

A group of trainers and consultants, Patterson, Grenny, McMillan, and Switzler (2002), are working with organizations and individuals throughout the United States to provide people with the tools to manage crucial conversations. Crucial conversations are important to avoid missing opportunities, failing to advocate for

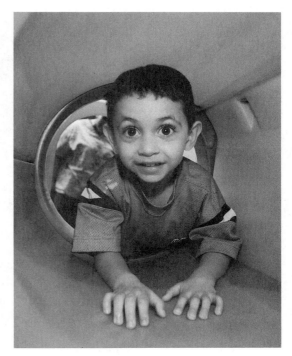

CASE STUDY: DIFFERING STYLES

As part of a mentor coach/protégé relationship, Kim and Carrie began to realize that they preferred receiving information in different ways. Kim, the mentor coach, used a traditional, almost lecture style of presenting material. Carrie, the protégé, was a full-time teacher in a busy Head Start program. By the end of the day, the last thing Carrie wanted was to hear a lecture. Carrie indicated that, for her, the relationship had to be a two-way sharing, with Carrie telling Kim how the past week had gone, including the positive moments as well as the negative ones. Although Kim initially believed she was losing control of the situation and was not doing what was expected of a mentor coach, she gradually accepted that this worked for Carrie and that was what was important.

Critical Thinking Questions

1. Is there one right way for a mentor coach/protégé relationship to work?
2. What do you think would have eventually happened if Carrie had not spoken up and indicated her preferred communication style?
3. With this style of communication, what recommendations do you have for Kim, the mentor coach, to express the points she thinks she needs to convey?

ourselves and others, and not understanding how and when to speak up. So often, in an organization or a relationship, the failure of people to speak up and clearly express personal feelings and thinking keeps organizations stagnant or results in failed marriages and relationships. Carrie, the protégé in the preceding case study, understood the value of crucial relationships by explaining to the mentor coach that, at the end of the day, she would prefer not to listen to a lecture. Instead, she shared her preferences for how to spend their time together.

COMMUNICATION IN ORGANIZATIONS

Communicating in organizations works differently from a one-on-one conversation; however, some basic considerations are part of both the one-on-one and the organizational approach. According to Kanter (2004), accountability is one cornerstone of building confidence and communication in an organization. When accountability fails, when challenges provoke denial and people cover up their mistakes, or, even more commonly, find someone else to blame, there is a downward spiral of positive activity. The second cornerstone of creating a productive work environment involves collaboration. Communication, open and across systems, builds trust and respect. The third cornerstone is continuing initiative and innovation. A telltale sign of an organization where communication and responsibility for outcomes is failing is apparent when an employee responds to a request for an action by saying "I am not doing that, it's not in my job description."

Kinslaw (1996), a consultant and trainer, has identified what he considers essential for good communication between the mentor coach and a protégé. These components include the following:

- balance
- being concrete
- shared responsibility
- shape
- respect

Kinslaw (1996) incorporated his approach to mentor coaching in his definition, which states that mentor coaches

- should strive for continuous improvement for the organization.
- should consider conversation an essential process.
- should believe the process must be disciplined.

SUMMARY

This chapter focused on the importance of communication and, specifically, appreciating a level of discussion that becomes dialogue. Dialogue involves the suspension of judgment to truly listen to another person's point of view. Another consideration for the mentor coach and protégé early on in the relationship involves spending time to develop an understanding of the work and behavioral styles of each other, as well as how each prefers to experience communication. Understanding another person's communication style and realizing that it may be different from one's own can improve the mentor coaching process.

▓ KEY TERMS

Aggressiveness	Extroverted
Behavioral	Four-quadrant behavioral model
Characteristics	Genetically
Collective unconscious	Hypothesize
Combativeness	Introverted
Communication	Pessimistic
Dialogue	Psyche
Dispositions	Synergy

▓ CHAPTER DISCUSSION QUESTIONS

1. What is the definition of communication?
2. What is the difference between dialogue and discussion?
3. Describe the differences between an extroverted person and an introverted person.
4. Is the protégé supposed to try to mimic the mentor coach?
5. How does communication in an organization differ from a one-on-one discussion?
6. What usually happens when two people have different styles of communicating?

▓ MENTOR COACH/PROTÉGÉ INTERACTION

Discuss the possible challenges that can occur when a mentor coach is an extrovert, highly verbal, and pushing for results and the protégé is an introvert, less verbal, and believes it is necessary to build a good relationship.

▓ REFLECTIVE PRACTICE

A parent has confronted the protégé in the classroom and is demanding to know the name of the child who has been biting her child as well as the child's parents' names. What suggestions can the mentor coach give the protégé?

■ LEARNING JOURNAL

Write a couple paragraphs about what you have learned as a result of reading this chapter. Can you apply any learning, personally or professionally? Describe any insights or "ah-has" that you have experienced as the result of reading and doing the activities suggested in this chapter.

_____

_____

_____

_____

_____

_____

_____

■ REFERENCES

Covey, Stephen. (2004). *The seven habits of highly effective people: Powerful lessons in personal change.* New York: Free Press.

DiSC Classic Instrument. (1986). Minneapolis, MN: Inscape Publishing. 1-800-398-3134.

Gerard, G., & Ellinor, L. P. (1999). Dialogue. San Francisco, CA: Berrett-Koehler Publishers, Inc. All rights reserved. www.bkconnection.com

Gonzalez-Mena, J. (2001). *Diversity in early care and education.* New York: McGraw-Hill.

Holman, P., & Devane, T. (eds.). (1999). *The change handbook: Group methods for shaping the future.* San Francisco, CA: Berrett-Koehler Publishers, Inc.

Jung, C., & Freeman, J. (ed.). (1964). *Man and his symbols.* New York: NY Dell Publishing.

Kanter, R. (2004). *Confidence.* New York: Crown Business Books.

Kinslaw, D. (1996). *The ASTD trainer's sourcebook—Coaching: Create your own training program.* New York: McGraw-Hill.

Patterson, K., Grenny, J., McMillan, R., & Switzler, A. (2002). *Crucial conversation tools for talking when the stakes are high.* New York: McGraw-Hill.

■ FURTHER READINGS

Gladwell, M. (2000). *The tipping point: How little things can make a big difference.* New York: Little, Brown & Company.

Nolan, M. (1984). Mentoring and its influence on administrators in California Community Colleges. Ann Arbor, MI: University Microfilms Int.

Parkin, M. (2001). *Tales for coaching*. Sterling, VA: Stylus Publishing.

Zeus, P., & Skiffington, S. (2005). *The coaching at work toolkit: A complete guide to techniques and practices*. Sydney, Australia: McGraw-Hill.

Zigarmi, D., Blanchard, K., O'Connor, M., & Edeburn, C. (2004). *The leader within: Learning enough about yourself to lead others*. New York: Pearson McGraw-Hill.

For additional information on research-based practice, visit our Web site at http://www.earlychilded.delmar.com

Additional resources for this chapter can be found on the Online Companion™ at http://www. earlychilded.delmar.com. Special features of this supplement include Web resources, additional case studies with critical thinking questions, and multiple choice questions for each chapter. The answers to each quiz, along with the rationale for the correct answers, can also be found on-line.

6

Mentor Coaching and Learning

INTRODUCTION

There are several recent theories of how people learn. One part of the following discussion introduces assessment of a personal learning style using the Learning Success System©. The Learning Success System is based on Carl Jung's (1994) four-quadrant behavioral theory. This understanding of learning styles is then expanded to align with multiple intelligences by Howard Gardner (1983). Further discussion addresses "situated learning," followed by Senge, Scharmer, Jaworski, and Flowers (2004), "U" theory of learning as well as the latest thinking on learning called "deep smarts." Identifying how one learns helps an individual understand one's teaching methods and patterns and why some children are easier to work with than others.

■ CHAPTER OBJECTIVES _____

After reading this chapter, you should be able to:

- Describe several theories of learning.
- Discuss personal learning styles and identify how they relate to personal teaching styles.

"To teach is to learn."

LATIN PROVERB

• Understand and describe learning that goes beyond acquiring new skills or practicing methods from new theories that involve deeper levels of learning.

DEFINITION OF LEARNING

According to *Webster's* dictionary (1999), learning involves acquiring knowledge of a subject or a skill by study, experience, or instruction. In early care and education, this seems to be a very narrow definition for children ages 0 to 5. The discovery of the world, including learning to love, explore, and talk while also developing empathy; also making friends. Another important pre-school age task is to develop the range of emotions from angry to happy that go well beyond the definition of learning as merely acquiring knowledge. Yet in teacher preparation course work at any level, very little—if any—time is spent on what learning is, when it occurs, and how it is measured other than by rote pen-and-pencil tests.

MENTOR COACHING AND LEARNING

As the concept of learning is discussed, it becomes apparent how little is actually known about learning and how it happens. Certainly, essential to the focus of a mentor coaching program is learning. A commitment and willingness to learn must be part of the relationship for both the mentor coach and the protégé. Learning is at the heart of a successful experience. When a person learns and how a person learns differ from person to person as a result of the uniqueness of the individuals involved.

Early in the mentor coach/protégé relationship, the mentor coach and protégé should discuss their learning preferences. Using the Jungian (1994) four-quadrant model discussed in Chapter 5, they can quickly determine learning preferences. Understanding and discussing learning preferences will serve to begin to build immediate rapport and trust in the relationship. Having the same learning styles will not contribute to the success of the relationship. What is important is to respect one another and discuss differences, which will provide rewarding dialogue. The Jungian (1994) model considers the four character types and how they influence the learning process.

STYLES OF LEARNING

Dominant or direct learners learn best when they can move around. They are kinesthetic learners; they prefer hands-on activities and learning by using their bodies. They tend to operate in the here and now and act spontaneously. This type of learner often is a good athlete and prefers being taught by someone who provides feedback, much like that of an athletic coach's style. This kind of leader often has high energy, can be a risk taker, is competitive, and likes a challenge. They are the children who want to sit up front, answer first, and demand to be heard. They are linear, logical-sequential learners. These children are always apparent in a room. They tend to be extroverts. If they are not involved and engaged in an activity, they become fidgety and may get into trouble.

As an early care and education teacher, the dominant/direct person likes the idea of children and teaching; however, she or he is easily bored by the structure and routine. These individuals usually seek management positions. Many program directors have this style of learning, or they leave the field in the first three to five years.

The interactive/social learner tends to be a visual learner. These character types need someone to show them how to do a puzzle rather than telling them how to do it. As children, these types are conceptual and global, and usually quite the storytellers. They demand personal attention and are extroverts; in fact, they are constantly talking. They enjoy multiple friendships and tend to be empathetic and concerned with other's feelings. As children, they tend to develop their vocabularies and are quite expressive. They are the children who will want to retell the story just read to them. These children are often random thinkers, "popcorning" with different ideas in their heads.

As teachers, they are wonderfully creative and usually have colorful, high energy classrooms with several ongoing projects that never seem to get finished. This type of teacher tends to be a packrat with a wonderful assemblage of materials that will someday be used, but they are not quite sure when.

Steady and stable learners enjoy school as children and, at early ages, decide to be teachers. These character types are good listeners, follow directions, and want others to do the same. They are the classroom managers who remind others of the routine; they easily transition to new activities, and generally try to please adults. They tend to be practical and realistic. They may play dress-up either as mothers or as teachers for their friends. They learn their numbers and letters of the alphabet earlier than others; memorization and drill is their kind of fun. They tend to be introverted with a few good friends. They are linear, logical-sequential learners and are good problem solvers. They sometimes need to be alone, reviving in a quiet area.

As teachers, they are well-organized; they prepare schedules and follow routines. This type of leaner is the most prevalent in the field of early care and education. Their reward in life is being of service to others and caring for children to whom they become attached.

The complex or cerebral type of learner tends to be a shy child who prefers to play by himself or herself. Often able to entertain themselves in the block area or with cars, these learners tend to get upset when someone moves into their space. They are curious and full of questions. They ask questions that seem to be beyond their age levels, especially questions about how things are built. They are the children who enjoy taking a clock or a toaster apart and often can put it back together with only a few spare parts left. They appear bright and usually are; however, they can be nontraditional learners and have trouble understanding why they have to do what all the other children are doing. They are slow to transition and prefer sticking to one activity for the day. They tend to learn quickly and seem to understand things quickly. They appear to learn both logically and globally simultaneously.

As early care and education teachers, complex or cerebral individuals enter the field interested in child development, but the routine and day-to-day programming quickly dissipate their interests, and they often go on to work in higher levels of education or leave the field for areas they believe will be more intellectually stimulating. See Appendix C for the complete Learning Success System.

Understanding and using learning styles during the mentor coach/protégé program will increase its effectiveness and help reduce miscommunications.

OBSERVING AND UNDERSTANDING CHILDREN'S LEARNING STYLES

In early care and education programming, daily stress can be reduced by observing and understanding each child's preferred learning style. Cherry (1998) outlined nine indicators that she thought were valuable in determining the kind of environment and learning style that a child prefers (see Table 6–1).

In each entry in Table 6–1, the first activity indicates that the child

---

TABLE 6–1   NINE CATEGORIES OF OBSERVABLE BEHAVIOR

- Reasoning—Observe children constructing something. Do they use materials in traditional ways, or are they innovative in their use of materials?
- Motivation—Observe children exploring how something works. Do they wait for directions from an adult, or do they just plunge ahead?
- Perception—Observe children creating faces with construction paper parts. Do they attempt to create a realistic shape, or do they just enjoy the process of working with the materials?
- Organization—Observe children playing with a puzzle. Do they proceed from a point and move in one direction, or do they experiment with different pieces all over the place within the boundaries of the puzzle?
- Language expression—Observe children retelling a story that has just been read to them. Do they go back to the beginning of the story when interrupted, or do they just keep going even if they have lost their train of thought?
- Temporal awareness—Observe children when "clean-up time" is announced. Do they immediately respond or are they slow to respond and clean up?
- Emotional expression—Observe children being told a humorous story. Do they laugh after others laugh, or do they clown around and want to make others laugh?
- Graphic expression—Observe children painting. Do they draw exactly what is expected, or do they expand from what is expected to include their own ideas?
- Musical expression—Observe children in a group singing. Do they express the music mechanically well, or do they express music spontaneously, often singing and humming to themselves?

Source: Cherry, C., Godwin, D., & Staples, J. (1998). *Is the left brain always right? A guide to whole child development.* Grand Rapids, MI: Frank Schaffer/School Specialty Publishing.

---

tends to be more logical and sequential in his or her thinking. The second activity in each entry indicates that the child tends to be more of a **global-holistic** thinker. Obviously, children are experiencing an intense period of development and can respond one way with one approach and, a few days later, exhibit a different way of thinking. However, when consistent observations are noted and analyzed, a pattern of predominance appears. Working with this information and creating environments that support the child's preferred ways of thinking will greatly reduce stress for both the child and the teaching staff.

■ **GLOBAL-HOLISTIC**
Looks at the big picture, nonlinear learner

SITUATED LEARNING

One of the more recent works on learning comes from England. Lavé and Wenger (1991) discuss in their research "deep learning," or what they call "situated learning." According to the concept, significant, deep learning occurs

---

CASE STUDY: THE NEW TEACHER

The program director began to get complaints about a fairly new teacher, Pam. The families were complaining that she was not academically prepared and that the activities she planned for the children in the classroom were inadequate. Philosophically, Pam believes that preschool is the time for playing, learning how to share, and acquiring a base for later learning. When the program director shared the families' complaints, Pam acknowledged that she had heard the complaints also and was not sure how to explain to parents how she works with the children. The program director suggested including some literacy and numeric activities in her daily plan and sharing these activities with families so they could work with their children at home. This idea proved successful and the families were pleased with the new approach.

Critical Thinking Questions

1. How can a mentor coach help a protégé deal with her feelings of inadequacy as a new teacher?
2. How can the protégé become comfortable explaining her philosophy of education? What goals and objectives could be set on which the protégé could work?
3. What kind of support could a mentor coach provide in a situation like this?

---

when the context includes an actual experience. In other words, learning goes beyond the mere acceptance of factual knowledge and information to an experience, for example, the development of a new skill to an understanding in a social context. For example, compare it to being told about riding a bike, being shown pictures of people riding bikes, and personally experiencing and learning to ride the bike. In this situation, the experience is necessary. The skill is not acquired until one has had the experience. The situated learning body of literature reflects a belief in the constructivists' view of learning.

Vygotsky (1962), an early childhood theorist, describes how children learn and indicates that an experienced person can help the child to bridge the gap in his or her learning. Vygotsky's (1962) concept, called the **zone of proximal development** (ZPD), describes the learner as an individual with a learning base that is supplemented by another person, peer, or adult who guides the learner to the next level of learning. Teachers are encouraged to consider what would be the highest level a child could reach with assistance and, most likely, something she or he would not be able to do on her or his own without a lot of trial and error. Vygotsky (1962) encouraged teachers to understand and identify the child's potential for learning and not to use testing as a predictor of what the child could learn.

■ **ZONE OF PROXIMAL DEVELOPMENT (ZPD)**
Vygotsky's theory that a child develops a new skill as the result of an adult or peer helping him or her bridge the gap

Vygotsky (1962) also promoted the idea of scaffolding. Scaffolding is a communication technique that invites learners to collaborate and participate in their own learning by asking open-ended questions and building on what they already know. An instructor then provides assistance or support in helping the student move to the next level of skill or knowledge development.

This concept mirrors what happens in the mentor coach/protégé relationship. The mentor coach's availability is at the "heart" of the successful mentor coach process.

MULTIPLE INTELLIGENCES: A THEORY OF LEARNING

Harvard professor Howard Gardner (1983) presented his view on learning as a pluralistic system rather than following a single focus in his book *Frames of Mind,* which was the case with learning theory until that time. The traditional view of intelligence is usually discussed in terms of a person's ability to solve problems, use logic, and think critically. Gardner's (1983) work refuted the bell curve theory of learning, which asserts the following:

- Intelligence is a single entity.
- People are born with a certain amount of intelligence.
- It is difficult to alter a person's amount of intelligence—it is in the individual's genes so to speak.
- Psychologists can determine how smart a person is by administering intelligent quotient (IQ) tests.

Gardner's (1983) understanding of intelligence is a more holistic, mind/body approach where everyone has a **biopsychological potential** to process specific forms of information in certain kinds of ways. Gardner (1983) outlined a framework of intelligences to which he continues to add; however, his initial work presents seven intelligences (see Table 6–2).

Gardner's (1983) work is aligned with the Learning Success System presented at the beginning of the chapter and available in Appendix C. The Learning Success System examines four of the Gardner (1983) intelligences:

1. Bodily-Kinesthetic intelligence or "body smart" as the dominant learner
2. Linguistic intelligence or "word smart" as the interactive learner
3. Logical Mathematical intelligence or "number/reasoning smart" as the stable learner
4. Spatial intelligence or "picture/art smart" as the complex learner

■ **BIOPSYCHOLOGICAL POTENTIAL**
Attributing physiological reasons to psychological responses

TABLE 6–2   GARDNER'S MULTIPLE INTELLIGENCES

- Bodily-Kinesthetic intelligence or "body smart"
- Logical-Mathematical intelligence or "number/reasoning smart"
- Linguistic intelligence or "word smart"
- Spatial intelligence or "picture/art smart"
- Interpersonal intelligence or "people smart"
- Intrapersonal intelligence or "self smart"
- Musical-Rhythmic intelligence or "music smart"

These four types of learning, which were discussed previously, are related to how people acquire information in a learning setting. The Musical-Rhythmic interpersonal and intrapersonal intelligence, seem to be universally distributed across all individuals to a greater or lesser degree.

Gardner (2004) continues to research and write in the field of learning. His recent book *Changing Minds: The Art and Science of Changing Our Own and Other People's Minds* examines how whole societies and large organizations learn and eventually change directions. Building on his theory of multiple intelligences, he states that all learning also must be set in a community context that values learning. As he considered changing minds, he indicated levels where change occurs (see Figure 6–1).

The mind is fascinating, and this is an area where the challenge of mentor coaching can have its greatest impact. People change their minds either because they want to change them or because something happens in the real world or their mental lives that requires a major change. Gardner (2004) identifies a framework for changes of the mind, which is presented in Table 6–3.

Large scale changes for diverse populations of a region and/or a nation
Large scale changes for homogenous groups
Changes brought about through works of art or science
Changes within formal instructional settings
Intimate forms of mind changing
Changing one's own mind

FIGURE 6–1   Gardner's Levels of Change

Gardner, H. (2004). *Changing minds: The art and science of changing our own and other people's minds.* Boston: Harvard Business Review Press.

TABLE 6–3   GARDNER'S CHANGING ONE'S MIND

- Content: an idea, theory, or skill
- Desired change: content desired
- Counter content: an idea, theory, or skill that runs counter to existing conditions
- Type of audience/arena
- Format
- What levers tipped the change

Source: Excerpted and reprinted by permission of Harvard Business Review.
From Gardner, H. (2004). *Changing minds: The art and science of changing our own and other's minds.* Boston: Harvard Business Review Press. Copyright © 2004 by the Harvard Business School Publishing Corporation; all rights reserved.

BRAIN RESEARCH

Much work is being done in the area of brain research. Researchers are discovering that children have "windows of learning" that need to be accessed earlier than was done in the past. If these windows of learning do not receive proper stimulation at an appropriate time, it is still possible to recover them in a limited way and with intense levels of activities. Amen (1998) used spectrographic equipment to examine the brain and determined that lack of connectors and missing brain matter seriously affects one's learning and behavior. He asserts that the brain is the hardware of the soul and the very essence of being a human being.

Critical to functioning is an area of the brain known as the deep limbic system, which is about the size of a walnut; however, it is power packed with emotions and feelings. This area of the brain is thought to be the oldest and closest to the mammalian brain that allowed animals to experience and express emotions and supported their survival skills.

HOW ONE'S MIND CHANGES

In today's organizational environment, making decisions based on past experience is no longer optimal or wise. According to Senge, Scharmer, Jaworski, and Flowers (2004), business leaders need to stand back, suspend thinking, and reflect on how new learning and knowledge can sustain the organization. The acceleration of technology, the pressures of consumerism, and other global challenges affect organizations' behavior and their leaders' perspectives and behaviors. Overall, businesses are operating less and less like the halls of production of the old, repetitive manufacturing industries and more and more like casinos of technology.

Beginning with John Dewey, theorists have maintained that learning builds on past experiences in cycles of action and reflection followed by new actions. Dewey's (1915) original explanation of the learning cycle involved four stages:

- observe
- discover
- invent
- produce

According to recent theories and research, there is still much to discover and explore about learning and the cognitive sciences. Society is changing rapidly, and preparing students for global experiences requires rethinking the factory model of education currently in effect.

The assembly line influenced the industrial age school design with the aim of producing uniform, standardized products as efficiently as possible. However, educators know now that they need to develop thoughtful, knowledgeable, compassionate global citizens in the twenty-first century, which differs profoundly from the need to train factory workers in the nineteenth century. However, educators continue to be largely unaffected by the realities of children growing up in the present day.

Most learning today involves what is known as "reactive learning," which is based on previous experiences and actions, "downloading" habitual ways of thinking and seeing the world only in the categories with which one is comfortable. This kind of learning keeps educators in the cocoon of being right and inevitably ends up reinforcing outdated, preestablished mental models.

In "situated learning," a level of superficial thinking exists in today's schools, marketplaces, and relationships. The idea of "presence" was to dig in more deeply and follow a theory of thinking that begins with an image of a "U" in order to distinguish different depths of perceiving reality and different levels of action that follow. The process entails three major stages, or elements, as illustrated in Figure 6–2.

The three basic components of this "U" movement reflect what happens in all learning processes. That is why they bear superficial similarities to standard models of planned change. In a sense, more superficial learning and change processes are appreciated versions of the "U" movement. Most change efforts do not move very far down the "U." The deep learning occurs when the learner combines traditional reactive learning with suspending judgment, listening

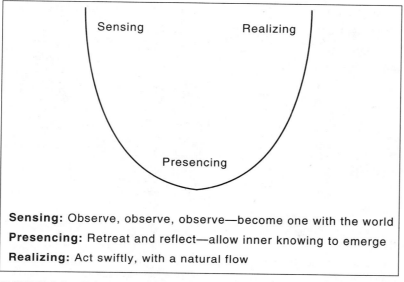

Sensing: Observe, observe, observe—become one with the world

Presencing: Retreat and reflect—allow inner knowing to emerge

Realizing: Act swiftly, with a natural flow

FIGURE 6–2   Theory of Deep Learning

Source: Senge, P., Scharmer, O., Jaworski, R., & Flowers, B. S. (2004). *Presence: Human purpose and the field of the future.* Cambridge, MA: Society of Organizational Learning. Reprinted by permission.

with the heart, and being willing to seek out new and deeper meanings for actions and knowledge.

PROCESS LEADERSHIP MODEL

Following along with Gardner's (1983) approach are the constructs of learning described in the Grove Facilitation Model (2001), see Figure 6–3. Although this model is designed for facilitating groupwork, the same interactive learning processes and stages occur in an effective mentor coaching experience.

In practice, the strategies in the Grove Facilitation Model tend to flow into one another interchangeably, appear throughout the process, and take on different and usually deeper meanings. The first and critical stage involves getting the attention and awareness of the protégé as to what the process is all about and what both the mentor coach and protégé hope to accomplish as a result of time spent together. The energy stage, or connecting, with the protégé requires an open heart and a willingness to empathize, listen, and become available to this person on the part of the mentor coach.

Once rapport has been established, outcomes determined, and an action plan set in place, it is then time to provide the protégé with information. The mentor coach provides information based on his or her experience and from written

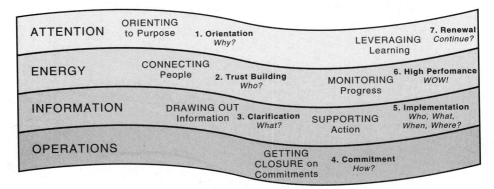

FIGURE 6–3   Grove Facilitation Model

Source: "The Grove Facilitation Model"™. "The Grove Consultants International" (2001). *Principles of facilitation*. San Francisco, CA: Grove Publishing Co. www.grove.com. Reprinted with permission.

materials. The mentor coach may also probe the protégé to determine what he or she may already know. This is a time for providing validation of the knowledge the protégé already has and determining how best to build on it.

At the operational point, the project direction, or plan formulation, begins to take place. As the protégé begins to take charge of his or her own learning, the power in the partnership begins to shift and the role of the mentor coach becomes one of monitoring performance by supporting, refining, and validating the actions of the protégé. At this point in the process, the mentor coach and the protégé engage in some reflective practice where constructive feedback and perhaps additional resources are provided.

This cycle of activities can occur over time and across several different projects; however, an important task of empowering the protégé is to set up the process of letting go; a time will come when the protégé is ready to move on.

This separation occurs at a different time and in different ways in each relationship. It is not so much a complete separation from the relationship but rather a detachment that involves gradually moving back out of the relationship. This sometimes can be difficult for the mentor coach because of ego-needs and needs to be handled diplomatically by both in the relationship.

MENTOR COACHING AND "DEEP SMARTS"

Organizations are learning the hard way that they have some excellent employees who have deep knowledge about the business, including how things are accomplished and how to make appropriate decisions, that is not that easily transferred to new employees. Understanding deep smarts and how to transfer the critical skills and information is more challenging than it first appears.

Deep smarts occurs when a person evaluates a complex situation and comes to a rapid decision that proves to be not only good but brilliant. Almost intuitively, these people can make the right decision, at the right level, and with the right people. Those who have deep smarts can see the whole picture and zoom in on a specific problem others have not been able to diagnose. Their insights are based more on know-how than on facts; they involve a system view as well as expertise in individual areas.

Deep smarts are experience based. They cannot be developed overnight or imported readily as many companies pursuing new strategies have discovered. In most organizations, deep smarts develop more by chance than by intent, often in spite of the organization's practices rather than because of them. Organizations assign people to new situations, incurring the costs of trial-and-error learning, instead of preparing a carefully thought-out transition that might occur through a dedicated mentor coaching program.

Most organizations' practices are not grounded in a fundamental understanding of how people learn. Furthermore, most organizations' training and development programs are designed to transfer explicit technical or managerial knowledge—not deep smarts.

Experienced employees with deep smarts encounter a wide variety of situations over many years and accumulate storehouses of knowledge. With this knowledge, they also develop the ability to reason swiftly and without a lot of conscious effort. See Table 6–4.

Receptors receiving information is not enough; it must be internalized and acted upon. The most valuable part of deep smarts is the know-how (and often know-who) that a person builds up during years of experience (see Table 6–5).

TABLE 6–4   MOVING TOWARD DEEP SMARTS

Directives, presentation, lectures	Rules of thumb, stories with a moral	Socratic questioning	Guided practice, guided observation	Guided problem solving	Guided experimentation

Passive Reception ——————————————————➤ Active Learning

TABLE 6–5   DEEP SMARTS LEADERSHIP APPROACHES

Situations	Examples
The skills to be learned involve interpersonal relations, so there is no set of absolute steps but rather an array of possible responses to the actions and emotions of others.	• Working with a board of directors • Negotiating a lease • Handling a talented, yet difficult staff person
There are many tacit dimensions to the skills, so even an expert cannot make all of them explicit.	• Closing a facility purchase • Dissipating tension in a meeting • Coming up with new solutions to old problems
The knowledge context is specific, so it's appropriate to be adaptive rather than explicit.	• Starting a new program • Remodeling a facility

Source: Excerpted and reprinted by permission of Harvard Business Review. From "Deep Smarts Leadership Characteristics" by Leonard, D., & Swap, W. (2004, September). Copyright © 2004 by Harvard Business School Publishing Corporation; all rights reserved.

This knowledge cannot be easily documented and transferred as information documentation in a filing cabinet or on a CD.

Early care and education programs that have experienced directors exhibit these kinds of deep smarts because they have successfully completed an experiential learning curve. Even if a new event is not exactly the same as a previous one, they can search their reservoir of ideas and solutions to determine what a good decision would be. However, a person may have an excellent education and seem to be well prepared, but still find it difficult to be confident and make decisions quickly in urgent situations.

In their research, Leonard and Swap (2004) found that the most efficient way to share deep smarts in an organization was to use knowledge coaches, those who could transmit experience-based expertise. Because deep smarts is an experience-based process, one cannot merely describe experiences, tell staff what to do, or give them rules; rather, deep smarts must be re-created in order to be effective. This can be accomplished by practice, observation, problem solving, and experimentation, and with the facilitation of knowledge in the process, both partners' learning is deepened.

Table 6–6 indicates some of the tasks that involve decision making that help develop different levels of experience, revealing the direction people with deep smarts thinking will follow.

TABLE 6–6   CHARACTERISTICS AND LIMITATIONS OF DEEP SMARTS

Tasks	Novice	Expert	Expert's limitations
• Making decisions	Needs to review facts	Makes decisions	Overconfidence
• Considering context	Relies on rules of thumb that minimize context	Takes context into account when solving problems	Difficulty transferring expert knowledge due to faulty context
• Extrapolating information	Lacks receptors, thus has limited basis for extrapolation	Can extrapolate from a new situation to find a solution	May base on inappropriate pattern
• Exercising discrimination	Not able to see the fine distinctions	Can make the fine distinctions	Not able to communicate to novice about fine distinctions
• Being aware of knowledge	Doesn't know what he doesn't know	Knows when rules don't apply	May assume expertise where it doesn't exist
• Recognizing patterns	Has limited experience from which to draw patterns	Has large inventory of patterns drawn from experience	Without patterns, expert and novice no better off
• Using tacit knowledge	Relies largely on explicit knowledge	Uses extensive tacit knowledge to drive decision making	May have a hard time explaining and transferring knowledge

Source: Excerpted and reprinted by permission of Harvard Business Review. From "Characteristics and Limitations of Deep Smarts" by Leonard, D., & Swap, W. (2004, September). Copyright © 2004 by Harvard Business School Publishing Corporation; all rights reserved.

One frustration in many organizations is the continual employee turnover and the process of remaking the wheel. The most successful transfer of knowledge occurs when a person learns by doing. This requires active dialogue between the mentor coach and the protégé. Deep smarts reflect an experienced repertoire. Merely explaining experiences is not nearly as powerful as actually having the experiences and reflecting about them.

Guided practice can be significant in closing the knowledge gap. Another strategy is guided observation, where the mentor coach observes the protégé in action and provides reflective dialogue about recognizing patterns and avoiding pitfalls.

In addition, guided problem solving requires active participation of the protégé, and the knowledge transfer from the mentor coach may be more about "know-how" than "know-what." Guided problem solving combines many of the transfer of knowledge techniques, including focusing attention, sharpening process skills, giving feedback, providing an opportunity to mimic the mentor coach, and having the protégé develop his or her own "deep smarts."

SUMMARY

Mentor coaches can be effective in providing guided experiences that can help protégés develop a deep understanding of a person's role and responsibilities much more effectively than in other types of learning. The mentor coach/protégé relationship provides the kind of setting where dialogue and the opportunity for deep learning should be something desired. Identifying personal learning and teaching styles can set the baseline for effective communication as protégés indicate how they prefer to receive information. It is important that protégés find their own voices and not think they have to mimic the mentor coach.

■ KEY TERMS

Biopsychological potential

Global-holistic

Zone of proximal development (ZPD)

■ CHAPTER DISCUSSION QUESTIONS

1. Whose four-quadrant theory is the basis for the Learning Success System?
2. Compare the "U" theory of learning with the situated learning theory.
3. Why is learning in new ways important for educators as well as business leaders?
4. List the four types of learning styles described in the Learning Success System.
5. Describe the meaning of "presence" as it relates to learning.
6. Provide a description of what is meant by deep smarts.

■ MENTOR COACH/PROTÉGÉ INTERACTION

The mentor coach and the protégé should take the Learning Success System together and compare notes. Each participant should then discuss how this affects the action plan and goals and objectives set for the project.

■ REFLECTIVE PRACTICE

Attend a board of directors, school board, or governing board meeting. Both the mentor coach and the protégé should take notes and then compare notes after the meeting, commenting on how power is used, what issues were addressed, and how the protégé would feel about presenting to a group such as this.

▓ LEARNING JOURNAL

Write a couple paragraphs about what you have learned as a result of reading this chapter. Can you apply any learning, personally or professionally? Describe any insights or "ah-has" that you have experienced as the result of reading and doing the activities suggested in this chapter.

_____

_____

_____

_____

_____

_____

▓ REFERENCES

Amen, Daniel. (1998). _Change your brain, change your life._ New York: Random House.

Cherry, C., Godwin, D., & Staples, J. (1998). _Is the left brain always right? A guide to whole child development._ Grand Rapids, MI: Frank Schaffer/School Specialty Publishing.

Dewey, J. (1915). _The child and the curriculum._ Chicago: University of Chicago Press. Re-issued 1991.

Gardner, H. (1983). _Frames of mind: The theory of multiple intelligences._ New York: Basic Books.

Gardner, H. (2004). _Changing minds: The art and science of changing our own and other people's minds._ Boston: Harvard Business Review Press.

Jung, C. (1994). Freeman, J. (ed.) _Man and his symbols._ New York: Dell Publishing.

Lavé, J., & Wenger, E. (1991). _Situated learning: Legitimate peripheral participation._ Cambridge, England: Cambridge University Press.

Leonard, D., & Swap, W. (2004, September). Deep Smarts. _Harvard Business Review_, 88–98.

Senge, P., Scharmer, O., Jaworski, R., & Flowers, B. S. (2004). _Presence: Human purpose and the field of the future._ Cambridge, MA: Society of Organizational Learning.

Webster's New World College Dictionary (4th ed.). (1999). New York: Macmillan.

Vygotsky, L. (1962). _Thought and language._ Cambridge, MA: MIT Press.

▓ FURTHER READINGS

Baker, A., & Manfred-Petit, L. (2004). _Relationships, the heart of specialty care: Creating community among adults in early care settings._ Washington, DC: NAEYC.

Sibbet, D. (2001). _Principles of facilitation guide._ San Francisco: Grove International Publishing Co.

Wenger, E. (1991). _Communities of practice: Learning, meaning and identity._ Cambridge, England: Cambridge University Press.

Zigarmi, D., Blanchard, K., O'Connor, M., & Edeburn, C. (2004). _The leader within: Learning enough about yourself to lead others._ New York: Prentice-Hall.

 For additional information on research-based practice, visit our Web site at http://www.earlychilded.delmar.com

Additional resources for this chapter can be found on the Online Companion™ at http://www. earlychilded.delmar.com. Special features of this supplement include Web resources, additional case studies with critical thinking questions, and multiple choice quizzes for each chapter. The answers to each quiz, along with the rationale for the correct answers, can also be found on-line.

CHAPTER 7

Mentor Coaching and Values

INTRODUCTION

This chapter includes a review of how values and motivation operate in one's life. The choices people make in deciding to continue working with children are facilitated by recognizing the values and motivators of individuals. The study of values and motivators can provide insight for both the mentor coach and protégé. Having in-depth discussions and using learning instruments to discover "hidden" motivators contributes to the development of a meaningful and appropriate action plan. If the goals and objectives of the action plan are aligned with the protégé's value system, they are likely to be accomplished.

■ CHAPTER OBJECTIVES _____

After reading this chapter, you should be able to:

• Understand and describe why values are important in a mentor coach/protégé relationship.

• Understand and describe two values models.

• Understand and describe personal value systems.

"Clarifying one's personal values, attitude, and habits is a prerequisite for understanding others."

JOANN HERREN
*Chief, Training
and Technical Assistance,
Head Start Bureau*

- Understand and describe the personal interests, attitudes, and values (PIAV) model incorporating Spranger's (1997) six attitudes: theoretical, utilitarian, individualistic, traditional, aesthetic, and social.
- Understand and describe the value systems of the traditionalist, in-betweener, challenger, and synthesizer (TICS).
- Understand the meaning of intrinsic and extrinsic rewards in a work setting.

DEFINITION OF VALUES

■ **VALUE**

An enduring belief that a particular means or end is more socially or individually preferable than another ends and means

A **value** is an enduring belief that a particular means or end is more socially or individually preferable than another means or end (Robbins, 1991). Values are those hidden motivators that make one choose a certain set of actions. Often these values are not understood until one takes the time to do some reflection around the choices one has made.

PERSONAL INTERESTS, ATTITUDES, AND VALUES

A nationally and internationally distributed learning instrument developed by Bonstetter (1997) and his Target Training International organization is the personal interests, attitudes, and values (PIAV) model. It is based on the theories of Edward Spranger (1882–1963). Later, building on Spranger's (1960) work, Allport, Lindzey, and Vernon (1960) all contributed to a work called the *Study of Values* that incorporated Spranger's (1960) six types of attitudes and created a values assessment tool. These six types (**utilitarian,** individualistic, traditional, aesthetic, social, and **theoretical)** were then incorporated into a learning instrument constructed and validated by Bonstetter (1997).

■ **UTILITARIAN**

The value of efficiency and practicality

■ **THEORETICAL**

The value of searching for knowledge

Understanding beliefs and attitudes is the baseline for understanding the importance and usefulness of values as they relate to a person's worldview, which is a way of looking at life or a mind-set and paradigm of thought. Attitudes, according to Spranger, (1960) determine positive values or negativity in life. Experiences result in a set of beliefs. A belief is a statement in which one has trust and confidence. A belief may or may not be true; it may be unchallenged or untested. It may change when challenged. Beliefs can be positive or negative.

Beliefs result from multiple experiences. Beliefs tend to cluster into similar categories and topics. Multiple experiences, either positive or negative, contribute to the intensity of a belief. Clusters of beliefs

evolve into a **hierarchy** of attitudes. Usually, individuals have two strong values that affect the other four values. The two strong values tend to decide what action a person takes, for example, who one votes for in a presidential election. These values determine the attitudes, direction, and purpose, and these values suggest how people, places, or experiences are evaluated.

Based on the brief descriptors in Table 7–1, it is easy to see that hidden motivators affect personal choices and decisions. Understanding an individual value system and then discovering and appreciating another's personal interests, attitudes, and values provides richness for the mentor coach/protégé dialogue. Although the stated goal for all early care and education professionals

■ **HIERARCHY**
A group of persons or things that are rank ordered from the highest to the lowest

---

TABLE 7–1   THE PERSONAL INTERESTS, ATTITUDES, AND VALUES MODEL

The following matrix provides a closer look at these six values:

World Attitude	Goal	Passion	Characteristics
• Theoretical	• Discovery of truth and knowledge	• Solving problems • Intellectual process • Pursuit of knowledge	• Objectivity • Values what can be rationally explained
• Utilitarian	• Searching for what is useful	• Uses resources to accomplish results • Getting a return on investments	• Practicality • Ability to maximize resources • Efficient
• Aesthetic • Experience joy and beauty	• Self-actualization	• Appreciation, enjoyment for form • Harmony and beauty	• Creative expression • Notices uniqueness of experience that others miss
• Social • Invest time, resources to help others	• To bring peace to the world	• Opportunities to develop potential in others • Being part of creating a better society	• Selflessness • Generosity with no expectation of return

(Continued)

TABLE 7–1   *(Continued)*

World Attitude	Goal	Passion	Characteristics
• Individualistic • Wants to lead and direct relationships	• To assert oneself and have personal-cause victories	• Leading others in carrying out a strategic campaign	• Attaining and using power to advance position
• Traditional • Pursue the highest meaning in life	• To search and find the highest value in life	• Pursuit of the divine • A worthy cause • Understanding the totality of life	• Living according to a predetermined system • Decisions made from principles held

Source: Bonstetter, B. PIAV © (Personal Interests, Attitudes, and Values). Scottsdale, AZ: Target Training International, Co. Reprinted by permission of Target Training International, Co.

is to serve children and families, there are different approaches even within one program.

THE TRADITIONALIST, IN-BETWEENER, CHALLENGER, SYNTHESIZER (TICS)© VALUES MODEL

There are several plans for understanding values. Another values model is based on the work of Massey and O'Connor (1981). There are four major descriptors to define this model: traditionalist, in-betweener, challenger, and synthesizer. Values are those hidden motivators that cause one to take action and make decisions of which one is often unaware. Surprisingly, these motivators are what an individual usually holds dearly throughout one's lifetime. These values are developed through childhood by family members, churches, and communities, who provide examples of acceptable behaviors and actions that, by the age of 12, have been either accepted or rejected. Values change, sometimes as the result of a **significant emotional event** (SEE). These events might include personal losses, such as the death of a family member or the loss of a close personal relationship.

■ **SIGNIFICANT EMOTIONAL EVENT (SEE)**

Having or expressing a serious emotional event, for example, loss, death of a loved one, immigration

TABLE 7–2   THE TICS VALUES MODEL

1. A value is chosen.
2. The action is chosen from alternatives.
3. The action is chosen with a knowledge of consequences.
4. The action is acted on over time.
5. The action is prized or "publicly owned."

Source: Zigarmi, Drea; Blanchard, Ken; O'Connor, Michael; & Edeburn, Carl, *The leader within: Learning enough about yourself to lead others,* 1st edition, © 2005. Adapted by permission of Pearson Education, Inc., Upper Saddle River, NJ.

The TICS Values Model and Criteria

The TICS values model has as a foundation the criteria presented in Table 7–2. A value is a belief that is chosen. Coerced or forced behaviors are not considered values based. To act under the threat of punishment may be the result of a specific value but not necessarily for the sake of the object or the act.

Actions are chosen from alternatives; people believe that certain ends or means are better for themselves and others in comparison to other possible ends or means. To act on one's values initially requires thoughtful reflection. It involves weighing what is better, what is right (or more right), against what might be worse or wrong.

A value is chosen in anticipation of the potential consequences of the choice. Beliefs and, therefore, values are formed by direct experience or derived through authority. A programmed value, poorly examined, is often formed without the direct experience that would facilitate a full appreciation of the consequences. A value or belief formed through direct experience often facilitates the examination of alternatives and the anticipation of possible consequences. These examined values are developed values.

A value is acted on over time. Values have behavioral components that are exhibited by repeatedly acting based on personal values.

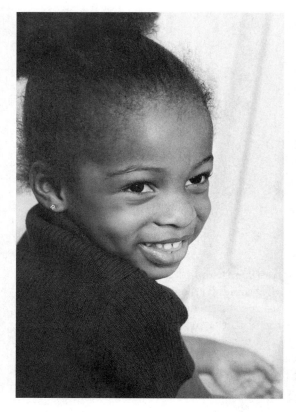

A value is also prized, or publicly owned. Most values should hold up to scrutiny, or stand in the light of day.

Developed values are shaped through a values process. If one chooses certain values, then the process becomes choosing among alternatives after deliberating and understanding potential consequences. If one continues to make the same choices, eventually the deliberation effort is minimized; the choices are made with little reflection, and decisions are automatically acted on.

Types of Values

There are two types of values: means and ends. The distinctions between the two are important; there are fewer ends values than means values. Think of an ends value as a goal state of existence for self and for others. These ends values are either social or personal in focus. A social ends value is concerned with how both the self and others should relate to others. Personal ends values are primarily concerned with what is desirable for the self and include only indirect implications for others. In other words, ends values can be other- or self-focused.

Means values are also either social or personal. Examples of social values include honesty, responsibility, and equality. These social means, values, or modes of behavior do not imply end states, but they do imply interaction with others. They are interpersonally focused and, when violated, cause a guilty conscience. The second type of means value is personal. A personal means is exemplified by values such as being logical, independent, and self-controlled. They are personally focused and do not seem particularly concerned with morality or socially acceptable behavior. However, failure to act in accord with these values could lead to feelings of shame or personal inadequacy. These ends and means systems are represented in Figure 7–1.

■ **INTERRELATED**
To make, be, or become mutually related

■ **SYSTEMIC**
An established way of doing things

■ **CONTINUUM**
A continuous whole, series, or quantity that cannot be separated

■ **PERIPHERAL**
Laying at the outside or away from the central part

ENDS AND MEANS VALUE SYSTEM

Each person holds a unique combination of ends and means values that are constantly used to sort experiences and make decisions. These combinations result in clusters of **interrelated** values and beliefs called a value system. It is **systemic** in the sense that certain beliefs and values depend on each other in a **continuum** from central to **peripheral.** It is not systemic in the sense that it has well-organized priorities that only occur with experience, application, and careful reflection.

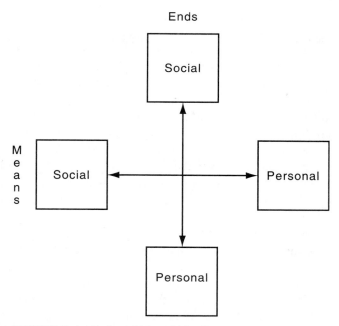

FIGURE 7–1   Ends and Means Value Systems

All people, regardless of whether they realize it, have some form of means and ends values; however, there is no hierarchy of values indicating that one is better than another. Some people are personally ends driven and socially means driven. Others are oriented to social ends and personal means. People do not function using only one value, rather, they have a schema, or cluster of interrelated values. A value system is a cluster of interrelated values that, when acted on over time, provide a sense of stability in decision making.

Values are formed in topical areas, such as politics, **economics, aesthetics,** morality, power, and social conduct. A well-integrated value system includes interrelated ideas and values that connect economics to power or to morality and so on. Means and ends are interconnected but not closely and naturally related. Ends do not dictate the means. One means might serve several ends, or several means might serve one end.

THE VALUE OF VALUES

Values serve several important functions. People use values as **ego defenses** or to present oneself in a social context. Values also may affect decision-making or conflict-resolution situations. Also, values are closely related to an individual's motivation.

■ **ECONOMICS**
Systems of business and finance

■ **AESTHETICS**
Systems for appreciating beauty and form

■ **EGO DEFENSES**
Mediators between the impulses of the id, the demands of environment, and the standards of the superego

■ RATIONALIZATION
To devise superficially rational or plausible explanations for an action, belief, or point of view

■ COMPETENCE
Ability or fitness for the task

Needs, feelings, and actions are part of the ego defense. If an individual's action or decision is socially unacceptable, the person may believe that his or her actions can become more acceptable by a process of justification or **rationalization.** Values allow the individual to rationalize certain actions that are unacceptable to others. By rationalizing, one can still feel a sense of morality or **competence.**

Values facilitate the social and personal interactions between a group and an individual. Values allow people to take particular positions on social, economic, legal, political, ethical, and aesthetic issues encountered in everyday living. They serve as guidelines for managing the self in light of others' expectations (values). Conversely, each individual uses his or her values to judge, evaluate, praise, or blame others. Values can be used to persuade and influence others.

Differences in values are at the base of all conflicts, regardless of whether they are national, interorganizational, or personal. Exploring and understanding a personal value system leads to one's ability to consider, understand, and appreciate another's value system. At a higher level, suspending personal judgments and understanding another's viewpoint facilitates true and honest dialogue and the possibility for collaboration.

As people mature, previously isolated values begin to integrate. A process occurs whereby an overriding value will drive an action or decision that originates from an orderly set of values that have priorities. Values also serve as means for self-motivation. Ends values are most often future oriented. The ends and means of attainment represent an individual's reasons for living. They keep one striving toward a life purpose and, ultimately, may provide the motivation to discover meaning in life. Adherence to ends values liberates energy. Motivation provides excitement, interest, and enthusiasm in work and life.

Values Model

■ FRAMEWORK
Structure, serving to hold parts together

Zigarmi, Blanchard, O'Connor, and Edeburn (2005) presented a **framework** for understanding and analyzing values that clusters four sets of values. It is called the TICS framework. The acronym stands for traditionalist, in-betweener, challenger, and synthesizer. These value types represent distinct ways a person deals with the world. In order to fully understand these perspectives, keep in mind the following considerations:

1. No values point of view is perfect or inherently better than another in its ability to guide an individual's actions.
2. The points-of-view framework may not predict an individual's specific position on an issue.

3. Experience, **socialization,** and significant life events may result in a shift in one's values' point of view.

4. Simply observing someone is not enough to identify an underlying point of view. Asking why a person made a decision or acted in a certain way provides insight into what values were acted on.

Another consideration in this discussion of values involves understanding that all four of these values (ends and means) clusters focus on either the self or others. An individual is either acting for a future state for humanity—peace on earth, better health care, and so on—or is interested in a comfortable life that only includes the self.

Knowing the source of control for power in one's life also affects these four value systems. Is power centered in the self or does it rest within a government, a religion, or some other organized institution with standards that apply to all? This responsibility **orientation** assumes that the entity will do what is right for the group rather than what is right for the individual. According to the responsibility orientation, other people's points of view are valid, but people following this orientation tend to compromise for the well-being of the group.

SOCIALIZATION
Adjust to or make fit for cooperative group living

ORIENTATION
Familiarization with and adaptation to a situation or environment

Traditionalists

The first value system to consider is that of the traditionalist. Traditionalists are oriented toward social ends and social means. They focus on responsibilities and expectations that others define as "goods and bads" of life. They care about responsibilities—theirs and others'. Traditionalists work to understand the rules, laws and customs, and beliefs of the group to which they belong.

The key end value for the traditionalist is responsible living at work and at home. They want what is best for the family, organization, church, or other special reference group with which they identify. They are motivated to contribute to other's well-being and that of society. They want to be of service to others and make the world a better place. They believe in the traditions of the past and will try to preserve age-old standards and values in keeping with the views of the group.

Traditionalists take a "we" orientation once the appropriate authority or process determines the group's goals and courses of action. They take a great deal of pride in meeting those obligations and standards. They value being role-players who contribute by steadily working because people can accomplish more together than they can individually.

The key means values of traditionalists are devotion, loyalty, and dependability. The value of devotion involves the commitment to work hard to achieve goals. They will work diligently to make responsible contributions to their identity groups. Traditionalists are found in churches, politics, and fraternal/service organizations. However, the primary identity group is always the family. The value of loyalty is seen in the importance that traditionalists attach to obedience. They work hard to maintain and strengthen the existing social order to which they identify. They follow the rules and expect others to do likewise. The value of dependability implies a dutiful work style in which "you do what you say you will do."

The traditionalist's values personally motivate him or her toward a proactive future. Acting on those values liberates positive energy and emotions, such as joy, peace, and delight. When acting out their value system of devotion, loyalty, dependability, and living responsibly, the traditionalist becomes the person he or she wants to be and, therefore, enhances and builds personal self-esteem.

The loss of social respect creates a self-esteem conflict for a traditionalist. They value their reputations, which are developed by living responsibly. Traditionalists are often concerned with carrying their fair share of responsibility. They worry about not meeting their obligations. The lack of self-esteem produced by not acting on these standards drives the traditionalist to be almost compulsive about devotion, loyalty, dependability, and responsible living.

Generally, the traditionalist's choices involve taking responsibility. They neither want nor expect a free lunch and are annoyed with others who do. They believe an individual should make do with what she or he has. They seek satisfaction with social restraint, often sacrificing immediate rewards for long-term gains. They believe the group is more important than the individual.

TWO-DIMENSIONAL
Having two dimensions, lacking in substance or depth

Traditionalists tend to view life from a **two-dimensional** mind-set of either/or choices. Their values' positions are typically a matter of right or wrong, for or against, or in or out choices. They work together to preserve what they, and others like them, have achieved. Their traditions, customs, institutions, organizations, and so on are the endowment that they are committed to leaving to future generations.

All four clusters of values face decisions about these basic issues of life in unique ways. The traditionalist addresses the basic life issues as presented in Table 7–3.

Work style refers to the way individuals derive meaning from what they do in a work setting. Traditionalists are company types; they want clear guidelines for themselves and others. They prefer constancy in their work roles with a singular or specialized purpose. They tend to work at one company all their lives out of devotion and commitment.

Because traditionalists are committed to rightness or correctness for the group to which they belong, they develop strategies to support their own beliefs. With the speed of change and new technologies, they need help being flexible, being open to new ideas, and accepting ideas from others who do not necessarily share their point of view.

TABLE 7–3   TRADITIONALIST'S VALUE SYSTEM

1. Political—The President is seen as "Commander in Chief," and patriotism is important.
2. Legal—They are law-and-order people, who believe that the laws are meant for everyone to obey.
3. Aesthetic—They see the "good life" as home, family, and taking care of business.
4. Social—They think people need to work together as a team.
5. Moral—They get their standards from religion or their organization; however, they will make decisions around how someone they respect would respond.
6. Economic—They believe hard work has its rewards, and they are not looking for a handout.

Source: Zigarmi, Drea; Blanchard, Ken; O'Connor, Michael; & Edeburn, Carl, *The leader within: Learning enough about yourself to lead others,* 1st edition, © 2005. Adapted by permission of Pearson Education, Inc., Upper Saddle River, NJ.

The traditionalist is oriented toward social ends and social means. This orientation leads to a point of view that focuses on responsibility for one's own and others behaviors. Individuals with the traditionalist's point of view build and care for practices, organizations, and systems that serve others and provide worth to society.

In-Betweener

The second value system to consider is that of the in-betweener. The name in-betweener is derived from their position in relation to the traditionalists and the challengers. They accept some of the beliefs of the traditionalists, such as sense of duty, responsibility, and tradition but focus on personal well-being. They are oriented toward personal ends and social means. However, similar to the challengers, they take a "rights" approach rather than a responsibility stance. They focus first on personal rights and then on the rights of others.

The key end values for in-betweeners are self-expression and happiness. With the primary focus on personal happiness, they believe their goals best can be served by cooperating with others. In-betweeners believe the key principle in life is the consideration of personal views and feelings. They are the best judges of personal fulfillment, but if it brings pain to others, it will not be satisfying. Happiness is important not only for self but also as it relates to its impact on others.

In-betweeners accomplish their goals with interpersonal interactions. In-betweeners differ from challengers and are more similar to traditionalists in that they believe hard work is the source of personal success. The key means values for the in-betweener are growth, equality, and helpfulness.

The belief in growth for in-betweeners is demonstrated by the desire to climb the highest mountain. "Attitude determines altitude." Often, in-betweeners find themselves caught between self-exploration and social traditions. Although they are not always decisive, they often take the position that whatever choices they make will contribute to a learning experience. They often are involved in self-help groups or reading self-help books.

The belief in equality is manifested by the in-betweener's concern for others. Although they tend to assess rules and regulations in light of personal experiences and beliefs, they are willing to accept the importance of authority figures and role models. The in-betweener is sensitive to the inequities in the world. Economic, social, and political inequalities are of concern to them; they seek ways to satisfy the wants of others without sacrificing personal happiness. When they are forced to choose, most often they will choose personal happiness.

The belief in helpfulness is demonstrated through friendly relationships and sensitive understandings of others' points of view. The in-betweener is a joiner and belongs to groups that advance his or her personal causes.

The in-betweener may get caught trying to satisfy personal desires with social means, wanting to be viewed as a socially responsible person. Actions ultimately are based on self-interests. In-betweeners want to be perceived as people who make a difference. They enjoy variety in life, so they sample different options. This may motivate them to be frequent job changers. In-betweeners typically want to have fun and enjoy life. Being forced to choose, they will endure social disapproval for personal satisfaction. The in-betweener addresses basic life issues as shown in Table 7–4.

In-betweeners derive meaning in the work setting by balancing personal rights with attempts to satisfy others. They search for ways to meet their own

TABLE 7–4   THE IN-BETWEENER'S VALUE SYSTEM

1. Political—They will take a stand rather than remain neutral.
2. Legal—They think all actions can be rationalized.
3. Aesthetic—Just having possessions is not an end goal for them.
4. Social—They make friends easily and work to maintain them.
5. Moral—Their conscience is only concerned if someone is watching.
6. Economic—They think money is meant to be circulated.

Source: Zigarmi, Drea; Blanchard, Ken; O'Connor, Michael; & Edeburn, Carl, *The leader within: Learning enough about yourself to lead others*, 1st edition, © 2005. Adapted by permission of Pearson Education, Inc., Upper Saddle River, NJ.

goals while meeting those of others. In-betweeners seek innovative ways to approach tasks. They often want to individualize work rather than conform to a set of rules.

The bind for in-betweeners involves their need to create unique, personal ends through social means. This requires a balancing between meeting one's own needs and being able to meet the expectations of others. For in-betweeners to reach their ends, they must use life experiences to substantiate what is "right" in light of present realities.

The in-betweener is oriented toward personal ends and social means. This perspective leads to being between self and other interests. End values, such as self-assertion and happiness, are goals. Mean values, such as growth, equality, and helpfulness, are the basis for the in-betweener's actions and viewpoints.

Challenger

The third value system to be discussed is that of the challenger. This value system takes the extreme position from the traditionalist's point of view. Challengers are concerned with personal, individual rights. They are oriented toward personal ends and personal means. Their ideas of what is good is self-defined based on experience, with the final goal being self-preservation and well-being.

The key end values for challengers are self-preservation and satisfaction. Challengers seek psychological and material satisfaction. As a result, they are continually searching for experiences and rewards that increase their sense of well-being. They are motivated by experiences that feel good and may seem self-indulgent to others. Challengers trust in their own experiences and may reject the norms and traditions of others.

Challengers take pride in their individualism and sense of self. They believe that they should do their own thing and want to be rewarded for it. For challengers, asking for what you want in life is a natural part of living.

The key mean values for challengers are independence, freedom, and ambition. The value of independence is demonstrated through a "my-way" approach to problems and choices. They enjoy the expression of individuality in unconventional clothes, mannerisms, and living habits. They change jobs, living patterns, and even relationships if they believe changes will contribute to growth and self-satisfaction.

The value of freedom is expressed in the challenger's reluctance to be **constrained** by obligations, customs, or expectations. **Conformity** to rules, policies, or traditions is acceptable only if they correspond with challengers'

■ **CONSTRAINED**
Compelled, forced, or obliged

■ **CONFORMITY**
The condition of being uniform or alike

outcomes and priorities. Individual freedom means freedom from restraint—freedom for self-expression, exploration, and achievement of a self-defined sense of well-being. They want the freedom to try new things, to explore new frontiers, and to accomplish their missions in life, no matter how unconventional they may be.

The value of ambition is expressed in the emphasis challengers place on self-preservation and well-being. They are willing to work for what they want, but they want to be rewarded for it, and they want those rewards immediately. Challengers may seem concerned with material success; however, that success is used primarily to serve their private sense of well-being. They strive to be upwardly mobile, to achieve power and status, and to live the good life as quickly as possible.

In living and achieving their desired sense of well-being, they seem to bring self-confidence and self-esteem along. Conflict arises if they sense a loss of well-being. They tend to be somewhat pessimistic about life and societies and do not want to be ruled by **constraints** or customs of the masses.

Challengers believe it is a "dog-eat-dog-world" and that only the strong survive. This means individuals must stand up for their rights. Challengers believe change is part of life. Their belief in independence results in their tolerance for individual differences in themselves and others. Challengers tend to be nonconformists who do things their way. The challenger addresses basic life issues as represented in Table 7–5.

Challengers like immediate rewards for their efforts. They want to be unconstrained in their work assignments. Therefore, they prefer being **entrepreneurs** rather than risking not being recognized for their contributions. When they are

■ **CONSTRAINTS**
Customs of repression of natural feelings or behavior

■ **ENTREPRENEURS**
People who organize and manage personal businesses

TABLE 7–5   THE CHALLENGER'S VALUE SYSTEM

1. Political—Power helps us become independent.
2. Legal—The fewer constraints there are, the better.
3. Aesthetic—The good life is following your bliss.
4. Social—They don't feel that they need to meet other's expectations.
5. Moral—The ends justify the means. Morality is situational.
6. Economic—Having money means that one is a wise and good person.

Source: Zigarmi, Drea; Blanchard, Ken; O'Connor, Michael; & Edeburn, Carl, *The leader within: Learning enough about yourself to lead others*, 1st edition, © 2005. Adapted by permission of Pearson Education, Inc., Upper Saddle River, NJ.

observed in organizational settings, they seem to be swimming upstream away from the group, thus they can become alienated.

The challenger is oriented toward personal ends and personal means; the result is a very self-focused point of view. Happiness, satisfaction, and personal well-being are the end values of the challenger. The mean values are independence, freedom, and ambition, which serve to assist them in reaching their goals.

Synthesizer

The fourth value system is described as a synthesizer. This value system is actually a by-product of all the other points of view. Synthesizers share with in-betweeners feelings of **optimism** and potential, with traditionalists concerns for the well-being of others, and with challengers a sense of independence and a will to do it their own way.

■ **OPTIMISM**
Taking a hopeful view, expects the best

■ **CONGRUENCE**
A way of coming together, being aligned

The key belief that motivates the synthesizer is the integration of self with others. Their approach to others is one of self-respect and they are responsibility oriented. They work to bring resolution to people, groups, and organizations without violating personal principles. They want win/win solutions and seek the common good of all. Synthesizers maintain a deep belief in themselves and their purpose in life.

The key means values for synthesizers are logic, justice, and inner competence. Their belief in logic is evident in their rational examination of all points of view. The good life evolves from rational, flexible actions. Careful consideration of risks, benefits, and actions results in greater equity and opportunity for all.

The synthesizer believes that justice results from a tolerance of other's viewpoints and an ability to appreciate others' perspectives. They try to make choices that result in fairness and justice for themselves and others.

The synthesizer's belief in inner **congruence** is evident in the constant examination of personal behavior and the behaviors of others. They believe each person has the right to personal viewpoints and that coexistence is possible with understanding and respect for others'

TABLE 7–6   THE SYNTHESIZER'S VALUE SYSTEM

1. Political—Politics is the art of the possible. Power should not be confused with greatness.
2. Legal—Law is the application and declaration of what is just.
3. Aesthetic—The good life is serving others with your abilities and knowledge.
4. Social—No man is an island; everyone is a part of the whole.
5. Moral—No one can be free until all are free.
6. Economic—A life simply and well lived is the sign of being rich.

Source: Zigarmi, Drea; Blanchard, Ken; O'Connor, Michael; & Edeburn, Carl, *The leader within: Learning enough about yourself to lead others,* 1st edition, © 2005. Adapted by permission of Pearson Education, Inc., Upper Saddle River, NJ.

value systems. They often are involved in issues that affect the welfare of themselves and others. They believe that reality is shaped by daily personal and collective action.

Conflicts occur for the synthesizer as a result of issues of integrity. To support something, yet not act on it, creates internal disharmony or incongruence, which can be stressful for synthesizers. Synthesizers actively participate in causes in which they believe. They view uncertainty as a part of life and are flexible and accountable. The synthesizer addresses the basic life issues as described in Table 7–6.

Synthesizers want to be aware of what is happening at work. They want to actively participate in issues that concern them. They tend to live simple lives and enjoy inner richnesses in highly personalized ways. They are often willing to give more than they get. As activists, they tend to be in demand and are frequently asked for help. They often overcommit and are disappointed when they cannot achieve all their goals.

The synthesizer is geared toward social ends and personal means. Self-respect and wisdom are core values for synthesizers. The mean values that are important include logic, justice, inner congruence, forgiveness, and self-control. People holding this point of view have lifelong passions and have made contributions that make the world a better place.

When examining the value clusters presented in Table 7–7, it becomes apparent that individuals' personal value systems can cloud their perceptions of others. Also, people may have a combination of value systems, depending on issues; however, most people have a predominate value system that determines the decisions and choices in life.

TABLE 7-7 SUMMARY OF VALUE CLUSTERS

	Traditionalist	In-Betweener	Challenger	Synthesizer
Ends values	Responsible living	Self-expression and happiness	Self-preservation and satisfaction	Integration of self with others
Means values	Decision, loyalty, and dependability	Growth, equality, and helpfulness	Independence, freedom, and ambition	Logic, justice, and inner congruence
Self-esteem conflict	Loss of others' respect	Not meeting self and others' goals	Loss of individual well-being	Loss of inner congruence
General perspective	Loyalty to others	Growth and optimism	Survival and pessimism	Pragmatic, idealism, and moderation
Work style	Hard work and conformity	Socially acceptable individuality	Self-expression and individuality	Personal activism
Growth action	Flexibility and collaboration	Self-understanding from past experience	Sensitivity to the impact of others	Greater self-tolerance

Source: Zigarmi, Drea; Blanchard, Ken; O'Connor, Michael; & Edeburn, Carl, *The leader within: Learning enough about yourself to lead others,* 1st edition, © 2005. Adapted by permission of Pearson Education, Inc., Upper Saddle River, NJ.

CASE STUDY: ACTION PLANNING

Allie, the mentor coach, and Pamela, the protégé, were developing an action plan for Pamela. Allie discussed goals and setting a timeline. Pamela's response to Allie was, "Oh, that's way too structured. I don't want to follow an action plan; that's too restrictive. I would rather read a book on curriculum design and then tell you how I might change things." Allie, being a conscientious type, has trouble not following the rules. Pamela, being a challenger, believes rules are for other people.

Critical Thinking Questions

1. What are your suggestions for resolving the issue?
2. What are the positive aspects of an action plan?
3. What are the negative aspects of an action plan?

SUMMARY

Values are important in the field of early care and education because motivation and passion will sustain an individual in the face of challenges and discouragement. If the mentor coach and protégé examine their personal value systems and share their ideas with each other, they may discover this is a productive exercise for developing action plans and setting goals.

■ KEY TERMS

Aesthetics	Interrelated
Competence	Optimism
Conformity	Orientation
Congruence	Peripheral
Constrained	Rationalization
Constraints	Significant emotional event (SEE)
Continuum	Socialization
Economics	Systemic
Ego defenses	Theoretical
Entrepreneurs	Two-dimensional
Framework	Utilitarian
Hierarchy	Value

■ CHAPTER DISCUSSION QUESTIONS

1. What is the importance of understanding values as part of a mentor coach/protégé interaction?
2. Provide the six descriptors that are described in the PIAV (1997) values model.
3. What are the four value clusters described in the TICS values model?
4. What are two kinds of means involved in the TICS values model?
5. Describe and give an example of what is meant by the term *intrinsic motivation.*

■ MENTOR COACH/PROTÉGÉ INTERACTION

The mentor coach and protégé could benefit from spending some time dialoguing about the values systems presented, identifying personal values, and examining how the values have affected their personal and professional lives. This value study can help align the action plan for the protégé as well as provide insights for the mentor coach.

▤ REFLECTIVE PRACTICE _____

Consider how values have been demonstrated in your life. Do values support your personal life/career plan?

▤ LEARNING JOURNAL _____

Write a couple paragraphs about what you have learned as a result of reading this chapter. Can you apply any learning, personally or professionally? Describe any insights or "ah-has" that you have experienced as the result of reading and doing the activities suggested in this chapter.

_____

_____

_____

_____

_____

_____

_____

▤ REFERENCES_____

Allport, G., Lindzey, G., & Vernon, M. (1960). *A study in values: A scale for measuring the dominant interests in personality.* New York: Houghton-Mifflin.

Bonstetter, B. (1997). *PIAV (Personal interests, attitudes, and values inventory).* Scottsdale, AZ: TTI (Target Training International).

Herren, J. (2002, July/August). *Leadership in action.* Head Start Bureau.

Massey, M., & O'Connor, M. (1981). *Values analysis profile.* Minneapolis, MN: Performax Systems International.

Robbins, A. (1991). *Awaking the giant within.* New York: Fireside Books.

Zigarmi, D., Blanchard, K., O'Connor, M., & Edeburn, C. (2005). *The leader within: Learning enough about yourself to lead others.* Upper Saddle River, NJ: Prentice-Hall.

▤ FURTHER READINGS _____

Bennis, W. (1989). *On becoming a leader.* Reading, MA: Addison-Wesley.

Bennis, W., & Nanus, B. (1985). *Leaders: Strategies for taking charge.* New York: Harper and Row.

Blanchard, K., & O'Connor, M. (1997). *Managing by values.* San Francisco: Berrett-Koehler.

Greenleaf, R. K. (1991). *The servant as leader*. Indianapolis, IN: Robert K. Greenleaf Center.

Jaworski, J. (1996). *Synchronicity: The inner path of leadership*. San Francisco: Berrett-Koehler.

O'Connor, M. (1986). *The professional trainer and consultant's reference encyclopedia to the TICS model*. Naples, FL: Life Associates, Inc.

O'Connor, M. (1985). *Values' instrument*. Minneapolis, MN: Carlson Company.

Rokeach, M. (1972). *Beliefs, attitudes and values: A theory of organization and change*. San Francisco: Jossey-Bass.

Wheatley, M. J. (1992). *Leadership and the new science: Learning about organizations from an orderly universe*. San Francisco: Berrett-Koehler.

For additional information on research-based practice, visit our Web site at http://www.earlychilded.delmar.com

Additional resources for this chapter can be found on the Online Companion™ at http://www.earlychilded.delmar.com. Special features of this supplement include Web resources, additional case studies with critical thinking questions, and multiple choice quizzes for each chapter. The answers to each quiz, along with the rationale for the correct answers, can also be found on-line.

8

Mentor Coaching and Cultural Competence

INTRODUCTION

In today's global society, an understanding of and appreciation for children and families of diverse backgrounds is important to caregivers. It is important to be sensitive to the concerns of parents, family values, and the importance of the family's first language. An appreciation of the family's values and the implementation of strategies that reinforce family values and cultures indicate that the caregiver is providing quality programming and services.

■ CHAPTER OBJECTIVES

After reading this chapter, you should be able to:

- Gain an appreciation of the importance of developing and **implementing** strategies for understanding and reinforcing families' values and cultures.

- Understand and discuss culture and values to ensure an appreciation of another's culture and values.

- Understand the importance of helping the child understand and appreciate the family of origin's language while acquiring a second language.

"If you have come here to help me, you are wasting your time.... But if you have come because your liberation is bound up with mine ... then let us work together."

ANONYMOUS
Australian Aboriginal Woman

■ **IMPLEMENTING**
A way of using a thing or person as a means to some end; to carry into effect, fulfill, or accomplish

DEVELOPING CULTURAL COMPETENCE

As part of a mentor coaching process, an important topic to consider involves one's background and culture. Developing effective intercultural communication skills is necessary in the quest to be a successful leader. Harris and Moran (1991) describe intercultural communication skills as a way of sharing perceptual fields. An individual's distinctive perceptual field consists of family, education, religion, and social backgrounds that enable a person to process information uniquely. Two individuals can receive the same information and interpret and filter it differently.

Caruso and Fawcett (1999) consider several specific cultural factors that affect communication and how one supervises. Considerations such as time sense vary by culture. For example, Americans in business expect promptness and rushing through business transactions; however, many cultures disagree with this style.

When talking with a colleague who speaks another language, it is best to use simple vocabulary and not use words that have multiple meanings, or stories or metaphors that might not be understood. In addition to using simple words when having a conversation to help clarify communication, consider such issues as pace (fast/slow) and tone (loud/softer), as well as facial expressions and proximity. Thinking through, observing, and sampling intercultural skills will be beneficial for both the mentor coach and protégé.

UNDERSTANDING PERSONAL CULTURE BEFORE APPRECIATING ANOTHER'S

In order to be effective with children and families of different cultures, it is helpful to consider one's own culture. A genogram tool helps to examine and understand family systems. Basically, a genogram is a family tree graph with extra details about relationships, occupations, illnesses, or other factors that can be identified. Examining at least four generations (grandparents, parents, siblings, and children) often yields repetitive patterns that, when analyzed, provide suggestions for discussions with family members.

Using a genogram as a family systems tool can help the caregiver understand a family having a different culture from the caregiver. Using one's own personal insights about his or her own culture through using the genogram can provide a baseline look at another culture's family strengths and similarities. Marlin (1989) provides additional formatting and diagramming techniques.

Components of Understanding Another's Culture

Looking introspectively, one can identify factors that can help an individual accept people who do not share the same ethnic or social background as oneself (culture). The promise of America involves the dreams of people from diverse cultures and backgrounds living in harmony. This dream has been difficult to achieve, and yet it remains the promise. In **cultural pluralism,** groups and individuals or families maintain personal culture and ethnicity while being a part of a larger cultural framework. Mutual respect is the goal.

Being culturally sensitive and wanting to understand other's cultures is important. As outlined in Table 8–1, there are six areas that are easily misunderstood and should be addressed (Gonzalez-Mena, 2005).

■ **CULTURAL PLURALISM**
Policy of favoring the preservation of groups within a given nation and/or society

---

TABLE 8–1   AREAS OF CULTURAL SENSITIVITY

1. Personal space—What is comfortable in the Western world is frequently uncomfortable for other cultures. In the Anglo-North European world, usually an arm's length is a comfortable stance. This arm's-length represents our "personal space" and our space feels invaded and threatened when anyone comes closer. The usual response is to back up. Other cultures feel very comfortable "being in your face" and can be easily misunderstood.

   Take a few moments and reflect about how close you sit or stand to communicate with someone you don't know well.

2. Smiling, touching, and eye contact also varies between cultures. North Americans tend to smile when they want to be friendly as well as when they are happy. Russians exhibit a smile only when they are happy. Conversely, the Vietnamese wear an enigmatic smile.

   Take a few moments and reflect about what a smile means and when to smile, and also what another person's smile means.

3. Eye contact is a very sensitive area that can easily be misunderstood, the look-you-in-the-eye approach can appear disrespectful and rude to Asians who tend to avert their eye contact until a level of relationship and understanding has been reached. Even looking at someone directly in the eye for too long a period of time can be understood as disrespectful.

   Take a few moments to reflect and consider what you expect the person you are communicating with to do—look you in the eye or avert his or her look out of respect.

4. Touch—Again, this is an area where cultures vary considerably. Touching between genders in North American society is up for scrutiny and is best to be avoided. The Vietnamese believed if you touch people on their head they lose their soul.

   Take a few moments and think about touching another person—is it a very sensitive action that brings a relationship closer or creates distance and challenges?

   (Continued)

TABLE 8–1   *(Continued)*

5. Silence—In North American society if a person suddenly stops talking, usually someone else will pick up the thought and continue the conversation. In some cultures, answering too quickly gives the appearance that not enough thought has been given to a person's conversation. Conversations around sports, and sports commentators, have developed a style of shouting and cutting each other off before the other has finished, which is influencing a generation of non-listening children. Good dialogue includes periods of silence and reflection.

   Take a few moments to think about the meaning of silence and how much is too much. Silence can have cultural meanings; what are they?

6. Time concepts—Time concepts vary not only between cultures but also within personal dynamics. Staff may feel the press of time and want parents to be there on time. Parents seem to have a different clock, and canceling appointments doesn't seem to matter as staff is always there. Again, perhaps related to individual differences as much as culture, the style of some people to get right to the point and others to always have to socialize and spend time on insignificant issues before they address the main issue or concern.

   Take a few minutes to think about your personal clock. What constitutes being late? How do you let others know what late means?

Source: Gonzalez-Mena, J. (2005). *Diversity in early care and education: Honorary differences* (4th ed.). New York: McGraw-Hill. Reproduced with permission of The McGraw-Hill Companies.

IMPORTANCE OF CULTURE IN CHILD-REARING PRACTICES

The family is a child's first culture and community. Learning begins with the family and the child begins to develop. Harkness and Super (1992) describe a child's earliest environment as a "developmental niche," or a place where developmental expectations and the child's daily life converge. There are three components of a child's cultural development: physical and social setting, customs and practices of care, and the psychology of caregivers. These cultural components influence child-rearing practices that are embedded in the values, beliefs, attitudes, and culture of a child's home and community.

Some specific cultural norms are influenced by religion, generational change, and shifts in cultural perspectives; the value of respect between children and parents; and the concept of independence versus interdependence. Cultures also vary in terms of specific attachment practices that encourage the emotional, cognitive, motor, language, and social development of children, such as feeding, carrying, touching, displaying affection, reading, singing, listening, playing, and teaching.

In studying cultures, a wide range of differences were found in the expectations of children one to four years of age related to the use of utensils, training cups, weaning, sleeping alone, dressing one's self, and playing alone. As early as three years old, children develop ideas about their own racial identity, as well as that of others.

Based on the research and what is generally understood about the importance of culture and child-rearing, it is clear that administrators, caregivers, and teachers must commit to partnering with parents, and engage in learning about one another and understanding each child's unique background, in order to provide the best possible services and ensure that every child is ready for school (Hepburn, 2004).

A widely misunderstood practice in the field of early care and education is the failure to understand and respect a child's **family of origin,** language, and culture. It is estimated that as many as 10 million children in the United States come from homes where English is not the primary language. Traditionally, it is expected that every child will speak English in the classroom, and they are chastised and corrected if they speak in another language. Children are labeled as challenging or disruptive if they do not understand adults who are asking for their cooperation. They are assessed and determined less intelligent if they do not respond correctly to the questions asked. Children are even assigned to special education classes as a result of not being able to respond to assessments that are given only in English.

FAMILY OF ORIGIN
Belonging to a family with a particular ethnic or cultural background

■ LINGUISTICS
The science of language, including phonetics, morphology, syntax, and semantics; the study of the structure and development of a particular language, and its relationship to other languages

■ PROFICIENT
Highly competent, skilled, or adept

■ BILINGUAL
Using or capable of using more than one language with equal or nearly equal facility

■ INTERPRETER
A person who explains the meaning of things, makes things understandable to, or translates from one language to another

■ INDIVIDUALIZATION
To consider as a separate entity, mark as different from others

TABLE 8–2   NAEYC STATEMENT ON ENGLISH LANGUAGE LEARNERS

NAEYC's statement encourages early care and education programs to

- Recognize that all children are cognitively, **linguistically,** and emotionally connected to the language and culture of their homes.
- Understand that second-language learning can be difficult. It takes time to become linguistically competent in any language. Although verbal **proficiency** in a second language can be attained in two or three years, the skills needed to understand academic content through reading and writing can take four or more years. Children who do not become proficient in their second language in two to three years usually are not proficient in their own language either.
- Recognize that children can and will acquire the use of English even when their home language is respected.

Traditionally, the approach has been to prepare children for life with English as the primary language. **Bilingual** programs that help children learn a primary language and then begin instruction in English have proven successful. However, critics maintain that bilingual programs favor children's native languages rather than preparing them to speak, read, and write correct English. Currently, the trend is to eliminate these programs. Legislators in California passed legislation against bilingual programs in school districts and funding is no longer provided for these programs.

The NAEYC organization has a policy statement on the importance of maintaining a child's native language as well as becoming fluent in English. (See Table 8–2.)

Generally, it was thought that children could not learn both their mother language and another language simultaneously. Now, there is evidence that children learn languages with greater speed when learning a second language. They retain the primary language, and it does not seem to inhibit their learning; rather, it appears to assist in learning the second language (Santrock, 2003, p. 414).

One of the greatest breakthroughs in early care and education occurs when staff learn to accept, appreciate, and arrange for **interpreters** and other resources so children and families feel accepted and understood. Developing a child's native language takes effort, and **individualization** benefits everyone, including the child, his or her family, other children, and staff. Appreciation for another's culture involves social skills increasingly needed by children as they move into a global society. Learning these skills early in life makes the acceptance and practice of them easier for the child than if they are learned later. The changing demographics of the United States show dramatic increases in the number of people with diverse ethnic backgrounds. Traditionally, African American, Hispanic, and Asian groups have been lower in the economic and social order. The American dream is fueled by education and opportunity, and it represents increasing challenges on how to provide equity of opportunity.

Culture refers to an individual's integrated pattern of human behavior, including thought, communication, language, beliefs, values, practices, customs, courtesies, rituals, manners of interacting, roles, relationships, and expected behaviors. It is essential to focus on the unique nature, strengths, and experience of any one individual, family, or community in order to avoid stereotyping about a culture.

Equally important to consider is **ethnicity,** which is based on cultural heritage, nationality characteristics, race, religion, and language. Central to the idea of ethnicity is the **ethnic identity,** which involves a sense of membership in an ethnic group, based on shared language, religion, customs, values, history, and race. This implies choice. A person may choose to belong to a group to which his or her ancestors were not a part.

Context is another factor of **diversity.** It is probably the aspect of early care and education that staff can influence the most because context refers to the setting in which development occurs. Historical, economic, social, and cultural factors of the family influence the setting. Caregivers' acceptance of diversity in a child's early development program can give the child and his or her family a sense of self-esteem and pride in his or her place in society.

HELPING CHILDREN UNDERSTAND AND APPRECIATE LANGUAGE

Helping children whose home language is other than English learn English is a shared responsibility among parents and caregivers. Young children have great capacity and developmental momentum to learn language. Language acquisition is considered a robust and resilient process that is, in fact, quite similar across cultures. Young children learn language as part of their daily routines and in relationships with caregivers. Early communication and language are rooted in the home culture and the nonverbal aspects of appropriate social behaviors, demonstrating respect, and showing affection toward others. Language and its social context make it one of the most significant tools for interaction, learning, and conveying **cultural messages.**

There have been, and continue to be, differences of opinion in approaching **English language learners** (ELL). The issues concern how best to honor and preserve the child's first and native language while simultaneously

---

CULTURE
Ideas, customs, skills, arts, and so on of a people or group that are transferred, communicated, or passed along

ETHNICITY
Common cultural heritage developed by custom, characteristics, language, and common history

ETHNIC IDENTITY
Designating a population subgroup having a common cultural heritage or nationality

DIVERSITY
Different cultures

CULTURAL MESSAGES
Ideas, customs, or skills of a group of people who pass on their identity and customs through oral and written traditions

ENGLISH LANGUAGE LEARNERS
People whose primary language is other than English and who are learning English as a second language

TABLE 8–3   WORKING WITH ENGLISH LANGUAGE LEARNERS
• Young children's first language (especially before age five) is not fully developed and children are, therefore, working toward two milestones at the same time. • Children need to develop their native language along with English so that they can maintain communication and relationships with their parents, extended family members, and community. • Learning English is an additive process. The children's native language must be respected in the early learning setting to preserve self-esteem and encourage the use of the native language. • Involving parents is essential to support learning at home, explore language and literacy patterns in the home, and integrate culture and language into classroom learning.

facilitating English language learning. Cultural and linguistic continuity is extremely important for infants, toddlers, and preschoolers. Table 8–3 presents several things to keep in mind when working with English language learners.

DELIVERING APPROPRIATE CULTURAL AND LINGUISTIC PROGRAMS

In the early care and education setting, educators should consider how they can incorporate a variety of aspects of diverse cultures in the classroom. As the child transitions into center care, the learning environment should continue to support learning about culture and diversity. The multicultural perspective requires knowledge about the meaning of culture and its impact on child development; attitudes and behaviors that value respectful, open discovery of differences; and skills to design and implement learning experiences that support multicultural learning. Strategies for caregiving and technical tools for teaching with a multicultural perspective include preparation for the caregivers; involving families; and using developmentally appropriate curricula, educational materials (books, games, and toys), and other childcare and classroom aids.

The goals of a multicultural **antibias curriculum** should involve empowering all children to become knowledgeable, caring, and active citizens in a multicultural and linguistically diverse world. According to Banks (1993), children must be comfortable and develop a sense of identity before they can begin to learn. The child should be comfortable and experience empathic interactions with people of diverse backgrounds. As the child develops in a multiculturally sensitive environment, the child should develop the ability to think critically about bias and, as a result, be able to stand up for him- or herself and others in the face of bias. Early care and education staff may perceive culture as an "add-on." However, this is not the case; understanding culture involves integrating a teaching approach that makes all learning experiences complete, accurate, and sensitive.

Educators should discuss openly with all students differences and diversity rather than feeling that these discussions may divide and create conflict for children. It is important to teach the values of understanding and negotiating differences toward mutual understanding and acceptance of diversity. The early care and education caregiver should be careful not to erroneously reinforce stereotypes and generalize about ethnic groups but rather should teach the value of appreciating each family for its uniqueness as part of a cultural group. One approach to be avoided is the "tourist" approach to multicultural activities, which involves providing multicultural activities only around holidays rather than incorporating them as part of everyday learning. Another limitation involves implementing a "cultural curriculum" separately from regular daily lessons rather than understanding and including a truly multicultural curriculum as an ongoing dynamic process that evolves daily as new experiences for children and their families arise. When implementing a multicultural antibias curriculum Hohensee and Derman-Sparks (1992) suggest the strategies outlined in Table 8–4. Guidelines for antibias curriculum materials can be found in Table 8–5.

■ **ANTIBIAS CURRICULUM**
A method of presenting activities to children to help them avoid ways of perceiving a person or a group as less than equal due to race, gender, or disabilities

---

TABLE 8–4   IMPLEMENTING AN ANTIBIAS CURRICULUM

Preparation of Personnel

Early Care and Education caregivers understand the rationale and benefits in implementing a multicultural curriculum.

Early Care and Education caregivers are committed to a multicultural approach.

Early Care and Education caregivers are aware and knowledgeable of their own biases.

There are strategies in place for Early Care and Education caregivers to learn about cultures other than their own.

(Continued)

TABLE 8–4   (*Continued*)

Early Care and Education caregivers are familiar with and prepared to implement a multi-cultural approach.

There is continuous learning and support opportunities for Early Care and Education caregivers to build self-awareness, learn new skills, problem solve, and evaluate implementation.

Curriculum

There is a curriculum development/selection and review process with parents and classroom staff involved.

The curriculum is developmentally appropriate.

Cultural and linguistic diversity permeates the curriculum.

The curriculum portrays a culture as a dynamic characteristic that is shaped by new learning and experiences as social, political, and economic conditions evolve.

The curriculum includes people of various cultural and class backgrounds throughout.

The curriculum shows respect and offers affirmation for each child's cultural and class backgrounds throughout.

The curriculum shows respect and offers affirmation for each child's cultural and linguistic background.

The curriculum helps children learn to understand experiences and multiple perspectives other than their own.

Classroom Practices and Activities

There are various types of learning situations available—working in groups, pairs, or individually.

Language and communication style (verbal and nonverbal) is tailored to be culturally and linguistically sensitive.

All children are equally encouraged to participate in classroom activities and discussion.

The classroom models a **democratic** and **equitable** decision-making process.

Early Care and Education caregivers have integrated the curriculum so that "teachable moments" can be used to reinforce concepts from the formal curriculum.

Parents are involved in classroom practices and activities to bring their cultural and linguistic strengths into the learning environment.

Source: Hohensee, J., & Derman-Sparks, L. (1992). *Implementing an anti-bias curriculum in early childhood.* (Web site: http://ecap.crc.uiuc.edu/eecearchive/digests/1992/hohens92.html). Early Childhood and Parenting Information Technology Group, University of Illinois at Urbana-Champaign. Used with permission.

■ **DEMOCRATIC**
Treating persons of all classes the same way

■ **EQUITABLE**
Characterized by equity, fairness, and justice: said of actions or results of actions

TABLE 8–5   ANTIBIAS CURRICULUM MATERIALS

Books and classroom materials reflect the cultures of the children in the program.

Play materials represent the cultures of the students in the program and are relevant to each child's life and experiences.

Materials are displayed that reflect the cultures of all the students in the program and include pictures or photographs of the children in the program or other people who are similar to themselves.

Bilingual materials (books, signs, posters, etc.) are all available for English language learners.

DEVELOPING CULTURAL SENSITIVITY FOR CHILDREN AND THEIR FAMILIES

Lynch and Hanson (1990) outlined some important guidelines for cultural sensitivity with children and families. These guidelines are not intended to be a checklist or an interview protocol but rather a way to assist caregivers in determining the kinds of questions that are helpful. They provide meaningful insights for understanding a particular family's attitudes, beliefs, and values in order to develop appropriate services and supports. The guidelines (presented in Table 8–6) may also provide the foundation for asking more

TABLE 8–6   DEVELOPING CULTURAL SENSITIVITY

Family Structure and Childrearing Practices

Family Structure

- Family composition
  Who are the members of the family system?
  Who are the key decision makers?
  Is decision making related to specific situations?
  Is decision making individual or group oriented?
  Do family members all live in the same household?
  What is the relationship of friends to the family system?
  Where is the hierarchy within the family? Is status related to gender or age?

- Primary caregivers
  Who are the primary caregivers?
  Who else participates in the caregiving?
  What is the amount of care given by the mother versus others?
  How much time does the infant spend away from the primary caregiver?
  Is there conflict between caregivers regarding appropriate practice?
  What **ecological/environmental** issues impinge upon general caregiving (i.e., housing, jobs, etc.)?

Childrearing Practices

- Family feeding practices
  What are the family feeding practices?
  What are the mealtime rules?
  What types of food are eaten?
  What are the beliefs regarding breastfeeding and weaning?
  What are the beliefs regarding bottle-feeding?
  What are the family practices regarding transitioning to solid food?
  Which family members prepare the food?
  Is food purchased or homemade?
  Are there **taboos** related to food preparation and handling?
  Which family members feed the child?
  What is the configuration of the family mealtime?
  What are the family views on independent feeding?
  Is there a discrepancy among family members regarding the beliefs and practices related to feeding an infant/toddler?

Family Perceptions and Attitudes

- Family's perceptions of health and healing
  What is the family approach to medical needs?

■ **ECOLOGICAL/ ENVIRONMENTAL**
Study of the relationship and adjustment of human groups to their geographic and social environments

■ **TABOOS**
Social prohibitions or restrictions that result from convention or tradition

Do they rely solely on Western medical services?
Do they rely solely on **holistic** approaches?
Do they utilize a combination of these approaches?
Who is the primary medical provider or conveyer of medical information? Family
   members? Elders? Friends? Folk healers? Family doctor? Medical specialists?
Do all members of the family agree on approaches to medical needs?

- Family's perceptions of help seeking and intervention
From whom does the family seek help—family members or outside agencies/individuals?
Does the family seek help directly or indirectly?
What are the general feelings of the family when seeking assistance—ashamed, angry,
   demanding help as a right, or do they view help as unnecessary?
With which community systems does the family interact (educational/medical/social)?
How are interactions conducted (face to face, telephone, or letter)?

Language and Communication Styles

- To what degree:
Is the caregiver or home visitor proficient in the family's native language?
Is the family, or at least some members, proficient in English?

- If an interpreter is used:
With which culture is the interpreter primarily affiliated?
Is the interpreter familiar with the **colloquialisms** of the family members' country or
   region of origin?
Is the family member comfortable with the interpreter? Would the family member feel
   more comfortable with an interpreter of the same sex?
If written materials are used, are they in the family's native language?

Interaction Styles

Does the family communicate with each other in a direct or indirect style?
Does the family tend to interact in a quiet manner or a loud one?
Do family members share feelings when discussing emotional issues?
Does the family ask you direct questions?
Does the family value a lengthy social time at each home visit unrelated to the service or
   program goals?
Is it important for the family to know about the caregiver or home visitor's extended
   family? Is the caregiver or home visitor comfortable sharing this information?

Source: Lynch & Hanson. (Eds.). (1990). From "Home-based early childhood services: Cultural
sensitivity in a family systems approach" by Wayman, K. I., Lynch, E. W., & Hanson, M. J. (1990).
Topics in Early Childhood Special Education, 10, 65–66. Copyright © 1990 by PRO-ED, Inc. Reprinted
with permission.

■ **HOLISTIC**
Concerned with the
whole or integrated
system rather than the
parts

■ **COLLOQUIALISM**
Local or regional use of
words or expressions

specific questions related to learning, school readiness, school entry, and family and school connections.

WORKING WITH FAMILIES FROM DIFFERENT CULTURES

The questions in Table 8–6 provide a good starting point for expanding one's understanding. These types of questions are valuable for caregivers or home visitors who provide services and interactions. They help service providers and those for whom they are caring build mutual trust and **empathy** and understanding even though there may be language and cultural barriers to overcome.

■ **EMPATHY**
The projection of one's own personality on another in order to understand the other person better; the ability to share in another's emotions, thoughts, or feelings

It is also important to understand that families living in poverty have different expectations from those not living in poverty. For example, those not living in poverty may ask, "What will we have for dinner?" but rather, "Will we have dinner?" People living in poverty are present focused; they are primarily concerned about the present moment. Thinking about and planning for the future are difficult without support and assistance. Payne (2005) discusses the importance of the poverty stricken having access to financial resources, as well as emotional, mental, and physical support systems; relationships; and role models. A mentor coach is able to provide the "hidden rules" of the middle class and how to get along in society.

DEALING WITH COLLEAGUES AND ADULTS WHO EXPRESS BIAS

In early childhood and education, it is easier to explain and redirect children's possible biases than those of adults. Carter and Curtis (1994), building on the work of Clarke (1989), suggest there are seven ways adults tend to react to someone who expresses a bias. They give the example of a father walking into his son's child care center and seeing him dressed up in a fluffy dress and high heels, feeding a baby doll. He is clearly upset and asks, "How could you let him play like this?" Table 8–7 presents possible responses.

> **TABLE 8–7   RESPONDING TO BIAS REMARKS**
>
> - Attacking—We let children play wherever they want, why don't you?
> - Defending—There's no way I can stop your child from playing dress-up.
> - Empathizing—It's hard for you to see your child do something you disapprove of.
> - Investigating—Are you concerned that he will get teased or picked upon?
> - Reframing—I'd like to understand what harm you think this might do to your child. From what I know, young children who are prevented from exploring their interests and identity in a supervised environment often grow up with confusion and shame about who they are.
> - Excusing—Oh, it's just harmless play.
> - Ignoring—I'm needed out on the playground.
>
> Source: From *Training teachers: A harvest of theory and practice,* by Margie Carter and Deb Curtis (Redleaf Press, 2003). Copyright © 1994 Margie Carter and Deb Curtis. Reprinted with permission from Redleaf Press, St. Paul, Minnesota, wwwredleafpress.org. To order, call 800-423-8309.

If you want to reassure the parent that you do not tolerate bias, the first two responses would be appropriate. If you want to build a trusting relationship and create more dialogue, some combination of empathizing, investigating, or reframing will work. The last two choices serve to avoid the subject and possible conflict.

> ### CASE STUDY: LONG-TERM SUBSTITUTE
>
> Maria Elena, a classroom teacher's assistant, was asked to fill in as a long-term substitute in a particular classroom. Maria Elena was unhappy about the assignment but was willing to give it a try. After the first couple of days, Maria Elena reported to her mentor coach that she was really unhappy with the new assignment because Bernie, the teacher in the classroom, had some obvious biases not only toward her as a Hispanic but also toward several Hispanic children. After a few days, she realized that Bernie seldom called on the Hispanic children, especially those who were still struggling to learn English. Finally, when Bernie made an unfortunate comment about children from poor, immigrant families to a parent, Maria Elena realized she needed to tell her supervisor about the situation. Before she made the appointment, she contacted her mentor coach, indicating she wanted the mentor coach to help her resolve this issue in a professional manner. The mentor coach
>
> *(Continued)*

(Continued)

suggested that she approach the supervisor with the attitude that she wanted this to be a win/win situation for all. Maria Elena was willing to stay in the classroom if Bernie was willing to understand and eliminate the biased attitude. The supervisor was a skilled mediator and suggested a three-way conference in which each person would be given the opportunity to present her perspective; the supervisor hoped they would be able to resolve the situation and learn from it. Bernie is a dedicated teacher and, when she was made aware of her biases, indicated that she had been unaware of them. She was willing to learn. The supervisor knew that even though Bernie now recognized her biased attitude, changing overnight was unlikely. The supervisor suggested that Maria Elena spend more time observing in the classroom, assisting Bernie with constructive feedback, and helping Bernie set goals for changing her behavior.

Critical Thinking Questions

1. Did Maria Elena take the right approach in handling her classroom challenge?
2. Do you have any suggestions for improving the approach?
3. Do you think Bernie, the teacher, completely changed? Why? Why not?

INCREASING CULTURAL COMPETENCIES IN A GROUP SETTING

It is not unusual for more than one staff member to be insensitive or consciously biased. An individual's culture and the sentiments of the community affect how a person responds to other cultures. Some effective staff training can be accomplished using learning instruments, role-play, or other kinds of awareness activities.

An informative and interesting classroom activity in a group setting might involve a learning instrument such as Discovering Diversity Profile® (2003). (See References at the end of the chapter on how to obtain.) This validated instrument can provide insight into humor and a deeper understanding of a person's awareness level of different cultures and ethnicity. Based on this evaluation, the individuals can assess their levels of biases as well as that of the group. Because it is a self-reporting instrument, no one tells the participants about their biases and stereotypes. Each individual discovers his or her own. As part of the group, each can assess the overall team's strengths and contribute to developing goals and objectives for the group or as part of the mentor coach/protégé process.

The diversity learning instrument is based on four major **constructs:** knowledge, understanding, acceptance, and behavior. Knowledge is the foundation of

■ **CONSTRUCTS**

Things built or put together systematically, a concept or theory devised to integrate in an orderly way diverse ideas or data all the other areas. Information about other people is necessary before one can understand someone else's feelings, thoughts, and motives. A subgroup of knowledge includes an item about **stereotypes.** These questions consider how an individual will respond to another with proper regard and respect, regardless of his or her cultural background. The second item examines information. Has the person made an effort to understand others and made an effort to interact with others appropriately as a result of that understanding?

Understanding builds on the knowledge base. Understanding is the intellectual recognition that people are the way they are because of their cultural backgrounds and influences. Subgroups are listed under awareness. Awareness explores understanding the effect of one's behavior on others. Empathy indicates that one has truly begun to appreciate another's perspective.

Acceptance is an expression of the feelings one develops about oneself and about diverse groups. Some level of understanding must precede any genuine acceptance of other people. This is particularly true for those with different physical abilities, customs, values, or sexual orientations. A subgroup considers receptiveness and examines whether an individual is willing to accept differences. Respect indicates the ability to trust others who are different.

Behavior refers to the ability to interact with different people; it includes the ability to perform tasks with comfort and ease with diverse people. Subgroups include several items about self-awareness and understanding behavior and how this affects the quality of relationships. When an individual develops the interpersonal skills that are effective with people of diverse backgrounds and cultures, he or she can effectively communicate with a wide variety of people.

Using the Discovering Diversity Profile participants gain insights, take action, and learn how to value diversity. In addition, participants discover personal comfort levels with people who are different from themselves. Participants begin to understand the impact of particular behaviors on others as well as assess the accuracy of their knowledge about the differences of others. As the participant becomes more involved in the process, he or she begins to understand how to reduce stereotypical behaviors in classrooms and the community. This self-analysis serves as the beginning of the process of transforming knowledge into acceptance and empathy, and truly embracing diversity as a source of an institution's strength.

■ **STEREOTYPES**
Unvarying forms or patterns; fixed or conventional motions or conceptions of a person, group, or idea

SUMMARY

In an increasingly complex and diverse world, educators need to spend time and make an effort to provide staff and families with the skills to appreciate diverse backgrounds. Celebrating diversity enriches everyone's lives. Originally in the United States, people wanted all the immigrants to blend in, to lose cultural identity, and to speak only English. Today, the United States is more aptly described using the concept of a "salad bowl," where all the parts make up a wonderful whole, which is the preferred goal. Understanding one's personal culture is the best way to begin to appreciate someone else's culture. Tools that can be used in appreciating diversity include a genogram and the Discovering Diversity Profile (2003) learning instrument.

■ KEY TERMS

Antibias curriculum	Equitable
Bilingual	Ethnic identity
Colloquialism	Ethnicity
Constructs	Family of origin
Cultural messages	Holistic
Cultural pluralism	Implementing
Culture	Individualization
Democratic	Interpreter
Diversity	Linguistics
Ecological/environmental	Proficient
Empathy	Stereotypes
English language learners	Taboos

■ CHAPTER DISCUSSION QUESTIONS

1. Why is being culturally competent important in early care and education programs?
2. Describe three components of culture and suggest strategies for handling differences.
3. What family patterns did you discover as part of the genogram process?
4. Provide an example from your own culture that you feel is unique.
5. With which of the seven responses for clarifying bias would you be comfortable?
6. Why is it easier to redirect a child's bias than an adult's?

■ MENTOR COACH/PROTÉGÉ INTERACTION

The mentor coach and protégé take the Discovering Diversity Profile 2003 learning instrument and discuss the results. Talk about strategies and ways of improving cultural competence.

■ REFLECTIVE PRACTICE

Use the genogram tools and answers to the questions that trigger your memories about your family. A genogram looks like a family tree; however, it includes information about family structure and relationships that influence family systems. Ask family members about family issues that have not been previously discussed. Reflect on your own family and diagram four generations starting with yourself and your siblings, adding parents and grandparents, and then adding any children and cousins. Think about family members that are close and those that have strained relationships and why. Also consider the occupations of different family members. Consider instances of leadership, how they occurred, and what relevance they have for you. Share your reflections with your mentor coach.

▓ LEARNING JOURNAL

Write a couple paragraphs about what you have learned as a result of reading this chapter. Can you apply any learning, personally or professionally? Describe any insights or "ah-has" that you have experienced as the result of reading and doing the activities suggested in this chapter.

▓ REFERENCES

Banks, J. (1993). Multicultural education: Development, dimensions, and challenges. *Phi Delta Kappan, 75*(1), 22–28.

Carter, M., & Curtis, D. (1994). *Training teachers: A harvest of theory and practice.* St. Paul, MN: Redleaf Press.

Caruso, J., & Fawcett, M. (1999). *Supervision in early childhood education: A developmental perspective* (2nd ed.). New York: Teachers College Press.

Clarke, J. (1989). *Growing up again: How to parent yourself so you can parent your children.* New York: Harper.

Discovering Diversity Profile (2003). Minneapolis, MN: Inscape Publishing. Available from the Mentor Group at 1-800-398-3134.

Gonzalez-Mena, J. (2005). *Diversity in early care and education: Honorary differences* (4th ed.). New York: McGraw-Hill.

Harkness, S., & Super, C. (Eds.). (1992). Parental belief systems. In Sigel, I., McGillicuddy-DeLiss, & Goodnow, A.V. *The psychological consequences for children.* Hillsdale, NJ: Erlbaum.

Harris, P., & Moran, R. (1991). *Managing cultural differences* (3rd ed.). Houston: Gulf Press.

Hepburn, K. S. (2004, May). *Building culturally and linguistically competent services to support young children, their families, and school readiness.* Baltimore, MD: The Annie E. Casey Foundation.

Hohensee, J., & Derman-Sparks, L. (1992). *Implementing an anti-bias curriculum in early childhood.* (Web site: http://ecap.crc.uiuc.edu/eecearchive/digests/1992/hohens92.html).

Lynch, E. W., & Hanson, M. J. (Eds.). (1990). Home-based early childhood services: Cultural sensitivity in a family systems approach. In Wayman, K. I., Lynch, E. W., & Hanson, M. J. *Topics in Early Childhood Special Education, 10,* 65–66.

Marlin, E. (1989). *Genograms: The new tool for exploring the personality, career and love patterns you inherit.* Chicago: Contemporary Books.

Payne, R. (2005). *A framework for understanding poverty.* Highlands, TX: AHA Press.

Santrock, J. (2003). *Children* (7th ed., pp. 412–413). New York: McGraw-Hill.

■ FURTHER READING

Harkness, S., & Super, C. (1996). *Parent's cultural belief systems: Their origins, expressions, and consequences.* New York: Guilford Press.

For additional information on research-based practice, visit our Web site at http://www.earlychilded.delmar.com

Additional resources for this chapter can be found on the Online Companion™ at http://www.earlychilded.delmar.com. Special features of this supplement include Web resources, additional case studies with critical thinking questions, and multiple choice quizzes for each chapter. The answers to each quiz, along with the rationale for the correct answers, can also be found on-line.

CHAPTER 9

Mentor Coaching and Creativity and Innovation

INTRODUCTION

Change is overdue in the field of early care and education. Practices in use today are just about the same as they were in the past. In order to bring some innovation and creativity into the field, educators need some dramatic breakthroughs in thinking. Some disciplines naturally spawn creative thinking, for example, engineering, architecture, music, and art. Early care and education attracts caregivers, people who support others and are comfortable following another's lead rather than being trailblazers of innovation. Creativity and innovation tend not to be rewarded in this field.

> "Man remains capable of finding a way out of any crisis as long as he is allowed to explore, to think, and to be creative."
>
> **MIKHAIL GORBACHEV, 1992**

■ CHAPTER OBJECTIVES

After reading this chapter, you should be able to:
- Involve participants in new ways of thinking.
- Engage participants with creative thinking skills.
- Encourage participants to consider early care and education in new ways.

DEFINITIONS OF CREATIVITY AND INNOVATION

■ **CREATIVITY**

The process of generating many ideas

Creativity, basically, is the process of generating many ideas. This can be accomplished by combining existing or new ideas in different ways. Or it can involve breaking an idea down to examine its parts. Another creative process involves making connections between the topics at hand, for example, combining them with seemingly unrelated facts, events, or operations (Ritter & Brassard, 1998). **Innovation** is the process of selecting, combining, refining, and turning the best creative practices into reality.

■ **INNOVATION**

The process of selecting, combining, refining, and turning the best creative practices into reality

Practitioners in early care and education programs have demonstrated very little creativity or new thinking. Funding requires extensive accountability, which perpetuates sameness and tends to discourage risk taking. In today's environment, there are usually three steps agencies take in their operating systems:

1. Quality control involves continual data analysis, examining process control policies and procedures, looking for problems, and determining root causes.
2. Planning involves developing plans, anticipating problems, analyzing resources, and allocating personnel.
3. **Continuous improvement** involves continually monitoring, assessing, and improving operations and systems.

■ **CONTINUOUS IMPROVEMENT**

A process that involves continually monitoring, assessing, and improving operations and systems

An additional step is needed in the planning process that includes creativity and innovation. This step would occur between step 2, planning, and step 3, continuous improvement, in which creativity and innovation are introduced. This step would serve to identify and reformulate problems using creativity tools, which would result in generating fresh ideas. These ideas might derive from a variety of disciplines, including early care and education. This reformulation would serve to gather diverse ideas and begin to implement plans, perhaps initially as pilot projects. These time-limited efforts would not be intended for a complete agency makeover but rather would earmark some resources and personnel to begin examining new approaches without fear of repercussions, criticism, or requiring the whole agency to change. These kinds of projects lend themselves to the mentor coach/mentor partner process because the dialogue and change process can be managed and addressed in a thoughtful way. The mentor coach/mentor partner can document what worked and what did not work and provide useful data for administrators to review.

An environment that supports creativity facilitates the trying out of new ideas without the fear of criticism. Connecting and building on ideas is encouraged; all involved team members are acknowledged and encouraged to build on existing ideas or contribute new ones. Individuals in this kind of environment usually have a good understanding of different people's talents and gifts and believe them to be assets. Participants in the creativity and innovation process are encouraged to look beyond their own field and examine the broader world. Instead of attending conferences and workshops in the field of early care and education, for example, they might attend events orchestrated by health providers, social workers, or **entrepreneurs.**

Playfulness and humor are often the basis from which new ideas spring. They serve to maintain perspective on serious issues. Adding lightness may serve to present a new solution.

Being a **catalyst** for creativity requires respecting others. One way to show respect involves asking for help. Another is to be an active listener, seeking clarification and repeating what has been shared in order to encourage people to continue contributing. Not every idea has to be believed or acted on; however, appropriate consideration should be given to all ideas because even the most obtuse answers may contain a grain of truth and be worthwhile.

Creative people spend much of their time interacting with others. Rather than struggling alone with a problem, they go out and find someone with whom to think. This obviously is an important area of dialogue between the mentor coach and the mentor partner. In order to keep creative juices flowing in conversations and meetings, it is important to avoid "killer" phrases such as, "We've already tried that and it doesn't work," or "We could never pull that off." If these comments arise, it is important not to let the idea fade, and instead extend the dialogue with such questions as, "Why didn't it work?" "Were enough time and resources provided?" Creative people tend to be explorers. They research the Internet, read professional journals, visit other programs, and continually ask questions.

Early care and education, as a field, tends to be isolated as a result of the demands of the job. In a classroom with 20 children everyday, there is little time for family and a lot of juggling is required. Organizations should consider paid time for the mentor coach process. The return on investment and quality of the project will be greatly enhanced.

■ **ENTREPRENEURS**
Individuals who start up and run their own businesses

■ **CATALYST**
A person or thing acting as the stimulus to bring about or hasten a result

CREATIVITY AND INNOVATION TOOLS

Mentor coaches and protégés may explore creativity and problem-solving tools and choose from among them those they consider most valuable to incorporate into projects and approaches for solving problems in new ways. Using creativity and innovation tools provides a structured way for individuals, groups, or teams to combine intuition, imagination, and personal experiences to create interesting and, eventually, innovative concepts and solutions. These tools enhance the creativity process by breaking routine ways of thinking and helping to bring to the surface the creative potential of all employees. Innovative programs can serve to harness all of the staff's creativity and experiences across the board. However, change without reason or adequate training and support for change is not recommended.

Table 9–1 includes a problem-solving model that easily can be adapted for a mentor coaching process or, for that matter, any task force or committee charged with developing new approaches and systems. A mentor coach might ask the protégé how she or he could use the Seven-Step Improvement Model

---

TABLE 9–1   SEVEN-STEP IMPROVEMENT MODEL

Plan

1. Select the problem/process that will be addressed first (or next) and describe the improvement opportunity.

   - Ask, "What's wrong?" and "What's not working?"
   - Look for changes in important agency indicators.
   - Assemble and support the right team.
   - Collect and review agency data. Define the organization's challenges and opportunities.
   - Narrow down the focus.
   - Develop a purpose statement.

2. Describe the current process surrounding the improvement opportunity.

   - Map out and describe the current process.
   - Validate with current process users.
   - Collect data.
   - Select the relevant process or segment to further refine the scope.

3. Describe all of the possible causes of the problem and agree on the problem.

   - Ask "why" five times.
   - Identify causes of the problem.

4. Develop effective and workable solutions and plans including targets for improvement.

- Generate potential solutions.
- Define, rank, and analyze solutions.
- Select solutions that best meet customer needs.
- Plan change process.
- Do contingency planning when dealing with new and risky plans.
- Determine resources.
- Set targets for improvement and establish monitoring methods.

Do

5. Implement the solution or process change.

- Implement.
- Collect additional data for subsequent assessment.
- Follow the plan and monitor the milestones and benchmarks.

Check

6. Review and evaluate the result of the change.

- Review the results of the change. Is the solution having the desired effect? Are there any unintended consequences?
- Revise the process as necessary.
- Standardize the improvement for monitoring the process for change.
- Establish measures for monitoring the process for change.

Act

7. Reflect and act on learnings.

- Assess the results and problem-solving processes and recommend changes.
- Continue the improvement process where needed and standardize where possible.
- Evaluate the lessons the team learned from the experience; decide what can be improved.
- Don't forget to celebrate success!

Source: Ritter, D., & Brassard, M. (1998). *The creativity tools memory jogger: A pocket guide for creative thinking* (pp. 10–11). Salem NH: Goal/QPC. Reprinted with permission. The Creativity Tools Memory Jogger™, Goal/QPC, Salem, NH, www.goalqpc.com.

when presiding at a team meeting. The purpose would be to move the team away from circular thinking ideology ("we tried that last year and it didn't work") to an agreed-on problem-solving model that they could work through together. Ritter and Brassard (1998) provide an easily adapted model titled the Seven-Step Improvement Model.

The demand for and use of creativity and innovation has increased since the 1950s, and a variety of models, theories, and programs has evolved. The tools of using creative thinking fall into four basic areas:

1. identifying and restating the problem
2. generating new ideas
3. transferring knowledge from other fields
4. combining different creative approaches and tools

Brainstorming

A classic creativity tool involves a process known as brainstorming, which was developed and practiced by Alex Osborn. Osborn (1953) was an advertising agency executive at Batten, Barton, Durstin, and Osborn (BBDO), which specialized in developing products, logos, and advertising campaigns for Fortune 500 companies, such as General Mills, Northrup King, and others.

Osborn (1953) identified the process his organization used and developed it into a training program and a book. Brainstorming is a way of generating "waves" of ideas. The simplest form of brainstorming consists of the following format:

1. State the problem or challenge in the simplest possible terms.
2. Convene a group of six to eight people who represent all parts of the organization.
3. Assign a recorder. The recorder does not participate in the discussion but contributes by recording ideas as presented and then promoting a discussion and prioritizing the ideas to be pursued.
4. Explain the ground rules of brainstorming:
   - Avoid criticizing anyone's ideas. Suspend judgment.
   - Produce as many ideas as possible. Quantity is critical.
   - Encourage a "free-wheeling" atmosphere.
   - Listen to each other's ideas and extend ideas by "piggybacking," adding to another's suggestions.
   - Avoid discussing the merits of one's ideas but do ask questions that clarify and sharpen the ideas presented.

The results of brainstorming can be amazing, and they often result in getting the team enthusiastic about change. Brainstorming helps energize the team involved in the process and tends to discourage some of the routine ("we've always done it this way") approaches.

Think Like a Genius® Creativity and Innovation Tool

Albert Einstein wrote, "Some things we can count, don't count. Some things we can't count, really count." No one really knows quite how a genius works or develops; however, certain creativity and innovation techniques, such as the Think Like a Genius approach, can transform an organization's knowledge, resources, services, and successes in amazing ways. Siler (1999), an innovative process consultant, developed Think Like a Genius with three major purposes:

1. to develop natural abilities to create, invent, discover, learn, and communicate
2. to act as a catalyst for breakthroughs and innovation
3. to see the factors that really matter in improving an organization's success

The process is designed to open minds and remove mental barriers that block creative and feasible solutions. Participants share knowledge through a simple yet sophisticated model-building activity that stimulates collaborative learning.

Think Like a Genius involves a four-step process known as **metaphorming:**

1. Connection—Make a comparison connecting two or more things.
2. Discovery—Explore the connections in depth to generate fresh insights and discoveries.
3. Invention—Create or invent something based on the insights and discoveries.
4. Application—Apply the solutions in innumerable ways and contexts.

Discovery, interpretation, analysis, and broad application are important aspects of collaborative learning through model building. Connecting different ideas or knowledge is only part of the creative process. Applying imagination

■ **METAPHORMING**
A change process conveying an idea, started by expressing a vision or belief or realizing a dream; works by helping people see similarities among perceptions rather than dwelling on differences

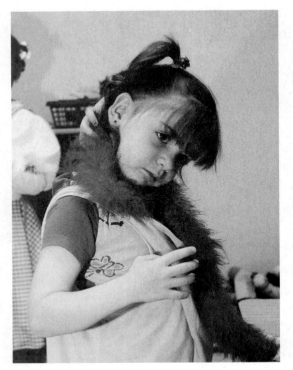

and personal knowledge to the ideas tends to be the more difficult part because an individual must reach into and explore the furthest depths of the mind. It has to work harder to make a discovery about a connection or to generate insights. The further one explores, the more creative energy is expended. Words alone do not increase everyone's depth of understanding. Models do. The four-dimensional model building process allows for a sharing of nonverbal communication that is often deeper, richer, and more memorable than the verbal ones. An exciting part of the Think Like a Genius process is the development of "expert novices." These are people who have learned to suspend what they know in order to discover what they do not know with open and fresh minds.

Creativity and Leadership

According to Bleedhorn and Clyde (1993, p. 19), "Events in human affairs in the 'new world order' call for designated leaders to work in new ways." Not only designated leaders but also undesignated leaders need to move away from old allegiances and limiting stereotypes toward "transformational" work where all, as part of human society, have freedom of speech, opportunities for decent housing, and satisfying work that provides a worthy wage. It is now evident that these ways of thinking creatively can be taught and learned by almost anyone and are desperately needed at all levels and in all disciplines as the pace of the world continues to change rapidly.

Nelson Mandela is an extraordinary example of how "transformational and creative" thinking can dramatically change a whole country. Mandela frequently comments on the mentors he worked with in his early years. They encouraged

CASE STUDY: EARLY CARE AND EDUCATION NETWORKING

Judy, a seasoned early care and education leader, attended a chamber of commerce meeting and heard that a new company with 3,000 employees would be moving into town close to her center. Her center is always full and has a waiting list. Judy wants to be able to serve at least some of these new families. She called a network of private and public childcare providers, some local politicians, and some business people together. She included a suggestion in her invitation that they be prepared to "think outside the box" about a community opportunity. At the meeting, Judy posted on a flip chart the challenge of how to accommodate these new-to-the-community children and their families. The group began brainstorming. They creatively thought of several workable solutions, including using an abandoned storefront location, developing a home-based visiting option, developing space at an assisted-living center for seniors that would create an intergenerational program, and using space at the local hospital to run a late-day program for parents who worked in shifts. The group, new to the brainstorming process, was amazed at how many workable solutions they generated in a short amount of time.

Critical Thinking Questions

1. What kind of leadership was Judy using with her community team?
2. What factors contribute to helping the brainstorming process generate a lot of ideas in a short amount of time?
3. Did Judy face risks by being proactive in addressing the challenge of meeting the needs of 3,000 new families? Describe some possible challenges.

and helped him create the vision of one South African country where people of all backgrounds could be treated equally. His vision sustained his 27 years of imprisonment, and despite his hardships, he never lost sight of his goals.

TRADITIONS IN EARLY CARE AND EDUCATION

Early care and education could surely benefit from using creative and innovative approaches. The field and its practices have not changed significantly in 50 years. A schedule is available from the Child Development Group of Mississippi, the federally funded pilot program that became Head Start in July 1965, that describes the activities and routines that should be available at every center. According to Greenberg (1969), every day should include group cozy time, where children share; outdoor play; free time for child-initiated play; mealtime, served family style; and nap time with at least 20 minutes of quiet.

Although curricula have evolved, it is interesting to note that these basic elements have not varied in more than 40 years of programming. It appears that some creativity and innovation could benefit not only the children but also the teaching staff.

The increasing demands on staff in the field of early care and education require flexibility and resilience. As Csikszentmihalyi (1996) in his landmark study of creativity comments, people with high levels of creativity can include a great variety of personality and behavior types from introverts to extroverts; however, the traits that present themselves most frequently are the level of complexity and perseverance one has. For successful administrators in the field, this certainly seems to be characteristic. People in the field have achieved incredible things with limited resources. They possess dogged determination, an ability to ask for help, and the vision of how important quality environments and services for children are. These are the people who light the way and, through mentor coaching, can pass on the torch.

SUMMARY

The field of early care and education is ready for the breakthroughs in which partners and teams use creativity and innovation tools. These tools and the use of creativity and innovation should be an integral part of an organization's operations. Opportunities for thinking creatively should be made available in planning, organizing, implementing, and evaluating a program in a cycle of continuous improvement. Once these tools become a part of an organization's infrastructure, the work of early care and education people will be refreshed instead of their considering the challenges in the same old routine ways. The mentor coach/mentor partner could bring this agenda of creativity and innovation to a program. They could lighten it up, examine opportunities, and try new techniques from other fields.

■ KEY TERMS

Catalyst	Entrepreneurs
Continuous improvement	Innovation
Creativity	Metaphorming

■ CHAPTER DISCUSSION QUESTIONS

1. Can creativity and innovation be taught?
2. Why are creativity and innovation important in the field of early care and education?
3. Describe the Seven-Step Improvement Model.
4. Provide the key elements of brainstorming.
5. What is metaphorming and how does it work?
6. At what point in quality improvement planning in a traditional program should creativity and innovation tools be introduced?

■ MENTOR COACH/PROTÉGÉ INTERACTION

Review the creativity and innovation tools described in this chapter. Identify one that can be applied to a current work challenge and create an action plan for working with a team to develop new approaches. List goals and objectives of the process, timeline, and resources needed and describe how the project will be evaluated.

■ REFLECTIVE PRACTICE

Take some time to think about the daily routine in your program or one you have visited. What was the schedule? Were children engaged? What could be improved? Was the outdoor space used fully? Were child-initiated activities accessible? Write your observations and thoughts in your learning journal.

■ LEARNING JOURNAL

Write a couple paragraphs about what you have learned as a result of reading this chapter. Can you apply any learning, personally or professionally? Describe any insights or "ah-has" that you have experienced as the result of reading and doing the activities suggested in this chapter.

■ REFERENCES

Bleedhorn, B., & Clyde, R. (1993). *Creative and critical thinking: Reflections and applications. American behavioral scientist*. Thousand Oaks, CA: Sage.

Csikszentmihalyi, M. (1996). *Creativity: Flow and the psychology of discovery and invention*. New York: HarperCollins.

Gorbachev, Mikhail. (1992, May 11). *Time*.

Greenberg, P. (1969). *The devil has slippery shoes: A biased biography of the child development group of Mississippi*. London: Macmillan.

Osborn, A. (1953). *Applied imagination*. New York: Scribner's.

Ritter, D., & Brassard, M. (1998). *The creativity tools memory jogger: A pocket guide for creative thinking.* Salem, NH: Goal/QPC.

Siler, T. (1999). Think Like a Genius. San Francisco: Berrett-Koehler.

■ FURTHER READINGS

American Institutes for Research. (2001). *Putting the pro in protégé: A guide to mentoring in Head Start and Early Head Start.* Washington, DC: U.S. Department of Health and Human Services, Head Start Bureau Administration for Children and Families, Contract #105-94-2020.

Holman, P., & Devanne, T. (1999). *The change handbook: Group methods for shaping the future* (pp. 279–294). San Francisco, CA: Berrett-Koehler.

Parkin, M. (2001). *Tales for coaching: Using stories and metaphors with individuals and small groups.* Sterling, VA: Stylus Publishing.

For additional information on research-based practice, visit our Web site at http://www.earlychilded.delmar.com

Additional resources for this chapter can be found on the Online Companion™ at http://www. earlychilded.delmar.com. Special features for this supplement include Web resources, additional case studies with critical thinking questions, and multiple choice quizzes for each chapter. The answers to each quiz, along with the rationale for the correct answers, can also be found on-line.

10

Mentor Coaching and Emotional Intelligence

INTRODUCTION

Mentor coaching has the power to ignite leadership in the field of early care and education. This statement was made in the first chapter, and understanding and working with emotional intelligence defines and empowers great leadership. Emotional intelligence reaches into the limbic brain and activates primal emotions in order to develop teams, to create vision, and to move an organization forward. The mentor coach/protégé process in the field of early care and education includes a unique opportunity to probe the depths of the inner self and explore the significance of emotional intelligence.

▣ CHAPTER OBJECTIVES _____

After reading this chapter, you should be able to:

• Understand and describe the importance of and the connection between emotional intelligence and early care and education.

• Understand and describe six types of emotional intelligence leadership styles.

"Some people come into our lives and quickly go. Some people move our souls to dance. They awaken us with new understanding, with a passing whisper of their wisdom. Some people make the sky more beautiful to gaze upon. They stay in our lives for awhile and leave footprints in our hearts, and we are never the same."

UNKNOWN

■ EMOTIONAL INTELLIGENCE
The dimension of intelligence responsible for the ability to manage one's self and interpersonal relationships

■ DISSONANCE
Lack of harmony, or agreement; an inharmonious sound

■ RESONANCE
In terms of brain function, people's emotional centers are in synch in positive ways

■ DE FACTO
Existing, but not by official recognition

- Understand and describe the four competency clusters—self-awareness, self-management, social awareness, and relationship management, as well as the 13 competencies associated with them and their importance to the field of early care and education.

DEFINITION OF EMOTIONAL INTELLIGENCE

Emotional intelligence is the dimension of intelligence responsible for the ability to manage one's self and interpersonal relationships. Organizations traditionally have relied on IQ as the success factor, with its emphasis on the analytical details and strategies based on fact and data, processes, and procedures. Although IQ is important, it is the emotional quotient (EQ), or emotional intelligence, that leaders use to create the vision, be passionate, and energize and create purpose in the organization.

One of the most valuable gifts a mentor coach can give a protégé is the insight into how emotional intelligence works within organizations and why it is so important for a leader to have. In any human group, it is the leader who has the maximum power to sway emotions. When a leader fails to lead effectively, **dissonance** takes effect. If the leader is able to generate enthusiasm, performance can soar, and when leaders drive emotions positively, **resonance** takes effect.

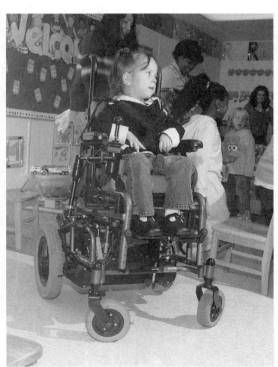

In organizations, everyone is watching the leader. Leaders tend to talk more in meetings, for example, they comment on new topics or respond to another's remarks. In some organizations, there is a **de facto** leader who sets the pace and the tone, especially if an assigned leader fails to lead effectively. Leaders' emotional states are easily perceived by how they express emotions in their faces, voices, and gestures. The more effective leaders are, the more they are magnets—people naturally gravitate toward them. This is one reason emotionally intelligent leaders attract talented people. Conversely, leaders who are cold, domineering, irritable, and grouchy repel people. Optimistic, enthusiastic leaders tend to retain staff compared to those who have a propensity to be negative. When people feel good, they work at their best. Feeling good lubricates mental efficiency, making people better at understanding information and using decision rules in complex judgments. The "group IQ" is the sum total of every person's best talents combined at full force, depending on the group's emotional intelligence. A leader skilled in

CASE STUDY: A NEW DIRECTOR TAKES OVER

A woman with a fresh, young face, Dawn Leonard, was hired to take over a large privately owned preschool in a pleasant, middle-class suburb. The previous director had ruled with an iron hand—she opened every piece of mail, trusted only an inner circle of staff with whom she consulted, and barked out orders one day and took them back the next day.

Staff was dispirited; many talented workers had left the organization. Dawn believed her first task was to raise the spirits of and create a vision for the people at the school. She approached this task by talking with all 280 employees. Her questions were simple: What was the purpose of their position? What helped them accomplish their tasks? What hindered them in accomplishing their tasks? Within a few months, the preschool had a new vibrancy, and performance efficiency had improved. The staff saw the direction in which Dawn was taking them and believed in her passion and enthusiasm for children and their families, as well as her true concern for all staff.

Critical Thinking Questions

1. What happens to staff when a leader orders something one day and changes her mind the next?
2. Are staff always aware of what the leader is doing?
3. Suggest an activity the mentor coach might present to the protégé in order to examine and understand the effect of two different types of leaders.

collaboration can maintain high cooperation levels and ensure a group's decisions are worthwhile. Such leaders know how to balance a group's focus on the task at hand with its attention to the quality of its members' relationships. They naturally create a friendly but effective climate that lifts everyone's spirits.

RESONANCE AND LEADERSHIP

Resonance, in terms of brain function, means that people's emotional centers are in synch in a positive way. Interestingly, one of the most powerful and direct ways to make that resonant brain-to-brain connection is through humor and laughter. Resonance does not stem only from a leader's good moods or ability to say the right thing but also from a whole set of coordinated activities that comprise particular leadership styles. Goleman, Boyatzis, and McKee (2002) have identified six distinct leadership styles and indicated the need for flexibility in their use as situations demand. These leadership styles have been described over the years in a variety of ways. These styles reflect a national survey of corporate leaders conducted by Goleman, Boyatzis, and McKee (2002). The survey has been analyzed and validated. Four of the leadership styles (visionary, coaching, affinitive, and democratic) generally have positive outcomes, whereas the other two (pacesetting and commanding) can be effective in the right situations but can also contribute to negative effects. (See Table 10–1.)

The six styles of leadership depend on a cluster of competencies that are used in groups of two to three in a flexible manner depending on the desired

■ VISIONARY

Leadership style of a person with strong and creative imaginary powers and often the ability to inspire others

■ AFFILIATIVE

Leadership style of a person with the ability to connect or associate one with

■ COLLABORATIVE

To work together

■ DEMOCRATIC

Leadership style of people who are popular with all or most people

---

TABLE 10–1   SIX EMOTIONAL INTELLIGENCE LEADERSHIP STYLES

1. **Visionary** Leadership Style

The visionary style tends to be the most effective, especially when combined with a triad of competencies: self-confidence, self-awareness, and empathy. It is necessary for the leader to be transparent and honest about believing in the vision, but it does not work in every situation.

- How it builds resonance: Moves people toward shared dreams
- Impact on climate: Most strongly positive
- When appropriate: When changes require a new vision or when a clear direction is needed

2. Coaching Leadership Style

The one-on-one approach to coaching helps people identify their unique strengths and weaknesses. This style encourages staff to establish long-term development goals and helps them conceptualize a plan for reaching those goals. Staff will gravitate toward the leadership style that ties into their own dreams, identity, and aspirations.

- How it builds resonance: Connects what a person wants with the organization's goals
- Impact on climate: Highly positive
- When appropriate: To help an employee improve performance

3. **Affiliative** Leadership Style

The affiliative style represents **collaborative** competence in action. Such leaders are most concerned with promoting harmony, fostering friendly interactions, and nurturing personal relationships that expand the connective tissue with people they are leading. When leaders are being affiliative, they focus on the emotional needs of employees over work goals. This focus creates empathy—the ability to sense the feelings, needs, and perspectives of others.

- How it builds resonance: Creates harmony by connecting people to each other
- Impact on climate: Positive
- When appropriate: To heal rifts in a team, motivate during stressful times, or strengthen connections

4. **Democratic** Leadership Style

A democratic approach works best when the leader is not sure what approach to take. Getting input from staff and stakeholders assures buy-in, but seeking staff's advice when they are uninformed can be disastrous. The best communicators are good listeners. A democratic leader combines the competency of a visionary with collaboration and teamwork.

- How it builds resonance: Values staff's input and gets commitment through participation

- Impact on climate: Positive

- When appropriate: To build buy-in or consensus or to get valuable input from staff

5. Pacesetting Leadership Style

The pacesetting approach can be very successful with a talented team that knows where they are going. When used with an inexperienced team, staff can feel pushed and become resentful, pushing down the performance.

- How it builds resonance: Meets challenging and exciting goals

- Impact on climate: Because too frequently poorly executed, often highly negative

- When appropriate: To get high-quality results from a motivated and competent team

6. Commanding Leadership Style

The commanding leader often uses the credo "Do it because I said to do it" without giving the background or reasons why. It casts a real pall over the organization and creates fear among staff. Even though this style has its obvious pitfalls, it is still the preferred method of managing for many organizations.

- How it builds resonance: Soothes fears by giving clear direction in an emergency

- Impact on climate: Because so often misused, highly negative

- When appropriate: In a crisis, to kick-start a turnaround, or with problem employees

Source: Excerpted and reprinted by permission of Harvard Business School Press. From *Primal leadership* by D. Goleman, R. Boyatzis, & A. McKee. Boston, MA 2002. Copyright © (2002) by the Harvard Business School Publishing Corporation; all rights reserved.

results. These competencies can be developed in individuals and provide a framework within which mentor coaches and protégés can work.

EMOTIONAL INTELLIGENCE COMPETENCIES

A successful leader has high emotional intelligence and is willing to continually examine him- or herself. These leaders understand why they are successful and whether their roles are suitable for themselves. Traditionally, in early care and education, the teachers who are well-organized, have developed staff, and have shown some initiative are promoted to administrative

TABLE 10–2   SELF-AWARENESS

- Emotional self-awareness—Leaders high in emotional self-awareness are attuned to inner signals, recognizing how their feelings affect them and their job performance. They are attuned to their guiding values and can often intuit the best course of action, seeing the big picture in a complex situation. Emotionally self-aware leaders are usually candid and authentic and are able to speak openly about their emotions and with conviction about their guiding vision.

- Accurate self-assessment—Leaders with high self-awareness typically know their limitations and strengths and exhibit a sense of humor about themselves. They exhibit a gracefulness, learning where they need to improve and welcoming constructive criticism and feedback. Accurate self-assessment lets a leader know when to ask for help and where to focus in cultivating new leadership strengths.

- Self-confidence—Knowing their abilities with accuracy allows leaders to play to their strengths. Self-confident leaders can welcome a difficult assignment. Such leaders often have a sense of presence, a self-assurance, that lets them stand out in a group.

Source: Excerpted and reprinted by permission of Harvard Business School Press. From *Primal leadership* by D. Goleman, R. Boyatzis, & A. McKee. Boston, MA 2002. Copyright © (2002) by the Harvard Business School Publishing Corporation; all rights reserved.

positions. Some teaching staff may not be given enough support, orientation, or training, in which case, these potentially good educators may change careers for other seemingly more suitable ones. Attrition is very high in education, and sadly, many young people who have dreamed of being teachers have difficulty the first few years and eventually leave the field. Tables 10–2 through 10–5 present emotional intelligence competencies. Table 10–2 presents self-awareness competencies that may help educators in the field of early care and education assist staff in becoming effective educators.

TABLE 10–3   SELF-MANAGEMENT

- Self-control—Leaders with emotional self-control find ways to manage their disturbing emotions and impulses and even to channel them in useful ways. A hallmark of self-control is the leader who stays calm and clearheaded under high stress or during a crisis—and who remains unflappable even when confronted by a trying situation.

- Transparency—Leaders who are transparent live their values. Transparency is an authentic openness to others about one's feelings, beliefs, and actions—it allows integrity. Such leaders openly admit mistakes or faults and confront unethical behavior in others rather than turn a blind eye.

- Adaptability—Leaders who are adaptable can juggle multiple demands without losing their focus or energy and are comfortable with the inevitable **ambiguities** of organizational life. Such leaders can be flexible in adapting to challenges, nimble in adjusting to fluid change, and limber in their thinking in the face of new data or realities.

- Achievement—Leaders with strength in achievement have high personal standards that drive them to constantly seek performance improvements, both for themselves and those they lead. They are pragmatic, setting measurable but challenging goals, and are able to calculate risk so that goals are worthy but attainable. A hallmark of achievement is in continually learning, and teaching, ways to do better.

- Initiative—Leaders who have a sense of efficacy. This means that this style of leader has what it takes to control his or her own destiny and excel in initiative. The leader seizes opportunities, or creates them, rather than simply waiting. Such a leader does not hesitate to cut through red tape or even to bend the rules when necessary to create better possibilities for the future.

- Optimism—A leader who is optimistic can roll with the punches, seeing an opportunity rather than a threat in a setback. Such leaders see others positively, expecting the best of them. And their "glass-half-full" outlook leads them to expect that changes in the future will be for the better.

Source: Excerpted and reprinted by permission of Harvard Business School Press. From *Primal leadership* by D. Goleman, R. Boyatzis, & A. McKee. Boston, MA 2002. Copyright © (2002) by the Harvard Business School Publishing Corporation; all rights reserved.

■ **AMBIGUITIES**

Having two or more uncertain reasons

TABLE 10–4   SOCIAL AWARENESS

- Empathy—Leaders with empathy are able to attune to a wide range of emotional signals, letting them sense the felt, but unspoken, emotions in a person or group. Such leaders listen attentively and can grasp the other person's perspective. Empathy makes a leader able to get along with people of diverse backgrounds and other cultures.

- Organizational awareness—A leader with a keen social awareness can be politically astute, able to detect crucial social networks, and read key power relationships. Such leaders can understand the political forces at work in organizations as well as the guiding values and unspoken rules that operate among people there.

- Service—Leaders high in service competence foster an emotional climate so that people directly in touch with the customer or client will keep the relationship on the right track. Such leaders monitor customer or client satisfaction carefully to ensure that they are getting what they need. They also make themselves available as needed.

Source: Excerpted and reprinted by permission of Harvard Business School Press. From *Primal leadership* by D. Goleman, R. Boyatzis, & A. McKee. Boston, MA 2002. Copyright © (2002) by the Harvard Business School Publishing Corporation; all rights reserved.

■ **CATALYST**
A person or thing acting as the stimulus in bringing about or hastening a result

> **TABLE 10–5   RELATIONSHIP MANAGEMENT**
>
> • Inspiration—Leaders who inspire both create resonance and move people with a compelling vision of shared mission. Such leaders embody what they ask of others and are able to articulate a shared mission in a way that inspires others to follow. They offer a sense of common purpose beyond the day-to-day tasks, making work exciting.
>
> • Influence—Indicators of a leader's powers of influence range from finding just the right appeal for a given listener to knowing how to build buy-in from key people and a network of support for an initiative. Leaders adept in influence are persuasive and engaging when they address a group.
>
> • Developing others—Leaders who are adept at cultivating people's abilities show a genuine interest in those they are helping along and an understanding of their goals, strengths, and weaknesses. Such leaders can give timely and constructive feedback and are natural mentors and coaches.
>
> • Change **catalyst**—Leaders who can catalyze change are able to recognize the need for the change, challenge the way things are currently handled, and champion the new order. They can be strong advocates for the change even in the face of opposition, making the argument for it compelling. They also find practical ways to overcome barriers to change.
>
> • Conflict management—Leaders who manage conflicts best are able to draw out all parties, understand the differing perspectives, and then find a common ideal that everyone can endorse. They surface the conflict, acknowledge the feelings and views of all sides, and then redirect the energy toward a shared ideal.
>
> • Teamwork and collaboration—Leaders who are able team players generate an atmosphere of friendly and respectful conduct and are themselves models of respect, helpfulness, and cooperation. They draw others into active, enthusiastic commitment to the collective effort and build spirit and identity. They spend time forging and cementing close relationships beyond mere work obligations.
>
> Source: Excerpted and reprinted by permission of Harvard Business School Press. From *Primal leadership* by D. Goleman, R. Boyatzis, & A. McKee. Boston, MA 2002. Copyright © (2002) by the Harvard Business School Publishing Corporation; all rights reserved.

Table 10–3 presents emotional intelligence competency clusters that increase self-awareness and help improve self-management skills. They benefit educators by promoting a disciplined approach; encouraging them to leaving emotional baggage behind; and setting boundaries for staff between being a friend, a good listener, and their mentor coach.

The next cluster of competencies are concerned with social awareness. (See Table 10–4.) They develop over time as the result of experiences and signal maturity. At this point, the staff person is aware of his or her strengths and limitations but is also able to empathize with another staff person's issues and can be effective as a mentor coach for this staff person.

The fourth cluster of emotional intelligence competencies, relationship management, is critical for the success of an administrator and is a sought-after competency when hiring new administrators (see Table 10–5). The ability to manage relationships requires good oral and written skills and sensitivity to a wide range of diverse people. In early care and education, there is a stigma associated with being political; however, if the profession is to grow and command respect, political know-how is a necessity.

By now you have gained quite a bit of knowledge about the mentor coach/protégé process and its unique vision and relationships. Mentoring may be one of the most exciting times in an individual's life. Remember every pair is unique, and each individual should follow his or her own path of discovery and growth. Table 10–6 provides Stoddard and Tamasy's (2003) view of ten powerful principles for mentoring.

TABLE 10–6   TEN POWERFUL PRINCIPLES FOR MENTORING
1. Effective mentors understand that living is about giving.
2. Effective mentors see mentoring as a process that requires perseverance.
3. Effective mentors open their world to their mentoring partners.
4. Effective mentors help mentoring partners align passion and work.
5. Effective mentors are comforters who share the load.
6. Effective mentors help turn personal values into practice.
7. Effective mentors model character.
8. Effective mentors affirm the value of spirituality.
9. Effective mentors recognize that mentoring + reproduction = legacy.
10. Effective mentors go for it!

Source: Quoted from *The heart of mentoring: Ten proven principles for developing people to their fullest potential* by D. Stoddard & R. Tamasy, copyright (2003). Used by permission of NavPress—www.navpress.com. All rights reserved.

SUMMARY

The field of emotional intelligence gained attention recently. It provides a new look at and validated research for leadership qualities that were understood but not necessarily well articulated. Descriptors of people would include phrases such as, "She has street smarts," "She relates to everyone well," and "She doesn't lose her cool." These feelings about people were discussed abstractly; however, now emotional intelligence provides a framework for a more concrete understanding of these qualities and the rationale for their importance for leaders in the field of early care and education.

Perhaps, after considering all the aspects of mentor coaching, the one thing that occurs during a successful mentor coach/protégé process is the closeness and the caring that develops between the mentor coach and the protégé as a result of their journey. Sometimes this makes it difficult for one or both in the process to understand when the time has come for the protégé to go on and the mentor coach to step back and let go, not unlike a parent.

After all is said and done, the words this work began with and the ones that run throughout the work are essentially about caring . . . about coming from the heart. Without caring and love, the process may provide some information, but it misses the power and potential of deep and life-changing possibilities for both the mentor coach and the protégé.

■ KEY TERMS _____

Affiliative	Democratic
Ambiguities	Dissonance
Catalyst	Emotional intelligence
Collaborative	Resonance
De facto	Visionary

■ CHAPTER DISCUSSION QUESTIONS _____

1. Define emotional intelligence.
2. Why is emotional intelligence important for leadership in the field of early care and education?
3. Discuss some of the qualities of a visionary leader.
4. Why is self-awareness important to a leader?
5. Why is self-management important to a leader?
6. Why is relationship management important to a leader?
7. Discuss three of the ten powerful principles of mentorship.

■ MENTOR COACH/PROTÉGÉ INTERACTION _____

After a year of mentor coach and protégé meetings, the protégé was promoted to a program director position from the classroom. Suddenly, the mentor coach began dropping in and interrupting important meetings with advice. How do you suggest the protégé handle this?

■ REFLECTIVE PRACTICE _____

Think back to supervisors you have had. Think about one who may not have appreciated you or given you recognition for your work, one who limited your scope of activities and never asked for input on doing the job. What feelings about that experience do you remember?

Hopefully, you have also had experiences with a good supervisor. Think about the ways that supervisor let you know that he or she appreciated your efforts. On what kinds of projects did you work? What made you feel a part of the team? What feelings about that experience do you remember?

■ LEARNING JOURNAL _____

Write a couple paragraphs about what you have learned as a result of reading this chapter. Can you apply any learning, personally or professionally? Describe any insights or "ah-has" that you have experienced as the result of reading and doing the activities suggested in this chapter.

_____

_____

_____

_____

_____

_____

_____

■ REFERENCES _____

Goleman, D., Boyatzis, R., & McKee, A. (2002). *Primal leadership*. Boston: Harvard University Business Press.

Stoddard, D., & Tamasy, R. (2003). *The heart of mentoring: Ten proven principles for developing people to their fullest potential*. Colorado Springs: NavPress.

■ FURTHER READINGS _____

Cherniss, C., Goleman, D., Emmerling, R., Cowan, K., & Adler, M. (1998, October 7). Bringing emotional intelligence to the workplace. *Technical Report: The Consortium for Research on Emotional Intelligence in Organizations*. New Brunswick, NJ: Rutgers University.

Hudson, F. (1999). *The handbook of coaching*. San Francisco: Jossey-Bass.

Lynne, A. (2002). *The emotional intelligence activity book*. New York: American Management Association.

Owen, Nick. (2001). *The magic of metaphor: Seventy-seven stories for teachers, trainers and thinkers.* Willistown, VT: Crown House Publishing, Ltd.

Parkin, M. (2001). *Tales for coaching: Using stories and metaphors with individuals and small groups.* Sterling, VA: Stylus Publishing.

Ruskin, M. (1993). *Speaking up: What to say to your boss and everyone else who gets on your case.* Avon, MA: Adams Publishing.

Warner, J. (2002). *The emotional intelligence style profile.* Amherst, MA: HRD Press.

Wenger, E. (1998). *Communities of practice: Learning, meaning and identity.* Cambridge, England: Cambridge University Press.

Zachary, L. (2000). *The mentor's guide: Facilitating effective learning relationships.* San Francisco: Jossey-Bass.

> For additional information on research-based practice, visit our Web site at http://www.earlychilded.delmar.com

Additional resources for this chapter can be found on the Online Companion™ at http://www.earlychilded.delmar.com. Special features for this supplement include Web resources, additional case studies with critical thinking questions, and multiple choice quizzes for each chapter. The answers to each quiz, along with the rationale for the correct answers, can also be found on-line.

A

Budget Template
for Mentoring

Budgeting for Mentoring		
Line Item	**Amount**	**Source of Funds**
Coordination of mentoring		
Mentor training (consultants, trainers, tuition for college course)		
Consultants and trainers		
Tuition reimbursement		
Travel to training		
Mentor stipend		
Mentor follow-up activities		
Salary increases for mentors		
Protégé training		
Travel to training		
Tuition reimbursement		
Recognition for protégés		
Substitutes provided during release time for mentors and protégés		
Technology for distance mentoring, such as telephone calls, video equipment, training on the use of equipment		
Travel costs (per diem) for visits to mentors or protégés		
Evaluation activities		
Other		
Total		

APPENDIX B

Decision-Maker's Guide

DEVELOPING YOUR MENTOR COACHING SYSTEM: A PLANNING TOOL

The following checklist summarizes important benchmarks in planning and implementing a mentor coaching system. The items are organized based on five sections of the Decision-Maker's Guide. Use this tool to monitor and document progress.

1. Selecting a model for early literacy mentor coaching
   - Assembled a decision-making team
   - Examined program philosophy regarding mentoring and supervision
   - Examined policy regarding the role of the mentor coach on the internal program career development system
   - Considered financial resources and organizational capacity
   - Selected a model:
     - Strengths of the model
     - Potential challenges

2. Finding financial resources
- Explored reallocation of funds in current Head Start budget
- Proposed a budget and services revision to the ACF regional office specialist
- Received ACF approval
- Identified need to secure additional funding
- Developed a plan for identifying and contacting potential funding sources

3. Selecting and matching mentor coaches
- Developed a job description
- Selected a mentor coach application process
- Designed interview strategies
- Developed and adopted criteria for mentor coach and protégé matching

4. Orienting and training mentor coaches
- Developed an orientation plan specifically for mentor coaches
- Individualized the plan for each mentor coach to meet his or her particular needs
- Established system of supervision and ongoing support for mentor coaches
- Designed and adopted a mentor coach and protégé agreement

5. Linking mentor coaching to program management systems communication
- Established protocols for communication between mentor coaches and supervisors and between mentor coaches and other program staff
- Defined confidentiality within the mentor coach and protégé relationship
- Provided training to staff on communication protocols
- Incorporated the protocols into the written program plans

6. Record keeping and reporting
- Designed forms to document the ongoing interactions between mentor coaches and protégés
- Designed form for tracking the work of the mentor coaches
- Defined the role of the mentor coach and other staff members in the record keeping process

- Developed protocols and timelines for completion and submission of written documents

7. Ongoing monitoring

- Incorporated the review and analysis of information about the mentor coach program into the system for ongoing monitoring

8. Self-assessment

- Determined the type of information about the mentor coaching program to be collected in the annual self-assessment
- Developed procedures and responsibilities for collecting these data

9. Planning

- Incorporated the review and analysis of information about the mentor coach program into the program planning system
- Developed a process for using the data to inform continuous quality improvement

Learning Success System©

LEARNING STYLES ASSESSMENT THAT HELPS YOU IDENTIFY HOW YOU PREFER TO LEARN

Work Version

A brain tool designed by Dr. Mary E. Nolan

Call 1-800-398-3134 for additional information, bibliography, and in-depth computerized version.

Roadmap© Learning Styles System

Directions: In each group, rank each of the four statements in order of its importance to you in a learning situation. Put an "X" over the numbers in the circle. Remember, use each number only once in each set.

"4" indicates the most important
"3" indicates the second most important
"2" indicates the next most important
"1" indicates the least important

Group One—Consider the following when rank ordering the statements:
When I am learning . . .

I like quick results	① ② ③ ④
I like to talk as I learn	① ② ③ ④
I like clear steps and to be told what is expected	① ② ③ ④
I like details and facts	① ② ③ ④

Group Two—Consider the following when rank ordering the statements:
When I am learning . . .

I want to know what's happening right now	① ② ③ ④
I want to experiment, come up with new ideas	① ② ③ ④
I want a routine	① ② ③ ④
I want time to finish my work	① ② ③ ④

Group Three—Consider the following when rank ordering the statements:
When I am learning . . .

I like to win	① ② ③ ④
I like to talk to others to solve problems	① ② ③ ④
I like to be told where and when to start	① ② ③ ④
I like to be alone so I can think	① ② ③ ④

Group Four—Consider the following when rank ordering the statements:
When I am learning . . .

I like action	① ② ③ ④
I like to know a lot of people	① ② ③ ④
I like the manager to tell me what to do	① ② ③ ④
I like clear written directions	① ② ③ ④

Group Five—Consider the following when rank ordering the statements:
When I am learning . . .

I like to be able to move around	① ② ③ ④
I like the big picture, not details	① ② ③ ④
I like others to follow the rules like I do	① ② ③ ④
I like to listen to what the manager has to say	① ② ③ ④

Group Six—Consider the following when rank ordering the statements:
When I am learning . . .

I prefer getting to the bottom line	①	②	③	④
I like to give presentations	①	②	③	④
I do well on teams	①	②	③	④
I like to work independently	①	②	③	④

Group Seven—Consider the following when rank ordering the statements:
When I am learning . . .

I do what I feel like doing most of the time	①	②	③	④
I am more interested in learning when I get recognition	①	②	③	④
I take good care of my work area	①	②	③	④
I prefer explaining ideas over memorization	①	②	③	④

Group Eight—Consider the following when rank ordering the statements:
When I am learning . . .

I can get bored sitting in one place	①	②	③	④
I like discussing projects with others	①	②	③	④
I like to be sure of the facts before talking	①	②	③	④
I often go into detail when talking about a subject	①	②	③	④

Group Nine—Consider the following when rank ordering the statements:
When I am learning . . .

I like to take charge	①	②	③	④
I like having a team approach	①	②	③	④
I like having things neat and clean	①	②	③	④
I like data and facts	①	②	③	④

Group Ten—Consider the following when rank ordering the statements:
When I am learning . . .

I want a challenge	①	②	③	④
I like to join others	①	②	③	④
I keep lists and lots of notes	①	②	③	④
I don't like interruptions	①	②	③	④

Name: _____ Date: _____

Results:

To Score the Learning Success System, add the statements in this order:

1. Add the first statement scores in each set of the groups, cumulatively. (Example: Group One, Statement 1 is 4, Group Two, Statement 1 is 3, the sum is 7, etc.) Place the total of all ten statements' score in the "D" box below.

2. Add the second statement scores in each set of the groups, cumulatively. (Example: Group One, Statement 2 is 3, Group Two, Statement 2 is 2, the sum is 5, etc.) Place the total of all ten statements' score in the "I" box below.

3. Add the third statement scores in each set of the groups, cumulatively. (Example: Group One, Statement 3 is 2, Group Two, Statement 3 is 1, the sum is 3, etc.) Place the total of all ten statements' score in the "S" box below.

4. Add the fourth statement scores in each set of the groups, cumulatively. (Example: Group One, Statement 4 is 2, Group Two, Statement 4 is 2, the sum is 4, etc.) Place the total of all ten statements' score in the "C" box below.

Does this style of learning describe you?   Yes _____   No _____

Learning Styles Descriptions

Following are descriptions for the four major learning styles.

D _____	I _____	S _____	C _____
DIRECT **Kinesthetic Learner**	**INTERACTIVE** **Visual Learner**	**STEADY** **Auditory Learner**	**COMPLEX** **Cerebral Learner**
• Actual-Spontaneous learner • Physically active • Realistic • Linear • Expends energy • Risk-taker • Competitive • Challenge • Likes excitement • Body smart • Logical-sequential • Motivated by task • Inductive • Extrovert • Left brain	• Conceptual-Global learner • Understanding self • Empathetic • Global • Develops relationships • Appreciative • Imaginative • Idealistic • Likes personalized learning • Word smart • Random-abstract • Motivated by people • Deductive • Extrovert • Right brain	• Actual-Routine learner • Caretaker • Practical • Linear • Service-oriented • Follow rules • Wants clear directions • Sensible • Likes routine • Number smart • Logical-sequential • Motivated by people • Inductive • Introvert • Left brain	• Conceptual-Specific learner • Appears "brainy" • Analytical • Global • Seeks approval for competence • Systems thinker • Explores ideas • Critical • Likes details • Art smart • Random-abstract • Motivated by task • Deductive • Introvert • Right brain
When not on task: fidgety, moving around	When not on task: talking	When not on task: daydreaming	On and off task: asks lots of questions

D

The Head Start
Child Outcomes
Framework

Domain	Domain Element	Indicators
Language development	Listening and understanding	Demonstrates increasing ability to attend to and understand conversations, stories, songs, and poems.
		Shows progress in understanding and following simple and multiple-step directions.
		*Understands an increasingly complex and varied vocabulary.
		*For non-English-speaking children, progresses in listening to and understanding English.
	Speaking and communicating	*Develops increasing abilities to understand and use language to communicate information, experiences, ideas, feelings, opinions, needs, questions; and for other varied purposes.
		Progresses in abilities to initiate and respond appropriately in conversation and discussions with peers and adults.
		*Uses an increasingly complex and varied spoken vocabulary.
		Progresses in clarity of pronunciation and toward speaking in sentences of increasing length and grammatical complexity.
		*For non-English-speaking children, progresses in speaking English.
Literacy	*Phonological awareness	Shows increasing ability to discriminate and identify sounds in spoken language.
		Shows growing awareness of beginning and ending sounds of words.
		Progresses in recognizing matching sounds and rhymes in familiar words, games, songs, stories, and poems.
		Shows growing ability to hear and discriminate separate syllables in words.
		*Associates sounds with written words, such as awareness that different words begin with the same sound.
	*Book knowledge and appreciation	Shows growing interest and involvement in listening to and discussing a variety of fiction and nonfiction books and poetry.
		Shows growing interest in reading-related activities, such as asking to have a favorite book read; choosing to look at books; drawing pictures based on stories; asking to take books home; going to the library; and engaging in pretend-reading with other children.

*Indicates the four specific domain elements and nine indicators that are legislatively mandated.

(continued)

Domain	Domain Element	Indicators
Literacy (*cont.*)	*Book knowledge and appreciation (*cont.*)	Demonstrates progress in abilities to retell and dictate stories from books and experiences; to act out stories in dramatic play; and to predict what will happen next in a story.
		Progresses in learning how to handle and care for books; knowing to view one page at a time in sequence from front to back; and understanding that a book has a title, author, and illustrator.
	*Print awareness and concepts	Shows increasing awareness of print in classroom, home, and community settings.
		Develops growing understanding of the different functions of forms of print such as signs, letters, newspapers, lists, messages, and menus.
		Demonstrates increasing awareness of concepts of print, such as that reading in English moves from top to bottom and from left to right, that speech can be written down, and that print conveys a message.
		Shows progress in recognizing the association between spoken and written words by following print as it is read aloud.
		*Recognizes a word as a unit of print, or awareness that letters are grouped to form words, and that words are separated by spaces.
	Early writing	Develops understanding that writing is a way of communicating for a variety of purposes.
		Begins to represent stories and experiences through pictures, dictation, and in play.
		Experiments with a growing variety of writing tools and materials, such as pencils, crayons, and computers.
		Progresses from using scribbles, shapes, or pictures to represent ideas, to using letter-like symbols, to copying or writing familiar words such as their own name.
	Alphabet knowledge	Shows progress in associating the names of letters with their shapes and sounds.
		Increases in ability to notice the beginning letters in familiar words.
		*Identifies at least 10 letters of the alphabet, especially those in their own name.
		*Knows that letters of the alphabet are a special category of visual graphics that can be individually named.

*Indicates the four specific domain elements and nine indicators that are legislatively mandated.

(*continued*)

Domain	Domain Element	Indicators
Mathematics	*Number and operations	Demonstrates increasing interest and awareness of numbers and counting as a means for solving problems and determining quantity.
		Begins to associate number concepts, vocabulary, quantities, and written numerals in meaningful ways.
		Develops increasing ability to count in sequence to 10 and beyond.
		Begins to make use of one-to-one correspondence in counting objects and matching groups of objects.
		Begins to use language to compare numbers of objects with terms such as *more, less, greater than, fewer, equal to.*
		Develops increased abilities to combine, separate, and name "how many" concrete objects.
	Geometry and spatial sense	Begins to recognize, describe, compare, and name common shapes, their parts, and attributes.
		Progresses in ability to put together and take apart shapes.
		Begins to be able to determine whether or not two shapes are the same size and shape.
		Shows growth in matching, sorting, putting in a series, and regrouping objects according to one or two attributes such as color, shape, or size.
		Builds an increasing understanding of directionality, order, and positions of objects, and words such as *up, down, over, under, top, bottom, inside, outside, in front,* and *behind.*
	Patterns and measurement	Enhances abilities to recognize, duplicate, and extend simple patterns using a variety of materials.
		Shows increasing abilities to match, sort, put in a series, and regroup objects according to one or two attributes such as shape or size.
		Begins to make comparisons between several objects based on a single attribute.
		Shows progress in using standard and nonstandard measures for length and area of objects.
Science	Scientific skills and methods	Begins to use senses and a variety of tools and simple measuring devices to gather information, investigate materials, and observe processes and relationships.

*Indicates the four specific domain elements and nine indicators that are legislatively mandated.

(continued)

Domain	Domain Element	Indicators
Science (*cont.*)	Scientific skills and methods (*cont.*)	Develops increased ability to observe and discuss common properties, differences, and comparisons among objects and materials.
		Begins to participate in simple investigations to test observations, discuss and draw conclusions, and form generalizations.
		Develops growing abilities to collect, describe, and record information through a variety of means, including discussion, drawings, maps, and charts.
		Begins to describe and discuss predictions, explanations, and generalizations based on past experiences.
	Scientific knowledge	Expands knowledge of and abilities to observe, describe, and discuss the natural world, materials, living things, and natural processes.
		Expands knowledge of and respect for their bodies and the environment.
		Develops growing awareness of ideas and language related to attributes of time and temperature.
		Shows increased awareness and beginning understanding of changes in materials and cause–effect relationships.
Creative arts	Music	Participates with increasing interest and enjoyment in a variety of music activities, including listening, singing, finger plays, games, and performances.
		Experiments with a variety of musical instruments.
	Art	Gains ability in using different art media and materials in a variety of ways for creative expression and representation.
		Progresses in abilities to create drawings, paintings, models, and other art creations that are more detailed, creative, or realistic.
		Develops growing abilities to plan, work independently, and demonstrate care and persistence in a variety of art projects.
		Begins to understand and share opinions about artistic products and experiences.
	Movement	Expresses through movement and dancing what is felt and heard in various musical tempos and styles.
		Shows growth in moving in time to different patterns of beat and rhythm in music.

*Indicates the four specific domain elements and nine indicators that are legislatively mandated.

(continued)

Domain	Domain Element	Indicators
Creative arts (*cont.*)	Dramatic play	Participates in a variety of dramatic play activities that become more extended and complex.
		Shows growing creativity and imagination in using materials and in assuming different roles in dramatic play situations.
Social and emotional development	Self-concept	Begins to develop and express awareness of self in terms of specific abilities, characteristics, and preferences.
		Develops growing capacity for independence in a range of activities, routines, and tasks.
		Demonstrates growing confidence in a range of abilities and expresses pride in accomplishments.
	Self-control	Shows progress in expressing feelings, needs, and opinions in difficult situations and conflicts without harming themselves, others, or property.
		Develops growing understanding of how their actions affect others and begins to accept the consequences of their actions.
		Demonstrates increasing capacity to follow rules and routines and use materials purposefully, safely, and respectfully.
	Cooperation	Increases abilities to sustain interactions with peers by helping, sharing, and discussion.
		Shows increasing abilities to use compromise and discussion in working, playing, and resolving conflicts with peers.
		Develops increasing abilities to give and take in interactions; to take turns in games or using materials; and to interact without being overly submissive or directive.
	Social relationships	Demonstrates increasing comfort in talking with and accepting guidance and directions from a range of familiar adults.
		Shows progress in developing friendships with peers.
		Progresses in responding sympathetically to peers who are in need, upset, hurt, or angry; and in expressing empathy or caring for others.
	Knowledge of families and communities	Develops ability to identify personal characteristics including gender and family composition.
		Progresses in understanding similarities and respecting differences among people, such as genders, race, special needs, culture, language, and family structures.
		Develops growing awareness of jobs and what is required to perform them.

*Indicates the four specific domain elements and nine indicators that are legislatively mandated.

(*continued*)

Domain	Domain Element	Indicators
Social and emotional development (*cont.*)	Knowledge of families and communities (*cont.*)	Begins to express and understand concepts and language of geography in the contexts of their classroom, home, and community.
Approaches to learning	Initiative and curiosity	Chooses to participate in an increasing variety of tasks and activities.
		Develops increased ability to make independent choices.
		Approaches tasks and activities with increased flexibility, imagination, and inventiveness.
		Grows in eagerness to learn about and discuss a growing range of topics, ideas, and tasks.
	Engagement and persistence	Grows in abilities to persist in and complete a variety of tasks, activities, projects, and experiences.
		Demonstrates increasing ability to set goals and develop and follow through on plans.
		Shows growing capacity to maintain concentration over time on a task, question, set of directions or interactions, despite distractions and interruptions.
	Reasoning and problem solving	Develops increasing ability to find more than one solution to a question, task, or problem.
		Grows in recognizing and solving problems through active exploration, including trial and error, interactions and discussions with peers and adults.
		Develops increasing abilities to classify, compare, and contrast objects, events, and experiences.
Physical health and development	Gross motor skills	Shows increasing levels of proficiency, control, and balance in walking, climbing, running, jumping, hopping, skipping, marching, and galloping.
		Demonstrates increasing abilities to coordinate movements in throwing, catching, kicking, bouncing balls, and using the slide and swing.
	Fine motor skills	Develops growing strength, dexterity, and control needed to use tools such as scissors, paper punch, stapler, and hammer.
		Grows in hand–eye coordination in building with blocks, putting together puzzles, reproducing shapes and patterns, stringing beads, and using scissors.
		Progresses in abilities to use writing, drawing, and art tools including pencils, markers, chalk, paint brushes, and various types of technology.

*Indicates the four specific domain elements and nine indicators that are legislatively mandated.

(*continued*)

Domain	Domain Element	Indicators
Physical health and development (*cont.*)	Health status and practices	Progresses in physical growth, stamina, and flexibility.
		Participates actively in games, outdoor play, and other forms of exercise that enhance physical fitness.
		Shows growing independence in hygiene, nutrition, and personal care when eating, dressing, washing hands, brushing teeth, and toileting.
		Builds awareness and ability to follow basic health and safety rules such as fire safety, traffic and pedestrian safety, and responding appropriately to potentially harmful objects, substances, and activities.

*Indicates the four specific domain elements and nine indicators that are legislatively mandated.

NAEYC Code of Ethical Conduct and Statement of Commitment

A position statement of the National Association for the Education of Young Children

Revised April 2005

PREAMBLE

NAEYC recognizes that those who work with young children face many daily decisions that have moral and ethical implications. The NAEYC Code of Ethical Conduct offers guidelines for responsible behavior and sets forth a common basis for resolving the principal ethical dilemmas encountered in early childhood care and education. The Statement of Commitment is not part of the Code but is a personal acknowledgement of an individual's willingness to embrace the distinctive values and moral obligations of the field of early childhood care and education. The primary focus of the Code is on daily practice with children and their families in programs for children from birth through eight years of age, such as infant/toddler programs, preschool and prekindergarten programs, child care centers, hospital and child life settings, family child care homes, kindergartens, and primary classrooms. When the issues involve young children, then these provisions also apply to specialists who do not work directly with children, including program administrators, parent educators, early childhood adult educators, and officials with responsibility for program monitoring and licensing. (Note: See also the "Code of Ethical Conduct: Supplement for Early Childhood Adult Educators.")

CORE VALUES

Standards of ethical behavior in early childhood care and education are based on a commitment to the following core values that are deeply rooted in the history of the field of early childhood care and education. We have made a commitment to:

- appreciate childhood as a unique and valuable stage of the human life cycle.
- base our work on knowledge of how children develop and learn.
- appreciate and support the bond between the child and family.
- recognize that children are best understood and supported in the context of family, culture,* community, and society.
- respect the dignity, worth, and uniqueness of each individual (child, family member, and colleague).
- respect diversity in children, families, and colleagues.
- recognize that children and adults achieve their full potential in the context of relationships that are based on trust and respect.

Culture includes ethnicity, racial identity, economic level, family structure, language, and religious and political beliefs, which profoundly influence each child's development and relationship to the world.

CONCEPTUAL FRAMEWORK

The Code sets forth a framework of professional responsibilities in four sections. Each section addresses an area of professional relationships: (1) with children, (2) with families, (3) among colleagues, and (4) with the community and society. Each section includes an introduction to the primary responsibilities of the early childhood practitioner in that context. The introduction is followed by (1) a set of ideals that reflect exemplary professional practice and (2) a set of principles describing practices that are required, prohibited, or permitted.

The **ideals** reflect the aspirations of practitioners. The **principles** guide conduct and assist practitioners in resolving ethical dilemmas.* Both ideals and principles are intended to direct practitioners to those questions which, when responsibly answered, can provide the basis for conscientious decision making. While the Code provides specific direction for addressing some ethical dilemmas, many others will require the practitioner to combine the guidance of the Code with professional judgment. The ideals and principles in this Code present a shared framework of professional responsibility that affirms our commitment to the core values of our field. The Code publicly acknowledges the responsibilities that we in the field have assumed and in so doing supports ethical behavior in our work. Practitioners who face situations with ethical dimensions are urged to seek guidance in the applicable parts of this Code and in the spirit that informs the whole. Often, "the right answer"—the best ethical course of action to take—is not obvious. There may be no readily apparent, positive way to handle a situation. When one important value contradicts another, we face an ethical dilemma. When we face a dilemma, it is our professional responsibility to consult the Code and all relevant parties to find the most ethical resolution.

*There is not necessarily a corresponding principle for each ideal.

SECTION I: ETHICAL RESPONSIBILITIES TO CHILDREN

Childhood is a unique and valuable stage in the human life cycle. Our paramount responsibility is to provide care and education in settings that are safe, healthy, nurturing, and responsive for each child. We are committed to supporting children's development and learning; respecting individual differences; and helping children learn to live, play, and work cooperatively. We are also committed to promoting children's self-awareness, competence, self-worth, resiliency, and physical well-being.

Ideals

I-1.1—To be familiar with the knowledge base of early childhood care and education and to stay informed through continuing education and training.

I-1.2—To base program practices upon current knowledge and research in the field of early childhood education, child development, and related disciplines, as well as on particular knowledge of each child.

I-1.3—To recognize and respect the unique qualities, abilities, and potential of each child.

I-1.4—To appreciate the vulnerability of children and their dependence on adults.

I-1.5—To create and maintain safe and healthy settings that foster children's social, emotional, cognitive, and physical development and that respect their dignity and their contributions.

I-1.6—To use assessment instruments and strategies that are appropriate for the children to be assessed, that are used only for the purposes for which they were designed, and that have the potential to benefit children.

I-1.7—To use assessment information to understand and support children's development and learning, to support instruction, and to identify children who may need additional services.

I-1.8—To support the right of each child to play and learn in an inclusive environment that meets the needs of children with and without disabilities.

I-1.9—To advocate for and ensure that all children, including those with special needs, have access to the support services needed to be successful.

I-1.10—To ensure that each child's culture, language, ethnicity, and family structure are recognized and valued in the program.

I-1.11—To provide all children with experiences in a language that they know, as well as support children in maintaining the use of their home language and in learning English.

I-1.12—To work with families to provide a safe and smooth transition as children and families move from one program to the next.

Principles

P-1.1—**Above all, we shall not harm children. We shall not participate in practices that are emotionally damaging, physically harmful, disrespectful, degrading, dangerous, exploitative, or intimidating to children. *This principle has precedence over all others in this Code.***

P-1.2—We shall care for and educate children in positive emotional and social environments that are cognitively stimulating and that support each child's culture, language, ethnicity, and family structure.

P-1.3—We shall not participate in practices that discriminate against children by denying benefits, giving special advantages, or excluding them from programs or activities on the basis of their sex, race, national origin, religious beliefs, medical condition, disability, or the marital status/family structure, sexual orientation, or religious beliefs or other affiliations of their families. (Aspects of this principle do not apply in programs that have a lawful mandate to provide services to a particular population of children.)

P-1.4—We shall involve all those with relevant knowledge (including families and staff) in decisions concerning a child, as appropriate, ensuring confidentiality of sensitive information.

P-1.5—We shall use appropriate assessment systems, which include multiple sources of information, to provide information on children's learning and development.

P-1.6—We shall strive to ensure that decisions such as those related to enrollment, retention, or assignment to special education services will be based on multiple sources of information and will never be based on a single assessment, such as a test score or a single observation.

P-1.7—We shall strive to build individual relationships with each child; make individualized adaptations in teaching strategies, learning environments, and curricula; and consult with the family so that each child benefits from the program. If after such efforts have been exhausted, the current placement does not meet a child's needs, or the child is seriously jeopardizing the ability of other children to benefit from the program, we shall collaborate with the child's family and appropriate specialists to determine the additional services needed and/or the placement option(s) most likely to ensure the child's success. (Aspects of this principle may not apply in programs that have a lawful mandate to provide services to a particular population of children.)

P-1.8—We shall be familiar with the risk factors for and symptoms of child abuse and neglect, including physical, sexual, verbal, and emotional abuse and physical, emotional, educational, and medical neglect. We shall know and follow state laws and community procedures that protect children against abuse and neglect.

P-1.9—When we have reasonable cause to suspect child abuse or neglect, we shall report it to the appropriate community agency and follow up to ensure that appropriate action has been taken. When appropriate, parents or guardians will be informed that the referral will be or has been made.

P-1.10—When another person tells us of his or her suspicion that a child is being abused or neglected, we shall assist that person in taking appropriate action in order to protect the child.

P-1.11—When we become aware of a practice or situation that endangers the health, safety, or well-being of children, we have an ethical responsibility to protect children or inform parents and/or others who can.

SECTION II: ETHICAL RESPONSIBILITIES TO FAMILIES

Families* are of primary importance in children's development. Because the family and the early childhood practitioner have a common interest in the child's well-being, we acknowledge a primary responsibility to bring about communication, cooperation, and collaboration between the home and early childhood program in ways that enhance the child's development.

*The term *family* may include those adults, besides parents, with the responsibility of being involved in educating, nurturing, and advocating for the child.

Ideals

I-2.1—To be familiar with the knowledge base related to working effectively with families and to stay informed through continuing education and training.

I-2.2—To develop relationships of mutual trust and create partnerships with the families we serve.

I-2.3—To welcome all family members and encourage them to participate in the program.

I-2.4—To listen to families, acknowledge and build upon their strengths and competencies, and learn from families as we support them in their task of nurturing children.

I-2.5—To respect the dignity and preferences of each family and to make an effort to learn about its structure, culture, language, customs, and beliefs.

I-2.6—To acknowledge families' childrearing values and their right to make decisions for their children.

I-2.7—To share information about each child's education and development with families and to help them understand and appreciate the current knowledge base of the early childhood profession.

I-2.8—To help family members enhance their understanding of their children and support the continuing development of their skills as parents.

I-2.9—To participate in building support networks for families by providing them with opportunities to interact with program staff, other families, community resources, and professional services.

Principles

P-2.1—We shall not deny family members access to their child's classroom or program setting unless access is denied by court order or other legal restriction.

P-2.2—We shall inform families of program philosophy, policies, curriculum, assessment system, and personnel qualifications, and explain why we teach as we do—which should be in accordance with our ethical responsibilities to children (see Section I).

P-2.3—We shall inform families of and, when appropriate, involve them in policy decisions.

P-2.4—We shall involve the family in significant decisions affecting their child.

P-2.5—We shall make every effort to communicate effectively with all families in a language that they understand. We shall use community resources for translation and interpretation when we do not have sufficient resources in our own programs.

P-2.6—As families share information with us about their children and families, we shall consider this information to plan and implement the program.

P-2.7—We shall inform families about the nature and purpose of the program's child assessments and how data about their child will be used.

P-2.8—We shall treat child assessment information confidentially and share this information only when there is a legitimate need for it.

P-2.9—We shall inform the family of injuries and incidents involving their child, of risks such as exposures to communicable diseases that might result in infection, and of occurrences that might result in emotional stress.

P-2.10—Families shall be fully informed of any proposed research projects involving their children and shall have the opportunity to give or withhold consent without penalty. We shall not permit or participate in research that could in any way hinder the education, development, or well-being of children.

P-2.11—We shall not engage in or support exploitation of families. We shall not use our relationship with a family for private advantage or personal gain, or enter into relationships with family members that might impair our effectiveness working with their children.

P-2.12—We shall develop written policies for the protection of confidentiality and the disclosure of children's records. These policy documents shall be made available to all program personnel and families. Disclosure of children's records beyond family members, program personnel, and consultants having an obligation of confidentiality shall require familial consent (except in cases of abuse or neglect).

P-2.13—We shall maintain confidentiality and shall respect the family's right to privacy, refraining from disclosure of confidential information and intrusion into family life. However, when we have reason to believe that a child's welfare is at risk, it is permissible to share confidential information with agencies, as well as with individuals who have legal responsibility for intervening in the child's interest.

P-2.14—In cases where family members are in conflict with one another, we shall work openly, sharing our observations of the child, to help all parties involved make informed decisions. We shall refrain from becoming an advocate for one party.

P-2.15—We shall be familiar with and appropriately refer families to community resources and professional support services. After a referral has been made, we shall follow up to ensure that services have been appropriately provided.

SECTION III: ETHICAL RESPONSIBILITIES TO COLLEAGUES

In a caring, cooperative workplace, human dignity is respected, professional satisfaction is promoted, and positive relationships are developed and sustained. Based upon our core values, our primary responsibility to colleagues is to establish and maintain settings and relationships that support productive work and meet professional needs. The same ideals that apply to children also apply as we interact with adults in the workplace.

A—Responsibilities to Co-Workers

Ideals

I-3A.1—To establish and maintain relationships of respect, trust, confidentiality, collaboration, and cooperation with co-workers.

I-3A.2—To share resources with co-workers, collaborating to ensure that the best possible early childhood care and education program is provided.

I-3A.3—To support co-workers in meeting their professional needs and in their professional development.

I-3A.4—To accord co-workers due recognition of professional achievement.

Principles

P-3A.1—We shall recognize the contributions of colleagues to our program and not participate in practices that diminish their reputations or impair their effectiveness in working with children and families.

P-3A.2—When we have concerns about the professional behavior of a co-worker, we shall first let that person know of our concern in a way that shows respect for personal dignity and for the diversity to be found among staff members, and then attempt to resolve the matter collegially and in a confidential manner.

P-3A.3—We shall exercise care in expressing views regarding the personal attributes or professional conduct of co-workers. Statements should be based on firsthand knowledge, not hearsay, and relevant to the interests of children and programs.

P-3A.4—We shall not participate in practices that discriminate against a co-worker because of sex, race, national origin, religious beliefs or other affiliations, age, marital status/family structure, disability, or sexual orientation.

B—Responsibilities to Employers

Ideals

I-3B.1—To assist the program in providing the highest quality of service.

I-3B.2—To do nothing that diminishes the reputation of the program in which we work unless it is violating laws and regulations designed to protect children or is violating the provisions of this Code.

Principles

P-3B.1—We shall follow all program policies. When we do not agree with program policies, we shall attempt to effect change through constructive action within the organization.

P-3B.2—We shall speak or act on behalf of an organization only when authorized. We shall take care to acknowledge when we are speaking for the organization and when we are expressing a personal judgment.

P-3B.3—We shall not violate laws or regulations designed to protect children and shall take appropriate action consistent with this Code when aware of such violations.

P-3B.4—If we have concerns about a colleague's behavior, and children's well-being is not at risk, we may address the concern with that individual. If children are at risk or the situation does not improve after it has been brought to the colleague's attention, we shall report the colleague's unethical or incompetent behavior to an appropriate authority.

P-3B.5—When we have a concern about circumstances or conditions that impact the quality of care and education within the program, we shall inform the program's administration or, when necessary, other appropriate authorities.

C—Responsibilities to Employees

Ideals

I-3C.1—To promote safe and healthy working conditions and policies that foster mutual respect, cooperation, collaboration, competence, well-being, confidentiality, and self-esteem in staff members.

I-3C.2—To create and maintain a climate of trust and candor that will enable staff to speak and act in the best interests of children, families, and the field of early childhood care and education.

I-3C.3—To strive to secure adequate and equitable compensation (salary and benefits) for those who work with or on behalf of young children.

I-3C.4—To encourage and support continual development of employees in becoming more skilled and knowledgeable practitioners.

Principles

P-3C.1—In decisions concerning children and programs, we shall draw upon the education, training, experience, and expertise of staff members.

P-3C.2—We shall provide staff members with safe and supportive working conditions that honor confidences and permit them to carry out their responsibilities through fair performance evaluations, written grievance procedures, constructive feedback, and opportunities for continuing professional development and advancement.

P-3C.3—We shall develop and maintain comprehensive written personnel policies that define program standards. These policies shall be given to new staff members and shall be available and easily accessible for review by all staff members.

P-3C.4—We shall inform employees whose performance does not meet program expectations of areas of concern and, when possible, assist in improving their performance.

P-3C.5—We shall conduct employee dismissals for just cause, in accordance with all applicable laws and regulations. We shall inform employees who are dismissed of the reasons for their termination. When a dismissal is for cause, justification must be based on evidence of inadequate or inappropriate behavior that is accurately documented, current, and available for the employee to review.

P-3C.6—In making evaluations and recommendations, we shall make judgments based on fact and relevant to the interests of children and programs.

P-3C.7—We shall make hiring, retention, termination, and promotion decisions based solely on a person's competence, record of accomplishment, ability to carry out the responsibilities of the position, and professional preparation specific to the developmental levels of children in his/her care.

P-3C.8—We shall not make hiring, retention, termination, and promotion decisions based on an individual's sex, race, national origin, religious beliefs or other affiliations, age, marital status/family structure, disability, or sexual orientation. We shall be familiar with and observe laws and regulations that pertain to employment discrimination. (Aspects of this principle do not apply to programs that have a lawful mandate to determine eligibility based on one or more of the criteria identified above.)

P-3C.9—We shall maintain confidentiality in dealing with issues related to an employee's job performance and shall respect an employee's right to privacy regarding personal issues.

SECTION IV: ETHICAL RESPONSIBILITIES TO COMMUNITY AND SOCIETY

Early childhood programs operate within the context of their immediate community made up of families and other institutions concerned with children's welfare. Our responsibilities to the community are to provide programs that meet the diverse needs of families, to cooperate with agencies and professions that share the responsibility for children, to assist families in gaining access to those agencies and allied professionals, and to assist in the development of community programs that are needed but not currently available. As individuals, we acknowledge our responsibility to provide the best possible programs of care and education for children and to conduct ourselves with honesty and integrity. Because of our specialized expertise in early childhood development and education and because the larger society shares responsibility for the welfare and protection of young children, we acknowledge a collective obligation to advocate for the best interests of children within early childhood programs and in the larger community and to serve as a voice for young children everywhere. The ideals and principles in this section are presented to distinguish between those that pertain to the work of the individual early childhood educator and those that more typically are engaged in collectively on behalf of the best interests of children—with the understanding that individual early childhood educators have a shared responsibility for addressing the ideals and principles that are identified as "collective."

Ideal (Individual)

1-4.1—To provide the community with high-quality early childhood care and education programs and services.

Ideals (Collective)

I-4.2—To promote cooperation among professionals and agencies and inter-disciplinary collaboration among professions concerned with addressing issues in the health, education, and well-being of young children, their families, and their early childhood educators.

I-4.3—To work through education, research, and advocacy toward an environmentally safe world in which all children receive health care, food, and shelter; are nurtured; and live free from violence in their homes and their communities.

I-4.4—To work through education, research, and advocacy toward a society in which all young children have access to high-quality early care and education programs.

I-4.5—To work to ensure that appropriate assessment systems, which include multiple sources of information, are used for purposes that benefit children.

I-4.6—To promote knowledge and understanding of young children and their needs. To work toward greater societal acknowledgment of children's rights and greater social acceptance of responsibility for the well-being of all children.

I-4.7—To support policies and laws that promote the well-being of children and families, and to work to change those that impair their well-being. To participate in developing policies and laws that are needed, and to cooperate with other individuals and groups in these efforts.

I-4.8—To further the professional development of the field of early childhood care and education and to strengthen its commitment to realizing its core values as reflected in this Code.

Principles (Individual)

P-4.1—We shall communicate openly and truthfully about the nature and extent of services that we provide.

P-4.2—We shall apply for, accept, and work in positions for which we are personally well-suited and professionally qualified. We shall not offer services that we do not have the competence, qualifications, or resources to provide.

P-4.3—We shall carefully check references and shall not hire or recommend for employment any person whose competence, qualifications, or character makes him or her unsuited for the position.

P-4.4—We shall be objective and accurate in reporting the knowledge upon which we base our program practices.

P-4.5—We shall be knowledgeable about the appropriate use of assessment strategies and instruments and interpret results accurately to families.

P-4.6—We shall be familiar with laws and regulations that serve to protect the children in our programs and be vigilant in ensuring that these laws and regulations are followed.

P-4.7—When we become aware of a practice or situation that endangers the health, safety, or well-being of children, we have an ethical responsibility to protect children or inform parents and/or others who can.

P-4.8—We shall not participate in practices that are in violation of laws and regulations that protect the children in our programs.

P-4.9—When we have evidence that an early childhood program is violating laws or regulations protecting children, we shall report the violation to appropriate authorities who can be expected to remedy the situation.

P-4.10—When a program violates or requires its employees to violate this Code, it is permissible, after fair assessment of the evidence, to disclose the identity of that program.

Principles (Collective)

P-4.11—When policies are enacted for purposes that do not benefit children, we have a collective responsibility to work to change these practices.

P-4.12—When we have evidence that an agency that provides services intended to ensure children's well-being is failing to meet its obligations, we acknowledge a collective ethical responsibility to report the problem to appropriate authorities or to the public. We shall be vigilant in our follow-up until the situation is resolved.

P-4.13—When a child protection agency fails to provide adequate protection for abused or neglected children, we acknowledge a collective ethical responsibility to work toward the improvement of these services.

NAEYC has taken reasonable measures to develop the Code in a fair, reasonable, open, unbiased, and objective manner, based on currently available data. However, further research or developments may change the current state of knowledge. Neither NAEYC nor its officers, directors, members, employees, or agents will be liable for any loss, damage, or claim with respect to any liabilities, including direct, special, indirect, or consequential damages incurred in connection with the Code or reliance on the information presented.

STATEMENT OF COMMITMENT*

As an individual who works with young children, I commit myself to furthering the values of early childhood education as they are reflected in the ideals and principles of the NAEYC Code of Ethical Conduct. To the best of my ability I will

- never harm children.
- ensure that programs for young children are based on current knowledge and research of child development and early childhood education.
- respect and support families in their task of nurturing children.
- respect colleagues in early childhood care and education and support them in maintaining the NAEYC Code of Ethical Conduct.
- serve as an advocate for children, their families, and their teachers in the community and society.
- stay informed of and maintain high standards of professional conduct.
- engage in an ongoing process of self-reflection, realizing that personal characteristics, biases, and beliefs have an impact on children and families.
- be open to new ideas and be willing to learn from the suggestions of others.
- continue to learn, grow, and contribute as a professional.
- honor the ideals and principles of the NAEYC Code of Ethical Conduct.

*This Statement of Commitment is not part of the Code but is a personal acknowledgment of the individual's willingness to embrace the distinctive values and moral obligations of the field of early childhood care and education. It is recognition of the moral obligations that lead to an individual becoming part of the profession.

GLOSSARY OF TERMS RELATED TO ETHICS

Code of Ethics defines the core values of the field and provides guidance for what professionals should do when they encounter conflicting obligations or responsibilities in their work

values qualities or principles that individuals believe to be desirable or worthwhile and that they prize for themselves, for others, and for the world in which they live

core values commitments held by a profession that are consciously and knowingly embraced by its practitioners because they make a contribution to society. There is a difference between personal values and the core values of a profession

morality peoples' views of what is good, right, and proper; their beliefs about their obligations; and their ideas about how they should behave

ethics the study of right and wrong, or duty and obligation, that involves critical reflection on morality and the ability to make choices between values and the examination of the moral dimensions of relationships

professional ethics the moral commitments of a profession that involve moral reflection that extends and enhances the personal morality practitioners bring to their work, that concern actions of right and wrong in the workplace, and that help individuals resolve moral dilemmas they encounter in their work

ethical responsibilities behaviors that one must or must not engage in. Ethical responsibilities are clear-cut and are spelled out in the Code of Ethical Conduct (for example, early childhood educators should never share confidential information about a child or family with a person who has no legitimate need for knowing)

ethical dilemma a moral conflict that involves determining appropriate conduct when an individual faces conflicting professional values and responsibilities

SOURCES FOR GLOSSARY TERMS AND DEFINITIONS

Feeney, S., & N. Freeman. (1999). *Ethics and the early childhood educator: Using the NAEYC code.* Washington, DC: NAEYC.

Kidder, R. M. (1995). *How good people make tough choices: Resolving the dilemmas of ethical living.* New York: Fireside.

Kipnis, K. (1987). How to discuss professional ethics. *Young Children, 42*(4), 26–30.

Reprinted, with permission, from the National Association for the Education of Young Children.

Glossary

A

advocacy the act of writing or speaking in favor of something

aesthetics systems for appreciating beauty and form

affiliative leadership style of a person with the ability to connect or associate one with

aggressiveness initiation of action

allocation a portion of resources that are identified and reserved for a purpose

ambiguities having two or more uncertain reasons

antibias curriculum a method of presenting activities to children to help them avoid ways of perceiving a person or a group as less than equal due to race, gender, or disabilities

appreciative inquiry the cooperative search for what is best in people

B

behavioral describing the way a person acts

bilingual using or capable of using more than one language with equal or nearly equal facility

biopsychological potential attributing physiological reasons to psychological responses

C

catalyst a person or thing acting as the stimulus in bringing about or hastening a result

characteristics distinguishing traits, features, or qualities

cocooning withdrawing; enclosing protectively

collaborative to work together

collective unconscious Carl Jung's theory involving the part of the unconscious mind that each human being inherits along with all other human beings; it contains certain patterns or archetypes

colloquialism local or regional use of words or expressions

combativeness ready to fight

communication two-way process that requires one person to provide a message or a stimulus and another person to receive the message and respond

competence ability or fitness for the task

competencies 1. condition or quality of being competent; ability, fitness, or legal capability; power or justification 2. set of skills that defines capabilities in a staff person

conferencing skills a two-way conversation that allows each person to contribute ideas

conformity the condition of being uniform or alike

congruence a way of coming together, being aligned

consensus agreement among all parties on an issue or activity

constrained compelled, forced, or obliged

constraints customs of repression of natural feelings or behavior

constructs things built or put together systematically, a concept or theory devised to integrate in an orderly way diverse ideas or data

context the whole situation, background, or environment relevant to a particular event, personality, or creation

continuous improvement a process that involves continually monitoring, assessing, and improving operations and systems

continuum a continuous whole, series, or quantity that cannot be separated

coordinator designated person responsible for a program's activities

creativity the process of generating many ideas

cultural messages ideas, customs, or skills of a group of people who pass on their identity and customs through oral and written traditions

cultural pluralism policy of favoring the preservation of groups within a given nation and/or society

culture ideas, customs, skills, arts, and so on of a people or group that are transferred, communicated, or passed along

D

de facto existing, but not by official recognition

democratic 1. leadership style of people who are popular with all or most people 2. treating persons of all classes the same way

descriptor describes, classifies, or identifies something

dialogue a form of communication used to gather information and learn from it

discernible able to see and examine separately

dispositions an individual's customary frame of reference

dissonance lack of harmony, or agreement; an inharmonious sound

diversity different cultures

E

ecological/environmental study of the relationship and adjustment of human groups to their geographic and social environments

economics systems of business and finance

ego defenses mediators between the impulses of the id, the demands of environment, and the standards of the superego

emotional intelligence 1. a set of behaviors that enables a person to survive and succeed, even in challenging and negative environments 2. the dimension of intelligence responsible for the ability to manage one's self and interpersonal relationships

empathy the projection of one's own personality on another in order to understand the other person better; the ability to share in another's emotions, thoughts, or feelings

English language learners people whose primary language is other than English and who are learning English as a second language

entrepreneurs individuals who start up and run their own businesses

equitable characterized by equity, fairness, and justice: said of actions or results of actions

ethnic identity designating a population subgroup having a common cultural heritage or nationality

ethnicity common cultural heritage developed by custom, characteristics, language, and common history

evaluation criteria for judging program activities

extrinsic coming from outside

extroverted outgoing personality

F

family of origin belonging to a family with a particular ethnic or cultural background

four-quadrant behavioral model a theory that has four major premises of observable behavior

framework structure, usually serving to hold parts together

G

genetically having to do with genetic (biological) inheritance

global-holistic looks at the big picture, nonlinear learner

H

hierarchy a group of persons or things that are rank ordered from the highest to the lowest

holistic concerned with the whole or integrated system rather than the parts

hypothesize to form groundwork, a foundation, a supposition

I

implementing a way of using a thing or person as a means to some end; to carry into effect, fulfill, or accomplish

individualization to consider as a separate entity, mark as different from others

initiation beginning of an activity without instructions or direction

initiatives set of authorizations promoted by an organization for programs and activities that support an approach

innovation the process of selecting, combining, refining, and turning the best creative practices into reality

intentionality having a focus or an intention

interpreter a person who explains the meaning of things, makes things understandable to, or translates from one language to another

interrelated to make, be, or become mutually related

intervening to come, be, or lie between

intervention to provide an activity, idea, or strategy that affects an outcome for someone

intrinsic coming from within

introverted passive, inwardly focused personality

L

leadership a set of skills that allows a person to lead a team of individuals to collectively work toward a goal

linguistics the science of language, including phonetics, morphology, syntax, and semantics; the study of the structure and development of a particular language, and its relationship to other languages

literature a body of written works, selected readings

M

mediated entry the medium that initiates and brings about results

metaphorming a change process conveying an idea, started by expressing a vision or belief or realizing a dream; works by helping people see similarities among perceptions rather than dwelling on differences

mnemonic a formula or means of improving one's memory

modeling skills activities that demonstrate how to correctly perform or teach

O

optimism taking a hopeful view, expects the best

organizational behavior a unified group of elements creating a systematized whole that describes behaviors in an organization

orientation 1. an overview and introduction 2. familiarization with and adaptation to a situation or environment

P

peripheral laying at the outside or away from the central part

pessimistic expecting the worst

pro forma budget a budget that estimates future costs

proficient highly competent, skilled, or adept

psyche the mind considered as a subjectively perceived, functional entity, based ultimately on physical processes but with complex processes of its own

R

rationalization to devise superficially rational or plausible explanations for an action, belief, or point of view

reengineering retooling and refining all systems; eliminating redundant reporting and work

reflective practice activity in which a mentor coach, supervisor, or peer takes time to listen to another's observations, interactions, or experiences and processes them for appropriateness or makes suggestions on how things might have been handled better

resonance in terms of brain function, people's emotional centers are in synch in positive ways

retention power or capacity to retain; ability to remember

S

sabbatical a period of rest that occurs in cycles

self-assessment skills methods of looking at how one is viewed by others as well as understanding one's own work and behavioral style

significant emotional event (SEE) having or expressing a serious emotional event, for example, loss, death of a loved one, immigration

socialization adjust to or make fit for cooperative group living

stakeholder a person with an interest in an activity or process

stereotypes unvarying forms or patterns; fixed or conventional motions or conceptions of a person, group, or idea

strategic planning planning for the future using key elements and timelines

symbiotic an association with mutual advantage among all parties

synergy interaction to accomplish tasks

systemic an established way of doing things

T

taboos social prohibitions or restrictions that result from convention or tradition

theoretical the value of searching for knowledge

two-dimensional having two dimensions, lacking in substance or depth

U

utilitarian the value of efficiency and practicality

V

value an enduring belief that a particular means or end is more socially or individually preferable than another ends or means

visionary leadership style of a person with strong and creative imaginary powers and the ability to inspire others

Z

zone of proximal development (ZPD) Vygotsky's theory that a child develops a new skill as the result of an adult or peer helping him or her bridge the gap

Index